# TRAFALGAR
# AND THE SPANISH NAVY

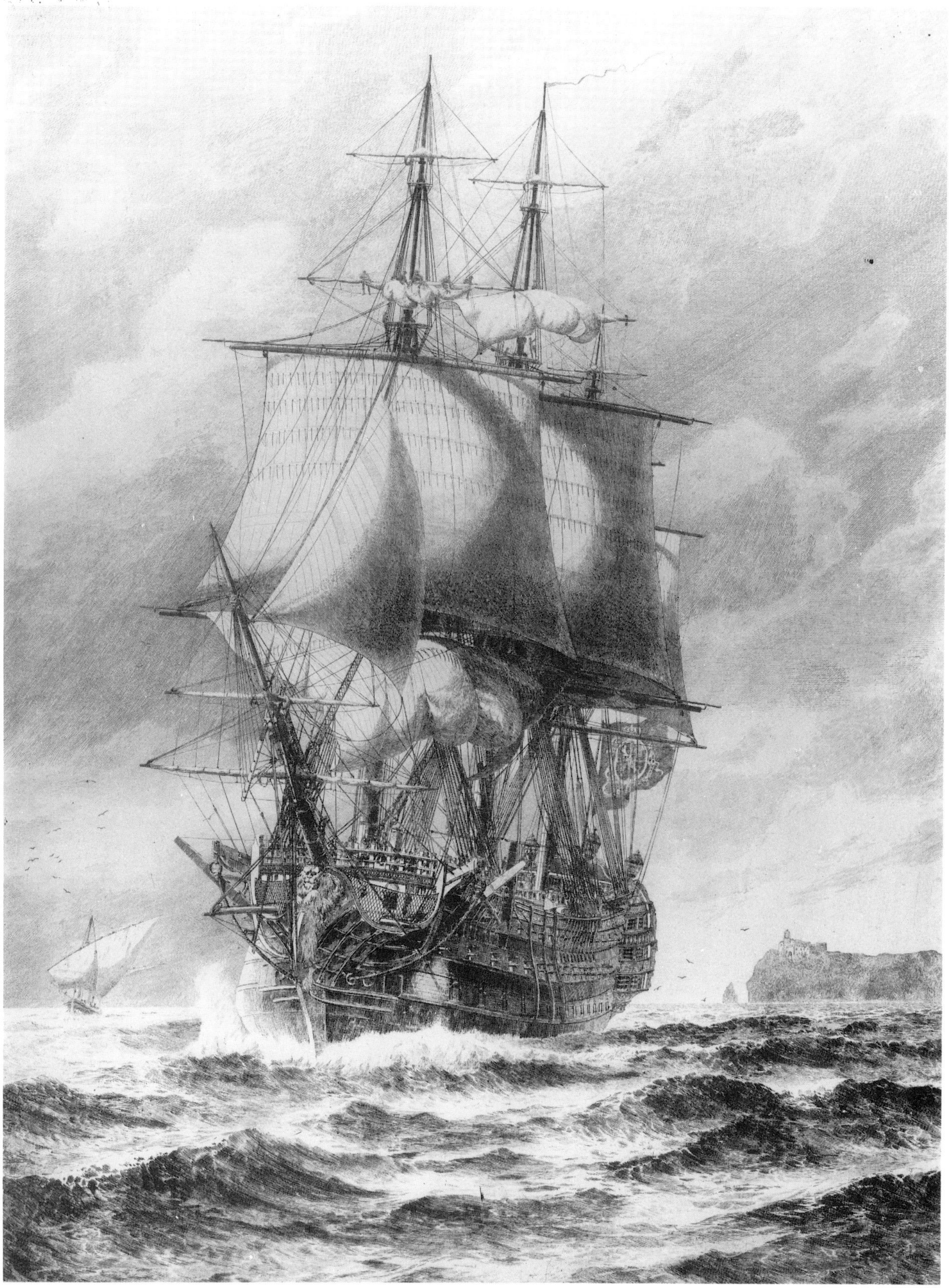

# TRAFALGAR
## AND THE SPANISH NAVY

by

John D Harbron

CONWAY

MARITIME PRESS

# DEDICATION

*My book is dedicated to its many heroes,*
*the warship designers and fleet administrators,*
*naval explorers, Spanish admirals, captains and their crews*
*who built, sailed and fought in the ships of*
*the eighteenth century* Armada Española.

HALF-TITLE PAGE
The royal crown and anchor of the eighteenth century
Spanish Bourbon kings as reconstituted by the modern
Bourbon monarchy of Juan Carlos I and used by the
modern Spanish Navy.

FRONTISPIECE
An engraving of the famous *Santísima Trinidad* by T Hägg.
(*National Maritime Museum*)

© John D Harbron 1988

First published in Great Britain in 1988 by
Conway Maritime Press Ltd,
24 Bride Lane, Fleet Street,
London EC4Y 8DR

ISBN 0 85177 477 6

Designed by John Mitchell
Typesetting by Witwell Ltd, Southport
Printed and bound at the University Printing House, Oxford

# CONTENTS

# FOREWORD

This book explores the renewal of Spanish sea power during the greatest period of Spanish naval expansion and the rejuvenation of the Spanish national spirit that took place near the end of the age of sail. Neither a definitive nor academic history of the Spanish Navy in the eighteenth century, nevertheless it is the first in which the naval history of that century is seen both through the records of Spain's great naval administrators as well as from the deeds of her shipbuilders, who constructed a new navy, and her best captains and admirals, who sailed and commanded the new warships which were among the best in Europe.

It also elaborates on why Spain at sea during the last full century of the long period of sail was not in chronic decline. Rather, during it Spain again became, if briefly, a dynamic sea power in which Spaniards excelled as they had done before during the age of exploration of the late fifteenth and early sixteenth centuries as major world explorers, navigators, ship designers and fleet administrators.

The many naval histories of the English-speaking world have inaccurately portrayed this period of Spanish maritime power in the century between the loss of Gibraltar in 1704 and Spain's defeat at Trafalgar in 1805 as one of unremitted decline. During that century, Spaniards were said to have been overwhelmed by their defeats in many of the major sea battles and weakened by the sense of loss that came with the decline of all the great European colonial and maritime empires. In fact, by 1783 – the year of the Treaty of Paris that formalized the British loss of her thirteen American colonies, which the Royal Navy could not prevent – Spain's overseas empire had reached its greatest geographical extent. At the same time, the Spanish Navy continued a naval renewal and expansion that both worried and impressed its English opponents.

Where Trafalgar is concerned, this book follows the same path as Spanish historians in writing about that battle from the Spanish point of view: that is, without rancour regarding the course of events. In this book, the fifteen Spanish warship captains and their four commanding admirals who fought at Trafalgar, emerge from the shadows of past history to appear as flesh and blood personalities. Many of them held responsible naval and governmental roles before and after that sea battle.

In modern times, the common bond of the sea links the modern Latin American maritime states to Spain's long imperial sea heritage. This is not unlike the similar linkages that have persisted between the navies of such successor states of the old British Empire as Canada, Australia and New Zealand with the modern Royal Navy. The existence of superb Spanish-built steel-hulled sail training ships in the contemporary Hispanic-American navies of Argentina, Chile, Colombia, Venezuela, Ecuador, Peru and Mexico also represent their living connections with Spain's long naval past.

During the 1970s and 1980s, the Tall Ships fleets that took part in historical celebrations of colonial events have included many of these modern sailing ships of Spain. Such events in which the Tall Ships participated included the Bicentennial sail-past in New York Harbour on 4 July 1976 to celebrate the 200th anniversary of the founding of the American Republic, the sail-past in front of Québec City in 1984 during the 400th anniversary year of the French discovery of Canada by Jacques Cartier and in Sydney harbour during January 1988 for the 200th anniversary of the founding of Australia. In many of these nautical showpieces, the modern Spanish-built sail training ships that were constructed in the historic shipyards of Bilbao and Cádiz, were joined by the *Juan Sebastián de Elcano*, the famous and well-travelled sail training ship of the contemporary *Armada Española*.

She is named, of course, for the first man (a Spaniard and a Basque) who circumnavigated the world, between 1520 and 1522.

# ACKNOWLEDGEMENTS

For granting me access since 1983 to the all-important archival material on the eighteenth century Spanish Navy in both the Museo Naval of the Spanish Navy Ministry in Mádrid and at Viso del Marqués and permission to reproduce selected prints and paintings held in the Museo Naval, I am greatly indebted to the distinguished Spanish naval historians Capitán de navío Ricardo Cerezo Martínez, Director of the Museo Naval, and his predecessor, Capitán de navío José María Zumalacárregui Calvo.

Of the Museo Naval staff I must thank in particular the archivists and directors of research, Doña María Vigon Tabar and Doña Lola Higueras Rodríquez as well as Jaime Jiménez and d Victoriano Ruíz, for their patience, enthusiasm and cheerfulness in their substantial assistance to me day by day.

I want to thank Vice-Admiral Fernando Moreno de Alborán y Reyna, retired director of the Instituto de Historia y Cultura Naval of the Spanish Navy Ministry, and Capitán de navío Juan Berenguer y Moreno de Guerra, its secretary-general, for their early suggestions on my book's theme.

I am also in debt to many senior officials in the Spanish Ministry of Foreign Affairs for their assistance and enthusiasm over the years. They include HE d Antonio Elias y Martinena and HE d Javier Oyarzun Iñarra, former Spanish Ambassadors to Canada, and HE Fernando Olivié, former Spanish Ambassador to Belgium, as well as the former Deputy Directors of Cultural Relations in the Foreign Ministry in Madrid, d Manuel González-Haba and d Mariano Alonso Burón, and especially Doña Gloria de Larrinaga, Secretary to the Ambassador of Spain, Ottawa, for her valuable and cheerful assistance to me over the years.

My special thanks and gratitude are extended to d José María de Areilza, Count of Motrico, the distinguished Spanish diplomat, historian and essayist, and his son d Enrique de Areilza Churruca, for granting me the first public access to the personal correspondence of Commodore Cosmé Damián Churruca, one of the best remembered of Spain's Trafalgar's captains. As a result of their family generosity, this book has been able to expand for the first time on the career and personality of Churruca.

My warm thanks also must go to one of my oldest personal friends, José A García Ordóñez y Montalvo of Concord, New Hampshire and formerly of Havana, Cuba, who gave me access to his private history of the Montalvo family that included data on his ancestor Lorenzo Montalvo, who played a central role in the development of the great eighteenth century Spanish naval shipyard in Havana.

Nor shall I forget the late parents of José Ordóñez who facilitated my path as a young graduate student at the University of Havana, Cuba in 1947 where my lifelong interest in the Spanish at sea began. My Cuban connection does not end here, but must include the distinguished Cuban historian Dr Herminio Portell-Vilá of Miami, Florida and formerly of Havana, Cuba. Not only did he open many doors for me at the University of Havana in the late 1940s, but gave me an appreciation of the enduring qualities of the Spanish colonial heritage, especially where his homeland is concerned.

In Canada, I am indebted to Peter Roberts, its Director, and the Canada Council for that agency's financial support in late 1986 during the concluding months of my archival research in Spain and Britain. Nor must I forget the willing staff of the Robarts Library of the University of Toronto who guided me through that library's collections of monographs of Spanish and Spanish-American history which are among the largest in the English-speaking world.

Many of my academic colleagues have helped me substantially, in particular: in Canada, J C M Ogelsby, Professor of Latin American History, University of Western Ontario, London, Ontario; and Gerald H S Jordan, Associate Professor of History, York University, Toronto; also my thanks go to Señora Laura Soto for her assistance in the preparation for publication of the letters of Commodore

1 Trafalgar and the Spanish Navy

Cosmé Damián Churruca. I am especially indebted to my employer Thomson Newspapers of Canada for granting me a leave of absence to complete my research; in Britain, Dr Roger J B Knight, Head of the Documentation Division of the magnificent National Maritime Museum at Greenwich; and naval historian Lieutenant Commander Peter Whitlock, MBE, RN (Ret), former commanding officer of HMS *Victory* at Portsmouth; in Spain, Victoria Stapells Johnson of Sevilla for granting me access to her unpublished MA thesis on eighteenth century Spanish corsairs in the Caribbean. In the United States, Dr Lewis Hanke, Emeritus Professor of Latin American History at the University of Massachusetts, Amherst, also deserves a special thanks from me. As Director of the Hispanic Foundation of the Library of Congress during the late 1940s, he took time from his busy life as one of the leading colonial historians of Latin America to direct me in my graduate student research work and later, to give me scholarly directions as a journalist. In fact, this book's theme was first outlined in a letter to Dr Hanke of 29 May 1962.

Finally, in both researching and writing my book, I owe so much to my ever-supportive wife, Sheila, not only for her patience and forbearance during my many absences from her between 1982 and 1987 to research material, but also for her expertise and patience in typing the manuscript into the now essential computer.

Toronto,
Ontario,
Canada.

March 1988

# AN EXPLANATORY NOTE
## ON NAVAL RANKS IN THE SPANISH NAVY
## OF THE EIGHTEENTH CENTURY

Despite the fact the word Admiral has come to the English language from both its Spanish and Arabic language versions, the *Armada Española*, the Spanish Navy of the eighteenth century, used mainly military titles for the ranks of flag officers from Commodore to Admiral of the Fleet. At the same time, contemporary middle rank and junior officers from Commander to Lieutenant bore identifiable naval ranks.

Because equivalent naval ranks exist for the military titles assigned to Spanish Navy flag officers of the eighteenth century, naval titles for all ranks will be used. The equivalent military and naval ranks of Spanish flag officers are as follows:

*Capitán General de la Armada* (Captain General of the Fleet) – Admiral of the Fleet.

*Almirante* (Admiral) – in this instance, the naval rank was preferred to General. Almirante is derived from the Arabic title *amir-al-bahar* 'prince or commander of the sea'. The rank of Almirante was first used by Fernando III, King of Castile in the thirteenth century. The Navy of Castile was the largest in the Spanish mediaeval Christian kingdoms and a distant predecessor of the eighteenth century *Armada Española*.

*Teniente General* (Lieutenant General) – Vice Admiral.

*Jefe de Escuadra* (Chief of Squadron) – Rear Admiral.

*Brigadier* – Commodore.

Middle and junior Spanish naval officers' ranks that maintained their naval identity are:

*Capitán de Navío* (literally Captain of the Ship of the Line) – Captain.

*Capitán de Fragata* (Captain of the Frigate) – Commander.

*Capitán de Corbeta* (Captain of the Corvette) – Lieutenant Commander.

*Teniente de Navío* – Lieutenant.

*Alférez de Navío* – Sub Lieutenant, or Ensign in the United States Navy. (In this rank there is a reversion to an ancient land title, namely Alferez Real, a junior town or village administrative official.)

*Alférez de Fragata* – in the Royal Navy, a Commissioned Warrant Officer.

*Guardia Marina* – Midshipman.

*Aspirante* – more properly the Spanish word for 'neophyte'. In naval parlance it is used appropriately enough for Naval Cadet.

In some ranks, such as Captain, several versions of it were used. For example, at the beginning of the eighteenth century a naval captain could be called *capitán de mar y guerra*, 'captain of sea and war'. *Capitán de bandera* or flag captain, was the commanding officer of a ship of the line or frigate that served as an admiral's flagship and which flew his flag.

*Capitana* was a ship's designation and not an officer's rank. *Capitana* was the correct naval term used during the seventeenth and eighteenth centuries for the fleet flagship – a title assigned to such a warship 'precisely and exclusively' by the *Real Cedula* or Royal Seal of 18 January 1654.

The title *Captain General* also was used for the shore-based commanding officer of a naval base and where it was applicable, such as at Cádiz, of the associated naval shipyard and arsenal. The Captain General of a major naval base – an experienced senior naval officer with considerable previous seatime and administrative experience – usually held the rank of Lieutenant General, that is Vice Admiral.

# A GLOSSARY
## OF THE MAIN EIGHTEENTH CENTURY SPANISH NAVAL SHIP TYPES

*Almiranta* (no exact English equivalent) – This was not a ship name but the title assigned to a warship that flew the flag of the second-in-command of a fleet. Such a ship could be a *fragata* or *navío*.

*Aviso* (English equivalent *dispatch vessel* or *packet*) – This designation is by function and not ship type, since *aviso* is the Spanish word for a 'Notice' or 'Message'. The *aviso* was a small and swift ship that carried messages between Spain and the Spanish New World and usually was a *bergantín* or *patache*.

*Azogue* (meaning mercury or quicksilver) – Not usually the name of a single type of ship, but one given to the small fleet that sailed from Spain to the New World which carried the mercury essential for refining silver from the big Peruvian and Mexican mines. An *Azogue* fleet could be composed of two to half a dozen ships of the *goleta*, *fragata* or *bergantín* type.

*Balandra* (the name is similar to the English *bilander* but the vessel is akin to a *hoy*) – A tiny flat-bottomed single-masted ship for moving supplies around a shipyard.

*Barco* – One of several terms for ships in general, more often used with merchant ships (see also *buque*, *embarcacion* and *baxel*). Despite the similarity in name, the *barco* was not the same as the later English and European *bark* or *barque*.

*Baxel* (English *vessel*) – A general term for a ship, but usually a larger one. Though it already was an archaic word in the eighteenth century, *baxel* was used nevertheless in official naval documents of that century. Also spelled *vaxel*.

*Bergantín* (related to English *brigantine*) – With fore and main mast and bowsprit; many with a poop often had a large mizzen sail in addition. About 200 tons. Because of her speed and small size, the *bergantín* often functioned as an *aviso*.

*Bombarda* (English *bomb ketch* or *bomb vessel*) – Had only fore and mizzen masts with two mortars forward port and starboard, in place of the fore mast. English bombs were ship-rigged from about 1760. Used to bombard low-lying shore positions.

*Brulote* (English *fireship*) – Expendable vessel loaded with combustibles for setting enemy ships on fire.

*Buque* (no direct English equivalent) – In wide use in documents. During the eighteenth century as today it means any type of ship or vessel, commercial and naval.

*Capitana* (English *flagship*) – Not a ship type *per se* but name given to the flagship of a Spanish naval fleet. The *capitana* could be a *fragata* or *navío*.

*Chambequin* (no English equivalent) – A *jabeque* rigged as a *fragata*.

*Corbeta* (English *corvette*) – A smaller version of the *fragata* or frigate three-masted. The *corbeta* was a Sixth Rate ship with a single gundeck, mounting up to 30 guns. It was sometimes larger than the British ship-sloop.

*Embarcación* (a curious use of the word which in English basically means what it sounds like, 'embarcation') – In Spanish documents of the period as well as personal correspondence, *embarcación* is used inter-changeably with *baxel*, *buque* and *navío* to mean a ship. Some eighteenth century state documents use the word specifically to mean *navío*, a ship of the line.

*Falucho* (no exact English equivalent but related to the word *felucca*) – A small ship that was used commercially in the coasting trade (*cabotaje*), and in coast guard defence. The *falucho* was usually identified by a fore mast inclined forward toward the prow and a small mizzen mast and sail.

*Fragata* (English *frigate*) – Three-masted full-rigged ship smaller than a *navío*, but larger than the *corbeta*. In terms of weapons, she was a Fourth or Fifth Rate carrying between 30 and 44 guns at this time, but later vessels carried more.

*Galeón* (English *galleon*) – Without doubt the most inaccurately applied ship-name in naval history. Anglo-Saxon writers have used it indiscriminately to mean almost any type of Spanish naval or commercial ship of the age of sail. During the sixteenth and seventeenth centuries, the *galeón* was indeed the major Spanish warship – for example in the Spanish Armada. However, during the eighteenth century, the type was used as a large commercial vessel. The eighteenth century *galeón* often was armed but needed the protection of Spanish Navy *navíos* in the North Atlantic and Caribbean convoys of the *Flotas* or commercial or trade fleets between Cadiz, Havana, Vera Cruz and Cartagena de Indias.

During the period of Spanish rule in the New World and the Philippines, the *galeón* was also identified specifically with the *Manila Galleon* that sailed regularly from about 1580 to 1800 between Acapulco on the west coast of Mexico and Manila. As such, the *Manila Galleon* maintained the longest-lasting trade route in history.

*Galera* (English *galley*) – Even in the eighteenth century oar- and sail-powered galleys were still in naval service but were used solely in the Mediterranean. As in earlier centuries, the *galera* also had two masts each with a lateen sail. In eighteenth century Spain, convicts still were assigned to the galleys for punishment.

*Goleta* (English *schooner*) – At this time usually a two-masted gaff rig.

*Guardacostas* (English *coast guard*) – A small armed ship, usually a *patache* or *polacra*, used for coast defence purposes in the eighteenth century for Spain's many Caribbean island colonies.

*Jabeque* (English *zebec* or *xebec*) – A three-masted ship based on Arab naval architecture, each mast having a large lateen sail. The *jabeque* was a truly ancient ship design used in the fleets of both the medieval Christian and Moslem kingdoms of Spain, and a ship most certainly known to Columbus. Incredibly, the *jabeque* continued to be built as a warship up to 1826 and was well known in the eighteenth century *Armada Española* as a smaller warship of about 200 tons, often heavily armed and carrying between 32 and 40 guns, the same number as a *corbeta* or *fragata*.

*Jabeque-bergantín* – A mix of both types usually with the square rig of the *bergantín* on fore and main masts and *jabeque*-style lateen on the mizzen.

*Navío* or *navío de línea* (English *ship of the line*) – This was the Spanish capital ship or battleship of the age of sail, three-masted with between two and three gun decks and carrying between 60 and 120 guns each. *Navíos* also were identified as First, Second and Third Rates, depending on the number of guns carried. First Rates had from 100 to 120 guns on three gun decks (*Santísima Trinidad* carried up to 144 on four gun decks, but in this was unique), Second Rates 80 to 100 guns also on three gun decks and the Third Rate with 74 to 80 guns on two decks – what was to become the ubiquitous '74-gun ship' in both the Spanish Navy and the other European navies of the mid- and late-eighteenth century.

*Navío* should not be used in an inter-changeable sense, as with *buque, barco* and *baxel*, to mean a 'ship'. When *navío* was used in eighteenth century documents and correspondence to mean a ship, it always meant a ship of the line.

*Patache* – A small fast-sailing two-masted vessel that functioned as a dispatch carrier or *aviso* for a fleet, coastal reconnoitring or as a guard ship for a naval base or commercial port.

*Polacra* (English *polacre*) – A two-masted ship with lower and topmasts in a single piece. This type of ship was often a mix of other types, with a hull similar to the *jabeque* and rig similar to that of the *goleta* or *bergantín*. Accordingly, this ship was often called a *polacra-goleta* or a *bergantín-polacra*.

*Registro* (no English equivalent) – Not the name of a special type of ship *per se*. Rather it was a merchant ship licensed by the Spanish Crown 'for a single voyage to a specified [Hispanic] American port, either on its own or in the company of other vessels' outside the *Flota*.

*Urca* (English *store ship*) – Originally of Dutch design she was often taken for a *galeón* because of her size which could be up to 750 tons, as large as a *fragata* or a *navío*. The *urca* was a cargo vessel, ungainly in design compared to a warship. From the era of the Spanish Armada into the eighteenth century the *urca* functioned as a stores and supplies vessel.

## CHAPTER ONE

# Imperial Values: Winners and Losers

*Day merges into day: the past is wide.*
*To the morrow, the morrow to the infinite*
*Men of Spain, no yesterday has died.*
*Future and past have yet no holy writ.*
Antonio Machado, *El Dios Ibero* (The Iberian God)

ON 3 MARCH 1769, the *Santísima Trinidad* (The Most Holy Trinity), the largest warship of the eighteenth century slipped gently into the warm waters of Havana harbour from her launching slip in the busy royal shipyard. She was the seventh Spanish ship to bear the name *Santísima Trinidad* since the distant era of the ill-fated Spanish Armada.

The English and the French preferred hardier warship names that spoke of courage, doughtiness and prowess at sea, though the Spanish at sea also displayed these qualities in abundance. Hence, there has been more than one *Renown* in the British Royal Navy and several *Redoutable*s in the French *Marine Royale*. By the mid-eighteenth century, only the Spanish continued to christen warships with names that implied other-worldliness, religious mysticism and a certainty that Spain could still count on God if not on great sea victories. The arrival of the *Santísima Trinidad* in 1769 was part of a surprising renewal of Spanish sea power in the century that the English-speaking world has both overlooked and underestimated.

Years later, the Royal Navy came to know the *Santísima Trinidad* as the impressive four-decker that twice eluded capture in England's two greatest eighteenth century sea battles against Spain. At Cape St Vincent on 14 February 1797, eighteen years after her launching, and again at Trafalgar on 21 October 1805, where she fought as a 36-year-old veteran, four years younger than the *Victory, Santísima Trinidad* almost, but not quite, became the chief prize of the ever-victorious Lord Nelson.

Like so many of the Spanish Navy's eighteenth century sister ships before her, it was the sea and not the British that at the last claimed *Santísima Trinidad*. Dismasted by Trafalgar's murderous cannon fire, she had surrendered but had to be sunk by her captors while under tow during the ferocious storm that followed that battle, the tempest that Nelson had predicted before the battle would wreak havoc on the British, French and Spanish fleets manoeuvring off the Spanish coast. It was the same storm, too, that denied the British so many of their Trafalgar prizes after their great victory against the Combined Squadron of the opposing Spanish and French navies.

On this warm mid-winter morning in a Havana restored to the Spanish crown after its brief, ignominious capture and occupation by the British in 1762, all eyes were on the massive ship as it slid effortlessly into the water of Havana harbour. For Spain's large colonial empire her naval captains and an effective naval administration, *Santísima Trinidad*'s launching was a positive event in Spain's centuries-long sea odyssey. Her launching was not a sign of the end of empire and the arrival of imperial decline: rather, it spoke of a new buoyancy for Spain at sea in the eighteenth century.

Comparative histories of the great European empires often define Spain's naval role as second or third best at sea. From formal studies to popular Hollywood movies about 'The Spanish Main', the Spanish as seamen, ship-handlers and administrators, too often come off as chronic losers and buffoons, ineffectually managing resources they could not control. Yet none of the many English, Dutch or French (when they were Spain's enemy) naval intrusions into the Spanish Caribbean, succeeded in bringing down the Spanish New World Empire. It lasted from the end of the sixteenth century until the early part of the nineteenth and included the continuous operations of two major commercial fleets between Spain and the Indies and a smaller locally-based Caribbean naval squadron. The two commercial fleets often needing naval escorts, were *La Flota a Nueva España*, 'The Fleet to New Spain' (modern Mexico) from Cádiz to Vera Cruz and Havana and the *Galeones a Tierra Firme y Perú*, 'The Galleons to the Continent and Peru', and later Havana. The naval squadron was the *Armada de Barlovento*, 'Windward Squadron', based in Havana or Vera Cruz depending on tactical needs.

The Manila Galleon which sailed regularly on the long Pacific Ocean voyage from Acapulco (in the eighteenth century the major west coast port of the Viceroyalty of *Nueva España*, New Spain) to Manila, capital of the Spanish Philippines, was taken only six times between 1580 and 1810 by the English enemy. The Manila Galleon transported Mexican silver to China in return for the luxury goods of Asia, with the economy of the Philippines almost entirely reliant on the cargoes of the single galleon arriving at Manila.

Sustaining these enlarged fleets and defending the vast coasts and many ports of the Spanish New World empire during the eighteenth century required up-to-date ship designs, able shipyard administrators and superior navigators, all with a sense of both continuity and change. These were stimulated and encouraged during the middle and late periods of the century by Carlos III, Spain's enlightened king who reigned from 1759 to 1788. Carlos III was an eighteenth century technocrat and modernizer. He was not the effete chief of state of a nation of incompetent 'Dons', as many English histories have derisively called Spanish leaders whom they charge failed in their missions as seamen, explorers and naval officers.

The unfortunate conclusions of such histories – that Spanish imperial institutions were naturally decadent while those of England were naturally reformist – were based to a large degree on deep-set residual biases about European Catholic societies that had survived from the religious wars of the sixteenth and seventeenth centuries. Such analyses of Catholic and Latin cultures saw them as being in various stages of political decline while those of Protestant Northern Europe were progressive and modern. The Spanish in history and in contemporary terms, call this *la leyenda negra* or 'the black legend' about Spain.

The extent to which *la leyenda negra* has survived to the present day emerged during the Falklands/Malvinas War of April-June 1982. Despite the use of missile-firing warships and aircraft, modern task forces and aircraft carriers, this was an eighteenth century-style Anglo-Spanish struggle. During that war Argentina, the successor Latin American republic to the Spanish Viceroyalty of La Plata, functioned as the surrogate 'Latin' enemy for Imperial Spain. For many in the English-speaking world, the insufferable 'Dons' of the 1780s had been replaced by the contemptible 'Argies' of the 1980s. Argentina's inherited Spanish claims to the Falkland Islands were brushed aside as historically inaccurate and irrelevant. The war of words about the Spanish-language name 'Malvinas' versus the English-language 'Falklands' which was aroused alongside the justifications for a shooting war, was reminiscent of the 'War of Jenkins' Ear', which broke out in 1739.

The former name for what in effect became another of the eighteenth century's dynastic wars was aroused by an inaccurate and highly-charged report to Parliament by one Captain Jenkins, the master of a British ship, that Spain must be punished for the atrocity committed against him in the Caribbean. Jenkins claimed that the Spanish captain who boarded his vessel, nailed him to the mast by his ear. To release him, a crew member had to sever his ear, the same one he claimed to have had in the box that he brought into Parliament.

Parliament needed little encouragement to avenge yet another atrocity by the 'cruel Dons', and at the same time to respond to the more honest English reaction for going to war, namely an excuse to break up and seize as much as possible of Spain's Caribbean empire. This, hopefully, could be done by mounting a very large expedition to storm and capture Cartagena de Indias, Spain's immense fortress and commercial centre on the north coast of South America (today the coast of Colombia). The assumption was that Cartagena was a ripe plum ready for the taking and that the Spanish would fail dismally in defending it. Britain was so certain of winning that the victory medal had been struck before the largest army and fleet ever sent by Britain to the Caribbean had set sail. How wrong the English were.

Unlike the Falklands/Malvinas War which resulted in the Argentine surrender – of islands over whose ownership the Spanish and English almost went to war as far back as 1770 – Britain did not take Cartagena. The British fleet penetrated Cartagena's defences but the army failed to storm the city and was later decimated by disease. The resourceful and wily Spanish admiral Blas de Lezo in command forced the English to withdraw without a victory. Indeed, the War of 1739–1748 saw few English naval victories in Spanish waters. The Spanish admirals, ship captains, shipbuilders and naval administrators who often were enemies of England at sea 200 years ago were men-of-the-sea whose lives were intertwined with maritime achievements that were in no way diminished by Trafalgar.

In the many sea wars and naval rivalries between England and France throughout history we have forgotten or know little about the role of Spain and the Spanish. The 'other side' in the many wars of the eighteenth century was understood to be the French, the enemy from centuries back in both land and sea warfare. Except, of course, for the Spanish Armada of 1588. Yet, many are not aware that the Spanish Navy joined the French fleet to form the *Escuadra Combinada* (the Combined Squadron) that Nelson defeated at Trafalgar.

Spain's empire and achievements at sea both reached their apogee and faced decline before those of England. Where the *Armada Española* (the Spanish Navy) was vanquished at Trafalgar, the Royal Navy had to wait until the naval disarmament treaties between the world wars formally ended its pre-eminence. In some respects the Royal Navy would hold out even longer, until the devastating losses of the *Prince of Wales* and *Repulse* off Malaya on 10 December 1941 ended forever British sea power in the Far East.

In time, all the great European empires built on sea power were to fade and die, swept away by defeats in battle or because of the rise of various nationalist and anti-colonialist movements: Latin American, African and Asian. Post-1945 Europe has witnessed the incredible and once unforeseen rise of Soviet sea power. In at least one instance, this newest of the great European naval powers has assumed a strategic role where Spain long ago held sway. Today close by the site of the royal shipyard in Havana which had become the largest and most productive Spanish naval shipyard by the mid-eighteenth century and which built some of the largest ships of the line in the age of sail, visiting Soviet warships and factory trawlers are

*(Map by Denys Baker, based on an original by the author)*

berthed alongside. Havana in the 1980s was a naval outpost of empire for the USSR as it was for Spain in the 1780s.

Spanish accomplishment lay in naval ship design and construction, not in winning sea battles, but almost overlooked were their continuous efforts at discovery and marine scientific investigations, especially in the Americas, where these were equal to or superior to similar English and French activities. Much is made in our history books of Commodore George

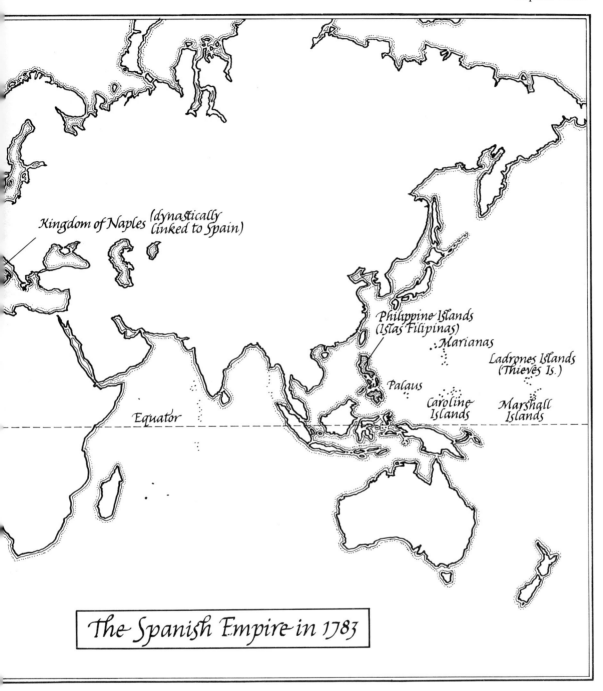

Kingdom of Naples (dynastically linked to Spain)

Philippine Islands (Islas Filipinas)

Marianas

Ladrones Islands (Thieves Is.)

Palaus

Caroline Islands

Marshall Islands

Equator

*The Spanish Empire in 1783*

Anson's circumnavigation of the world in the early 1740s, but little indeed of the equally, or perhaps more impressive global navigation and research functions of Captain Alejandro Malaspina. His two small scientifically-equipped naval vessels, at times commanded by young naval officers who would be among Trafalgar's Spanish ship captains, spent five years (1789–1794) sailing around the globe to fulfil navigational, botanical, mineral and other scientific studies, not unlike those of the much better known Captain James Cook.

HM King Carlos III, 1759–1788 (in Spanish, SM Su Majestad Carlos III El Rey – His Majesty Carlos III the King). (*From the Goya painting of Carlos III in hunting costume in the Museo del Prado, Madrid*)

Though Trafalgar wrote *finis* to the great fleet confrontations of the age of sail, the Caribbean basin continued as a cockpit of imperial struggle, like the Mediterranean during the European-Turkish wars that culminated at Lepanto in 1576. The Spanish Navy would continue to fight Berber pirates, Algerians and their privateers. However, it was in the Caribbean in the eighteenth century where both England and Spain would experience the defeats and victories which decided the future of the Spanish New World. Had the British captured Cartagena in 1741, that event might have hastened the disintegration of Spain's American empire sooner than it did, in fact, occur.

The major eighteenth century defeat for Spain in the Caribbean was the temporary British capture of Havana (1762–1763) which opened Cuba and much of the Spanish Caribbean to the concept of free trade. The British permitted ships of the world to trade with Cuba though they left intact the basic structures of Spanish government in the island, as indeed they had with French institutions in conquered Québec. Spanish victories in the region included the conquest of Florida from Britain in 1780 and defence against British privateer and Royal Navy attacks on Spanish commercial shipping by the new ships of the line that were coming from the royal shipyards.

The two most crucial sea battles of the eighteenth century period between Spain and

# DON CARLOS,

POR LA GRACIA DE DIOS,
Rey de Castilla, de Leon, de Aragon, de las dos Sicilias, de Jerusalèn, de Navarra, de Granada, de Toledo, de Valencia, de Galicia, de Mallorca, de Sevilla, de Cerdeña, de Cordova, de Corcega, de Murcia, de Jaén, de los Algarves, de Algecira, de Gibraltar, de las Islas de Canaria, de las Indias Orientales y Occidentales, Islas y Tierra-Firme del Mar Occeano, Archiduque de Austria, Duque de Borgoña, de Bravante y Milán, Conde de Abspurg, de Flandes, Tiról, y Barcelona, Señor de Vizcaya y de Molina, &c.

The full titles of Carlos III, translating as 'Don Carlos, by the Grace of God, King of Castile, of León, of Aragon, of the two Sicilies, of Jerusalem, of Navarre, of Granada, of Mallorca, of Sevilla, of Sardinia, of Cordova, of Corsica, of Murcia, of Jaén, and of the Algarves, of Algeciras, of Gibraltar, of the Canary Islands, of the West and East Indies, of the Islands and Continent of the Ocean Sea, Archduke of Austria, Duke of Burgundy, of Brabant and Milan, Count of Habsburg, of Flanders and of Tirol and Barcelona, Lord of Vizcaya and of Molina, etc.' Here, the title runs out – small wonder – since many of the above are either honorific, such as Duke of Burgundy and Count of Flanders and especially that of King of Jerusalem, or include territories over which Carlos III never ruled – most noticeably Gibraltar conquered by the English in 1704.

Curiously, the truly vast expanse of the Spanish Empire at the time of this title around 1770, is identified only by the honorific titles, 'the East and West Indies' and 'the Islands and Continent of the Ocean Sea', meaning all the stretches of the mainland and of the islands in Spanish America, (that is modern Mexico, Florida, the Southwestern USA, Central and South America, the Spanish Philippines, as well as the South Pacific island archipelagos of the Marianas, Marshalls (Ladrones) and Palaus.

England took place within miles of each other. These were the combined operations leading to the capture of Gibraltar in 1704 and Trafalgar, 101 years later. In fact, the greatest battle for the Spanish Navy in the eighteenth century, in terms of use of resources, was not Trafalgar but the colossal effort made over three years (1779–1782) by the Spanish army, navy and marines to recapture Gibraltar, an effort which ultimately failed.

Two centuries after the Spanish Armada sailed, the Spanish Empire was still the world's largest, with its zones of considerable influence in the Mediterranean and Caribbean seas, the Atlantic Ocean and, to a lesser extent, the Pacific Ocean. All of these had to be defended at one time. Therefore the biggest ongoing commitments of the Spanish Navy, by far, were the maintenance of the many vital sea lanes, both the commercial route to the Caribbean and the defence of those zones of influence, for which purposes the Spanish designed and built their warships in the eighteenth century. Added to these responsibilities for the navy between 1780 and 1800 were the greatly-increased number of scientific voyages assigned to Spanish captains and naval ships. The *Descubierta* and *Atrevida* of Alejandro Malaspina, the Sicilian sailor and aristocrat turned Spanish naval captain, were built for world-wide scientific exploration, new mappings and to support on-shore scientific explorations.

Though Carlos III was indeed the modernist who continued Spanish naval renewal, he

**Spanish Empire in America in the Late Eighteenth Century**

Viceroyalty

West and East Florida

Viceroyalty of New

Mexico

Acapulco

Vera Cruz

Spain

Havana

Captaincy General of Cuba

Santo Domingo
Puerto Rico

Boundaries of the Spanish Empire

Captaincy General of Guatemala

Viceroyalty of New Granada

Captaincy General of Venezuela

Audiencia of Santa Fe

GUIANA

Presidency of Quito

Equator

Audiencia of Lima

Lima

BRAZIL (PORTUGUESE)

PACIFIC

Presidency of Charcas

Potosi

0  200  400  600  800  1000 miles

0  400  800  1200  1600 kilometres

Viceroyalty of Peru

Audiencia of Buenos Aires

Santiago

Buenos Aires

Captaincy General of Chile

Viceroyalty of La Plata

OCEAN

SOUTH ATLANTIC OCEAN

Islas Malvinas (Falkland Islands)

*(Map by Denys Baker)*

[ 8 ]

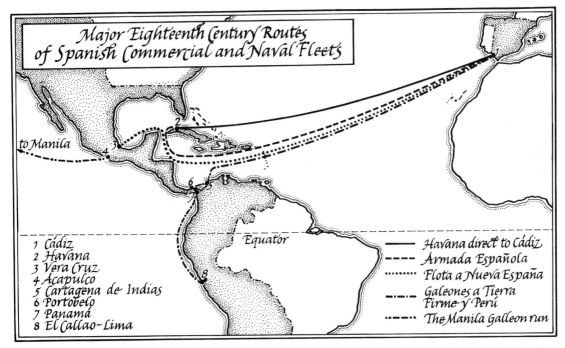

**Major Eighteenth Century Routes of Spanish Commercial and Naval Fleets**

1 Cádiz
2 Havana
3 Vera Cruz
4 Acapulco
5 Cartagena de Indias
6 Portobelo
7 Panamá
8 El Callao-Lima

to Manila

Equator

———— Havana direct to Cádiz
- - - - Armada Española
·········· Flota a Nueva España
—··—··— Galeones a Tierra Firme y Perú
—···—···— The Manila Galleon run

*(Map by Denys Baker, based on an original by the author)*

*Flota a Nueva España*, the Fleet to New Spain (Mexico), was one of the two commercial fleets of galleons that operated – with breaks – between Cádiz and Vera Cruz for two centuries ending in the 1780s. Like all western-bound fleets out of Cádiz, The *Flota*, usually leaving in May or June, had advantage of the prevailing north-east trade winds of the South Atlantic Ocean and into the Caribbean Sea. It usually joined the *Galeones* at Havana for the homeward treasure-carrying voyage. The *Flota* sailed from the 1540s until 1789 when Carlos III's free trade decree of 1778 finally killed it off, owing to foreign competition.

*Galeones a Tierra Firme y Perú* the Galleons to the Continent and Peru, usually left Cádiz in August. Unlike the Vera Cruz run, this route was not identified in documents as the *Flota*. The New World trade terminals of the *Tierra Firme* galleons were Cartagena de Indias in modern Colombia on the South American continent (hence, *terre firme*) and Portobelo with overland transport from it to Panamá to connect with the Pacafic Ocean-based commercial ships sailing to and from El Callao, the port of Lima. *Carrera de Indias*, the Indies' Run, was an important and constantly used Spanish expression of the era applying to the West Indies operations of any fleet sailing to the Caribbean. The *Galeones* were terminated in 1746 when the Spanish concentrated on developments in Venezuela and the Rio de la Plata. Towards the end of the Spanish imperial period the Crown replaced convoys with individual ships, or *registros*, that carried registered cargoes to the major Spanish American ports.

*Armada Española* Route from Cádiz to the naval base and shipyard of Havana. This was the usual – and longer route from Spain – sailing south of Santo Domingo and Jamaica and up the west coast of Cuba to Havana to avoid the shorter but perilous Florida–Bahamas Passage with its frequent bad weather as well as the traditional 'Black Hole' and shallow waters of the Bahamas region. Navy *navíos, fragatas* and *corbetas* functioned in the Indies either as convoy protection for the *Flotas* and *Tierra Firme* galleons or as part of the locally-based but small *Armada de Barlovento*, or Windward Fleet, for the protection of Spanish commerce. It came to an end in 1748 following the reduction in the convoy system.

*The Manila Galleon Run.* Operated for two centuries from 1580 to 1790 between Acapulco on Mexico's west coast and Manila, capital of the Spanish Philippines, as the longest continuous trade route in history. The basic trade flow of the Manila Galleon was Mexican silver shipped east in exchange for the fine brocades, silks and porcelain of China for both Spanish America and Spain – as well as basic goods and chattels, military and naval supplies shipped out to the Spanish colonials in the Far East.

*Havana Direct to Cadiz.* Despite its known navigational and weather dangers, both *Flota* galleons and *Armada Española* warships frequently attempted the Florida–Bahamas Passage if there were needs for urgency – in the case of the *Galeones* to meet cargo delivery dates in Cadiz as well as to ship the specie (gold and silver) as soon as possible to Spain from Mexico and Perú. Hence most of the individual New World Spanish ship losses from severe weather – and in one case during the eighteenth century of an entire fleet – took place along this passage before the fleets had reached the westerlies of the open Atlantic Ocean.

was a committed anglophobe, a reason in part for Spain's wars against England during his reign, 1759–1788. These in turn produced Spain's many lukewarm alliances with the French, the last of which at the end of this era in 1805, resulted in the disastrous Spanish involvement at Trafalgar.

The Spanish view of Trafalgar is not the French one, of a disastrous defeat at sea never to be forgotten. In Spain no continuous school of revisionist historians and unforgiving admirals has kept alive a sense of vengeance, the same one which was inculcated into successive generations of French naval officers to the present. In the mid-twentieth century, that tradition produced Admiral Jean Darlan who sooner would have surrendered his fleet in July 1940 to the victorious Germans than to have allied it with the Royal Navy. 'Glorious does not mean triumphant ...' wrote one of the leading Spanish historians of the battle, fifty years after Trafalgar in a Spanish rationale of not seeing failure in defeat.

The post-battle correspondence between Vice Admiral Ignacio María de Alava, the Spanish second-in-command at Trafalgar, and a British prisoner of war, and Admiral Collingwood is an outstanding example of the curiously close relationships which Spanish and English captains and admirals maintained after mortal combat. The Alava-Collingwood letters settled the hospitalization and inter-change of wounded English and Spanish sailors and officers.

Although defeat at Trafalgar did mean the decline of Spain's sea power, it was not the major reason by any means for the loss of most of Spanish America less than two decades later. In the Spanish New World what the Royal Navy failed to do both before and following Trafalgar – bring about the collapse of Spanish imperial power in the Americas – took place for other reasons. It was Napoleon's replacement of the Bourbon monarchy with his brother Joseph that triggered independence by removing the legitimate authority. In many of the Spanish colonies, the *criollos* or native-born leaders of Spanish stock, had to fill the vacuum. Independence became an option. The spirit of the Age of Enlightenment fuelled the move for independence as it had stimulated scientific and technological developments, some of which also had been employed in modernizing the Spanish Navy. Revolutionary ideas and not English sea power encouraged Spanish New World intellectuals and politicians to make the break with a Spain weakened by the Napoleonic invasion.

Finally, the Spanish view is that both the battle and the defeat that many of the Spanish captains predicted before Trafalgar, were imposed on them by the last of the many uneasy alliances between France and Spain, Europe's two largest and militarily most powerful Latin societies. Since Trafalgar – the last occasion when Spain and Britain fought each other – the Spanish and the British have seen the creation of separate commonwealths of nations shaped from the imperial systems of their two motherlands. For the Spanish, it is not inconsistent that they share with the British a common long view of the meaning of Trafalgar. Even at the hour of supreme victory for one and abject defeat for the other, the ultimate fate for both is that empires do not last forever.

# CHAPTER TWO

# *The Spanish Ship of the Line*

THE REBUILDING of a modern navy in the eighteenth century – literally from a new start – was unprecedented. Yet this is what Spain accomplished between 1700 and 1790. Moreover, it had to be done in a century during which Spain was more often at war than at peace, and when new ships of the line and frigates were constantly in demand to fight sea battles and protect that empire's global lines of communication.

Those Spanish historians who search for the reason for Spain's defeat at Trafalgar as other than the unparalleled fighting genius of Lord Nelson, have their own theory about a navy that built some of Europe's best warships but could not win its biggest sea battles. It is that Spain needed more than a century – and a mainly peaceful one at that – to restore her sea power to fight the British at sea on close to equal terms. Along with this reasoning goes a further theory that Spain no sooner had rebuilt her navy than a dynastic war intervened in which the existing new ships and their semi-trained crews were too soon committed to battle.

Since most wars of the eighteenth century were the result of dynastic quarrels, even the most professional of Spanish naval administrators and builders were frustrated by a course of events they could not control. In the language of modern management, Bourbon Spain during a century of great renewal and commitment, did not have enough time to create a learning curve of shipbuilding expertise, ship-handling and training to make its fleet equal to that of Britain, its chief maritime enemy in that era.

Without respite from intervening conflicts, no navy can be rebuilt quickly. With contemporary warships the most specialized ever built, the time sequence from approval of a warship design to active service for, say, a nuclear-powered submarine, can be as long as a decade. It was not so long in the eighteenth century, but the ship of the line was the most complex production unit of the pre-industrial era. A naval shipyard was the most complex gathering facility yet seen for equipment, inventory of parts, specialized manufacturing and the need for skilled manpower and management.

In his review of Dr N A M Rodger's *The Wooden World: An Anatomy of the Georgian Navy*, the novelist William Golding writes about the Royal Navy in a way that applies equally to Spain's navy of the same period:

> … The Georgian Navy was the largest industrial enterprise of its time in the world. Hundreds of ships, thousands of tons of food, tens of thousands of men had to be integrated whole over every ocean.[1]

Given the fact that Spain's eighteenth century navy had more extended roles to maintain around the world than the Royal Navy during most of the same period, the Spanish had to

Spanish frigate of 40 guns seen from the stern and running
before the wind. (*Museo Naval, Madrid*)

build a fleet that challenged but never equalled the size of the Royal Navy. In the Caribbean alone, the *Armada Española* often had to function on behalf of three distinct fleets. These were two commercial fleets and a locally-based small naval squadron. The commercial fleets were the *Flota a Nueva España*, the 'Fleet to New Spain' that operated between Cádiz and Vera Cruz (usually called simply *La Flota*, or The Fleet) and the *Galeones a Tierra Firme y Perú*, or 'Galleons to the Continent and Peru' from Cádiz to Cartagena de Indias in modern Colombia. Curiously, unlike the Vera Cruz squadron, it was rarely called *La Flota*.

Unlike the sixteenth century when the galleon functioned primarily as a warship, in the

Spanish *navío* of 112 guns seen broadside-on.

eighteenth century, a Spanish galleon was originally a cargo ship. However, the commercial galleons were often armed for self-protection since the eighteenth century Caribbean galleon usually carried the silver back to Spain from both Mexico and Peru – reaching Portobelo and then by sea to Cartagena de Indias via the overland route across the Isthmus of Panamá. However, often there were not enough *navíos* to escort these convoys, in which case *navíos* often carried specie back to Spain because as fully-armed warships, they could more easily ward off attack from marauding English and Dutch privateers and naval vessels.

The naval fleet in the Caribbean region called the *Armada de Barlovento* or 'Windward Squadron' was meant to defend both *La Flota* and the *Galeones* from attack. But at many periods during the eighteenth century when Spain was engaged in European dynastic wars, warships needed for the *Armada de Barlovento* were assigned to fleet duties in European and Mediterranean waters. The official Spanish records of the day often referred to the Caribbean fleet activities of *La Flota* and *Galeones* as the *Carrera de las Indias* or 'The Indies Run' without always specifying which fleet was indicated. In this regard, the rule-of-thumb was that 'The Indies Run' mainly referred to the trans-Atlantic movements of the two big commercial fleets and not those of the locally-based *Armada de Barlovento* .

The presence of Havana as fortress, port, point of arrival and departure for the Spanish commercial fleets as well as seat of the Spanish empire's largest overseas naval shipyard, constantly required a naval defence facility of a kind England never had to mount in the Caribbean. The same was true to a lesser degree of distant Manila which was connected to Mexico across the Pacific Ocean via the Acapulco-to-Manila galleon route. The British, by comparison, sent fleets to the Caribbean primarily in wartime.

Except for Spain, no major maritime state of the age of sail and during its imperial period – England, Holland, Sweden, Venice and France – had permitted its navy to wither away to the same extent. By the end of the seventeenth century and following one hundred years of national decline since the death of Philip II in 1598, there was no Spanish Navy.

In 1700, the French *Marine Royale* was still basking in the twilight of its largest expansion ever under the direction of Jean Colbert, Louis XIV's great administrator. According to John Robert McNeill's *Atlantic Empires of France and Spain: Louisburg and Havana, 1700–1763*, the French in the seventeenth century had built the most imposing navy Europe had yet seen. At its height it included 105 ships of the line, 358 ships in all, and 23,000 men.[2] By the beginning of the new century, Colbert's great fleet had dwindled in size. But it had not consumed the great oak forests he planted across France as a permanent source of timber supply for his monarch's fleet. To this day, many of these oaks have survived intact as sylvan monuments to one of the first European technocrats who understood the need for naval inventories.

During the century about to start, Spain too would find its own Colbert in the person of the Marqués de Ensenada, and great shipbuilders and designers, such as Antonio Gaztañeta, Jorge Juan, Gautier, Juan de Acosta and Romero y Landa, would build a large modern fleet. Although no Spanish king was to repeat Peter the Great's personal effort to learn shipbuilding, two of them, Felipe V (1700–1746) and Carlos III (1759–1788), played a central management role in Spain's naval rejuvenation during the eighteenth century. Nevertheless, it began badly for the Spanish Navy. It had disappeared as an effective force and had to be rebuilt almost from scratch.

While she remained the world's largest imperial and maritime power with colonies to be defended in Africa, Asia and the Americas, Spain had ceased building warships. At the Zorroza shipyard on the river mouth near Bilbao, the *El Salvador* and one other *navío* languished incomplete on the stocks for an astounding 14 years – 1686 to 1700 – because construction bills were not paid.

Capitán de navío Enrique Manera Regueyra, a former chief of the historical service of the Spanish Navy's general staff writes of these dismal times:

> Naval construction had suffered enormously in the dying years of the reign of Carlos II … the chief shipyards of the Cantabrian and Basque regions were in a great state of prostration as a result of the shortage of officials … delays in payments and attacks by [Spain's] enemies…

In 1700, there was no national navy, only several ineffectual 'regional fleets'. They failed utterly to defend both the Spanish Mediterranean and Bay of Biscay coasts as well as the vast

Jorge Juan y Santacilla, 1713–1773. (*Museo Naval, Madrid*)    Admiral Antonio Gaztañeta y de Iturribálzaga, 1656–1728.
(*Museo Naval, Madrid*)

and far-off maritime frontiers of Hispanic America. Where Christopher Columbus, at the dawn of Spain's imperial era, assumed the expansive title 'Admiral of the Ocean Sea' to search for unexplored oceans, 200 years later a Spanish aristocrat commanded one of Spain's regional fleets as 'Admiral of Castile'. Yet, by 1740 Spain had 46 ships of the line in service. By 1760, the second year of the reign of Carlos III, the navy's budget accounted for 18 per cent of the total expenditures of the Spanish crown. A series of naval administrators with experience as naval architects and planners designed and authorized the construction of the speedier and more seaworthy classes of *navíos* that, by the middle of the century, had aroused the interest of shipbuilders in the Royal Navy.

Before the new and much-expanded navy could be built, an infrastructure of larger *astilleros reales* (royal shipyards) had to be created. Between 1710 and 1740, the earliest technocrats and planners associated with naval renewal made do with a number of small and inadequate yards, most of them situated along the Basque coast. These included the old and small yards at Orio, La Graña, El Puntal on the Basque coast and San Feliu de Guixols in Catalonia on the Mediterranean. Before the openings of the larger modern and integrated shipyards and arsenals at Cartagena, Guarnizo (near Santander) and El Ferrol in the mid- and late-1740s, they had built a meagre 24 new *navíos*. This low and also slow production rate accounted for the Spanish need to purchase 9 *navíos* from France and Genoa in the years immediately before 1740.

Havana, which in the period 1700–1740 already had built the surprisingly large number of 33 *navíos* of between 52 and 70 guns, became the largest builder of *navíos* for the Spanish Navy during the eighteenth century. A total of 74 of the *Armada Española's* 227 *navíos* of the century were built in the distant but cost-competitive Havana *astillero real*. The new Guarnizo and El Ferrol yards that were considerably expanded later during the 1770s built another 88 *navíos*. La Carraca at Cádiz and Cartagena built 26 *navíos*. After 1740, the four smaller Basque yards and

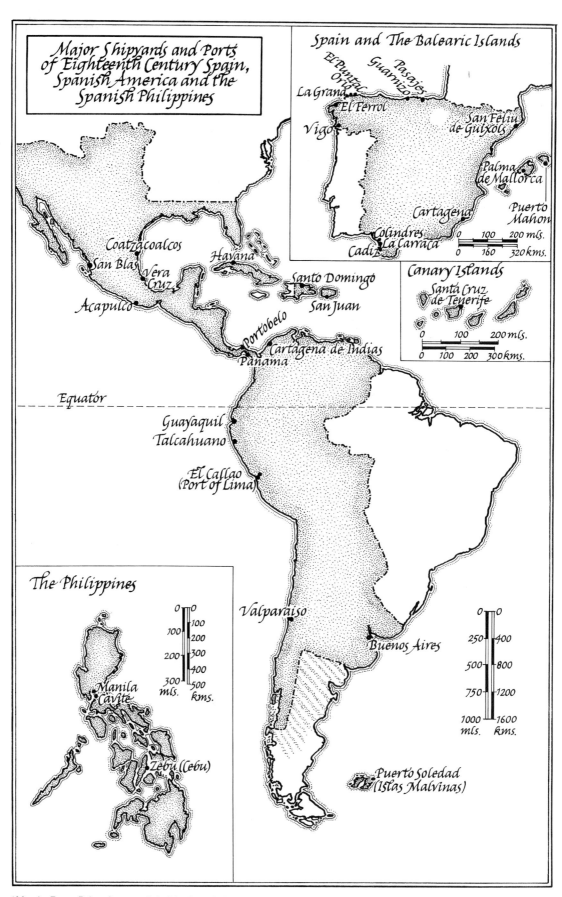

Major Shipyards and Ports of Eighteenth Century Spain, Spanish America and the Spanish Philippines

**Spain and The Balearic Islands**

El Puntal
Orio
Guarnizo
Pasajes
La Graña
El Ferrol
Vigo
San Feliu de Guixols
Palma de Mallorca
Cartagena
Puerto Mahon
Colindres
La Carraca
Cadiz
0 100 200 mls.
0 160 320 kms.

**Canary Islands**
Santa Cruz de Tenerife
0 100 200 mls.
0 100 200 300 kms.

Coatzacoalcos
San Blas
Vera Cruz
Havana
Santo Domingo
San Juan
Acapulco
Portobelo
Cartagena de Indias
Panama

Equator

Guayaquil
Talcahuano
El Callao (Port of Lima)

Valparaiso
Buenos Aires

**The Philippines**
0 0
100 100
200 200
200 300
300 400
mls. 500 kms.
Manila
Cavite
Zebu (Cebu)

0 0
250 400
500 800
750 1200
1000 1600
mls. kms.

Puerto Soledad (Islas Malvinas)

(Map by Denys Baker, from an original by the author)

### ORIGINS OF LINE OF BATTLE SHIPS IN THE EIGHTEENTH CENTURY ARMADA ESPAÑOLA

| | |
|---|---|
| Havana shipyard | 74 |
| El Ferrol shipyard | 50 |
| Cartagena shipyard | 19 |
| Guarnizo shipyard | 38 |
| La Carraca shipyard | 7 |
| Pasajes shipyard (before 1760) | 2 |
| Orio shipyard (before 1740) | 3 |
| La Graña shipyard (before 1740) | 4 |
| El Puntal shipyard (before 1740) | 2 |
| San Feliu de Guixols yard (before 1740) | 3 |
| Navíos bought in France | 4 |
| Navíos bought in Genoa | 5 |
| Other sources (see note 3) | 7 |
| Private purchases (unspecified) | 9 |
| Total | 227 |

NOTES:

[1]Output of *navíos* at the older and smaller shipyards of La Grana, Orio, Calindres and El Puntal ceased during the mid-1740s and at Pasajes in the 1750s as a result of the construction of the large and fully-integrated shipyards at El Ferrol, Guarnizo (near Santander) and La Carraca (Cadiz). San Felix de Guixols in Catalonia had also stopped production of *navíos* before 1740.

[2]Clearly, the overwhelming number of *navíos* for the eighteenth-century Spanish Navy were built in the four great Royal shipyards: El Ferrol, Cartagena, Guarnizo and Havana, which were a central part of the Spanish naval renaissance.

[3]'Others' represents a variety of sources, including two *navíos* built in Spanish America – one each at El Callao (Lima) and Coatzacoalcos (Mexico) – a further *navío* was 'gifted' by the people of Cádiz to the Navy in 1726, and one each was purchased from the Kingdom of the Two Sicilies in 1718 and Holland in 1728.

San Feliu de Guixols mentioned above built no new *navíos*. The smaller yard at Puerto Mahón in the Balearic Islands also could not build the larger *navíos* that were designed later in the century.

Havana launched its first ship, the 50-gun *Santa Rosa* in 1700 and its last, the 40-gun frigate *Anfitrite* in 1797. The *astillero real* at Havana built in all 198 naval vessels, from the giant 120-gun *Santísima Trinidad* to the tiny 12-gun *goleta* (schooner) *Nuestra Señora de Loreto*. In 1739, the Havana *astillero* also built the 70-gun *Princesa* whose single-handed action against a Royal Navy squadron of three ships during 1740, alerted the British to the high quality of Spanish ship design. After her capture she served in the Royal Navy under the same name until hulked in 1760, but was not sold until 1784.

La Carraca at Cádiz built its first *navío*, the 60-gun *Real Familia*, in 1732. Guarnizo at Santander constructed Spain's first three-decker, the pace-setting 114-gun *Real Felipe* in 1732. Guarnizo also built the second *navío* with the name *San José*. It was the 112-gun three-decker that Nelson captured in the Battle of Cape St Vincent on 14 February 1797. As the *San Josef* in the Royal Navy, she was his first flagship as a rear admiral (1800–1801). To El Ferrol goes the honour of building the long-lived 74-gun *Guerrero* in 1735. Her 89 years of continuous service until she was broken up in 1844 was probably the longest of any warship under sail.

After 1700, Spain's geographic proximity to France also became a dynastic one. From the time of the accession of Philippe Duc d'Anjou, the grandson of Louis XIV, in 1700 as King Felipe V of Spain, the two countries were linked dynastically for the rest of the century.

Indeed, it was Felipe's accession in 1700, linking the two giant European and colonial empires of France and Spain against Austria, Holland and England, that was the cause of the War of the Spanish Succession from 1701 to 1713. Spain's eighteenth century naval revival began before peace came with the Treaty of Utrecht in 1713. This revival owes much to the newly-introduced French administrative method in government as well as efficient Spanish practitioners in the navy.

A happy union of French method and Spanish managers was needed for the complete renaissance of a vanished navy. The basic evolution in the government of Bourbon Spain was the transfer of power from the councils of aristocrats that advised the Hapsburg kings, to the new specialized ministries with their teams of bureaucrats and experts. Jean Orry, an aggressive but prickly French financier and confidant of the now very old Louis XIV (more important, Orry was Colbert's pupil), was sent to Madrid to introduce the new administrative order.

Among the many new ministries created, the Ministry of the Navy and Indies was

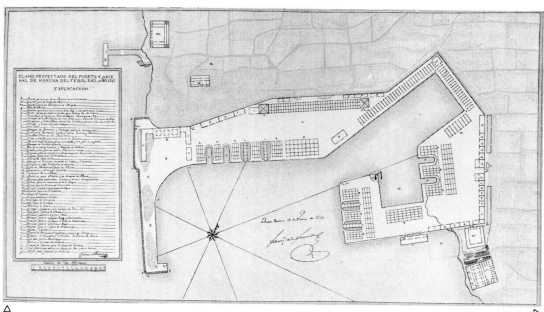

Photograph of the original plan of the Arsenal (including the shipyard) of El Ferrol, 1747, drawn by Cosmé Alvarez. (*Museo Naval, Madrid*)

Photograph of the original plan of the Arsenal (including the shipyard) of Cartagena of 7 August 1749, signed by Feringán. (*Museo Naval, Madrid*)

established in 1721. Where the navy was concerned, action to rebuild it had begun years earlier, in fact before hostilities ceased in 1713. A royal commission appointed by Felipe V in 1712 under his friend the Duque de Veragua, assigned the job of defining naval needs to Bernardo de Tinajero de la Escalera, then secretary to the old Council of the Indies.

Tinajero was the first of the able naval administrators – many of them with prior service at sea or as ship designers – who directed Spain's naval recovery during the eighteenth century. Orry early recognized Tinajero's abilities by appointing him in 1714 Secretary of the Navy independent of the Council of the Indies. In effect, Tinajero became Spain's first Minister of the Navy. Although Orry and his French planners felt the greatest need was to bolster Spain's naval defences in the Mediterranean, Tinajero emphasized the need to maintain naval strategic superiority in the Atlantic and Caribbean regions.

At a time when Spain was forced to buy its new *navíos* from foreign shipyards in France and Genoa, Tinajero recommended the following:
 – The founding and maintenance of a shipyard that could build and service large ships;
 – The use of American sources of timber from Mexico, Venezuela and Cuba;
 – Implement in new ships the naval construction theories of Admiral Antonio Gaztañeta y de Iturribálzaga, a senior Basque naval officer and naval architect born in the seaport town of Motrico in 1656, and at sea with the fleet since 1684.[3]
While Tinajero was not to stay in office long enough to introduce his own plans, they formed the basis of Spanish naval modernization when Gaztañeta became superintendent general of the shipyards in Cantabria. Long before his elevation in 1715 as shipbuilder to the king and for the navy – at that time called the *Armada Real* (Royal Navy) and not the *Armada Española* (Spanish Navy, as after 1775) – Gaztañeta already had an impressive naval service record.

The son of a naval captain, Gaztañeta was only forty-three when he was promoted and

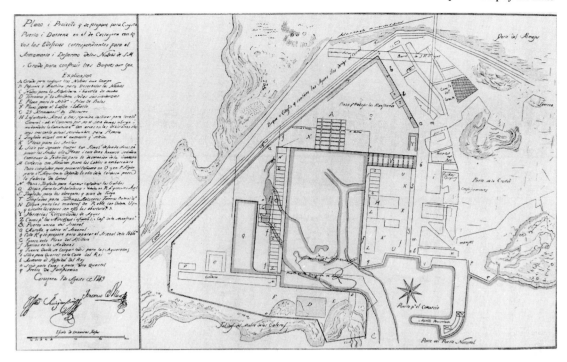

given command of the flagship *Capitana Real* with, as the record states, 'the honours of an admiral'. Prior to his promotion to captain, Gaztañeta as 'senior pilot' of the navy had written two major studies in navigation, as well as his seminal study on changes in warship construction. In 1699 a Caribbean squadron under his command dislodged a Scottish colony from its brief occupation of Darien in what is now the Republic of Panama, and he came to the influential post in the navy in 1715 that resulted in the design and construction of Spain's first new warships of the new century.

It was fortunate for the Spanish Navy that Gaztañeta's mixed career as a seagoing naval officer, administrator and naval architect was not unique. Rather, this kind of career was to be shared by many of the leading warship designers who followed after him during the rest of the century. If the Spanish were destined not to win the biggest sea battles during this century of naval rejuvenation, fate blessed their fleet and empire with a continuum of outstanding shipbuilders and naval administrators. Without them, the new navy would not have been built and Spain would not have experienced a final burst of excellence at sea before her empire succumbed to other winds – those of political change.

Despite the sharing of technology and the use of pragmatic methods in ship design and construction, shipbuilders of that period were unable to solve many of the basic problems associated with ship construction in the age of sail. Dry and wet rot and the teredo worm continued to disintegrate ships in all the European fleets until the arrival of the iron ship made wood rot in ships' hulls a thing of the past.

Some ships left the slipway better equipped than others to meet the fierce vicissitudes of ocean sailing. Where ships of one class might be too easily dismasted in a gale, others survived harsh weather undamaged. Some basic ship-handling problems, such as efficient launching methods, remained unsolved by both English and Spanish shipyards.

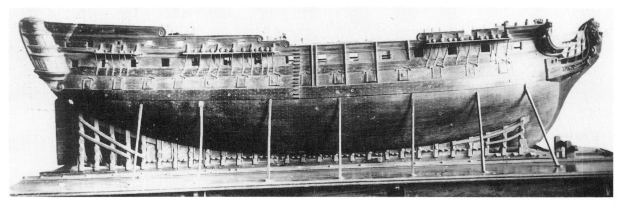

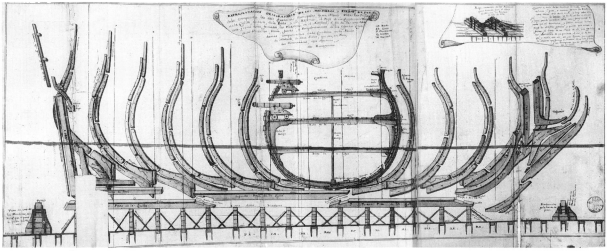

Scale model in the Museo Naval, Madrid of the hull of the *San Juan Nepomuceno*, Churruca's *navío* captured at Trafalgar and which served in the Royal Navy until 1808 as *San Juan*. (*Museo Naval, Madrid*)

The main timber components used in the construction of the hull of an eighteenth century *navío* or frigate. (*Marqués de la Victoria's Notebook*)

In his book *La Armada Española en el Siglo XVIII* (*The Spanish Navy in the Eighteenth Century*), Spanish economic historian José P Merino Navarro writes:

> The moment of entering the water ... the most dangerous during launching, produced deformities, and for this reason one hears of a sagging in the ship's hull or keel at the moment of hitting the water. It is easy to find a wide number of examples, *Newark* at Chatham in 1747 ... the *Alquilés* at Cádiz in 1754. The theme of launching, from slipway to final floatation was one of those that continued to dominate during the eighteenth century.[4]

During the eighteenth century, too, more Spanish *navíos* were lost in storms and hurricanes than were lost to the British. The ravages of disease on shore and afloat wreaked greater havoc on all the European navies of the century than either improper naval construction or fleet actions against each other. One of the greatest misjudgments made by Admiral Federico Gravina, the Spanish commander-in-chief whom Nelson would fight at Trafalgar, was not his agreement to go to sea with the French and fight that disastrous battle, but rather his indifference to the use of citrus juice in his navy. In 1793, during a rare visit to Portsmouth when the European monarchies were briefly united in war against revolutionary France, Gravina was advised by the British authorities to introduce lime juice into Spanish Navy diets as protection against scurvy. The Portsmouth naval officials knew what they were talking about. Fifty years earlier during the 1740s, only 145 of the 1955 officers and men who sailed with Commodore George Anson's squadron of eight ships to circumnavigate the globe saw England again. On-board epidemics of scurvy accounted for 1300 of his men.

As we shall discover later, both the eighteenth century Spanish ship of the line and frigate had a reputation for strength and staying power. They even survived Caribbean hurricanes. The English were aware of this fact, both from the pounding endured by Spanish *navíos* at the

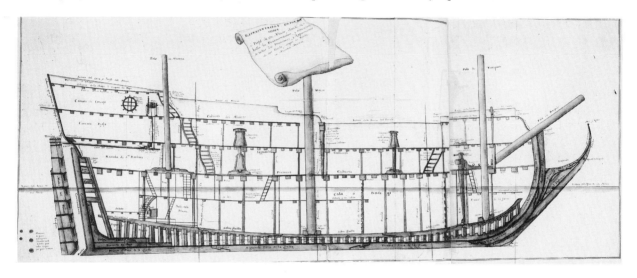

Internal profile of an early eighteenth century *navío*.
(*Marqués de la Victoria's Notebook*)

battles of Cape St Vincent in 1797 and Trafalgar in 1805 and the longevity of the prizes captured during these struggles.

How was the eighteenth century *navío* constructed? The techniques adopted by the Spanish were similar to those employed by other European powers. The backbone of the wooden ship's skeleton was the keel and the keelson, a supporting structure built above the keel to strengthen the surrounding framework. The keelson extended between the stem in the bow and the stern. Frames or ribs of the ship's skeleton were attached to the keel, and the entire structure was locked together with various kinds of planking both inside and outside the skeleton. The planking included wales – large timbers girding the skeleton around the frames – and transverse deck beams which fastened the frames on one side of the ship to their counterparts on the other side. The framework was held together by 'tree nails' or trunnels that were long dowels (not unlike steel nails as we understand them) as well as by bolts of wrought iron, all of which were made on site in the royal shipyards. In the largest *navíos*, such as *Príncipe de Asturias*, *Santísima Trinidad* or *Santa Ana*, the iron bolts measured up to 6 feet long. The bolts were driven through bored holes in the timber and held tight by iron or wooden nuts. As construction proceeded on the ship, sails were sewn by hand from flax canvas and hemp woven

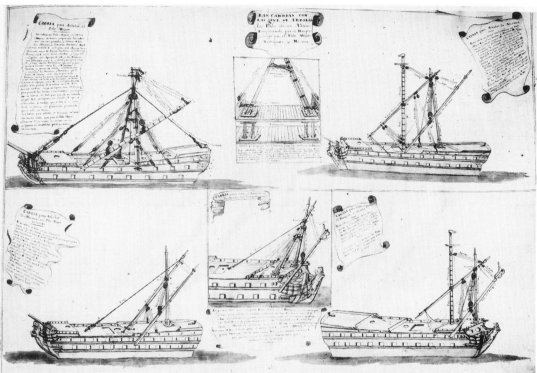

into rigging and lines that would guy the masts and secure the sails.

The most important factor was how the entire structure would work together at sea. The effect of constantly changing stresses from wind and waves on thousands of pieces of timber held together by wooden pegs and iron bolts was to make the *navío*, much more than today's sailing ship, a system under constant adjustment by the captain and crew. The *navío* creaked, groaned, splashed and heaved its way through the world's oceans in a manner no longer experienced by seafarers. Even those who sail today's tall ships enjoy the comparative rigidity of a steel hull.

◁ Representation of a frigate's hull under construction in a shipyard. (*Marqués de la Victoria's Notebook*)

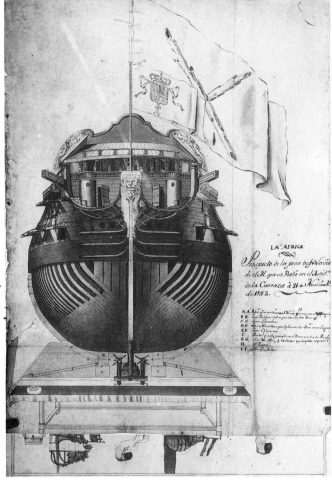

*Navío Africa*: 'Prospect of the bow of a *Navío* of His Majesty ▷ that was launched at the shipyard of La Carraca (Cadiz), 21 November 1752.' The *Africa* lasted until her breaking up fifty-seven years later. (*Marqués de la Victoria's Notebook*)

◁ Raising the masts in a new *navío*. (*Marqués de la Victoria's Notebook*)

The amount of wood consumed in the construction of warships was immense. About 3000 trees, each with a yield of 600 board-feet, were needed to build the 74-gun Third Rate warship, the workhorse of the mid-eighteenth century European navy. Merino estimates that during the eighteenth century, Spain's navy consumed three million trees. This is the equivalent of two million cubic metres of timber or about 65,000 hectares of forest. Pine for the masts and yards on which sails were rigged was grown largely in what is modern Mexico, or was imported from the Baltic monarchies. As many as 40 pine trees were needed to make the 22 yards and masts in a single Third Rate three-masted (fore, main and mizzen) warship. Where the other European navies relied almost entirely on oak and beech from quickly-depleting forests for ships' hulls, the Spanish had unlimited supplies of the longer-lasting mahogany and teak from Cuba and Central America in their New World empire.

One of the most effective developments in European navies, including the Spanish, was the movement towards ship design standardization, that was first used by the English as far back as the first Anglo-Dutch War of 1652–54. By the 1770s, standardization was well-advanced in Spain, having been introduced forty years earlier in the naval designs of Gaztañeta's first *navíos*. Naval ships were grouped into six major rates and then into classes, and ships within each class were constructed according to common architectural drawings. Designs for ships of differing

## SPANISH NAVY AS OF 24 MARCH 1794

| Ships of the line | | Armed | Disarmed | Total | | Armed | Disarmed | Total |
|---|---|---|---|---|---|---|---|---|
| Ships of the line | 80–112 guns | 14 | 6 | 20 | Cargo Vessels | | | |
| | 68–74 guns | 39 | 11 | 50 | Hookers | 10 | 3 | 13 |
| | 54–64 guns | 8 | 1 | 9 | Packets | 4 | 0 | 4 |
| | | 61 | 18 | 79 | Brigs | 13 | 2 | 15 |
| Frigates | 40–42 guns | 5 | 1 | 6 | Bilanders | 4 | 1 | 5 |
| | 30–36 guns | 39 | 8 | 47 | Schooners | 8 | 0 | 8 |
| | | 44 | 9 | 53 | Tenders | 1 | 2 | 3 |
| Minor Warships | | | | | Galliots | 3 | 0 | 3 |
| Xebecs | 14–36 guns | 5 | 5 | 10 | | 43 | 8 | 51 |
| Corvettes | 30 guns | 2 | 0 | 2 | Total Naval Vessels | 187 | 48 | 235 |
| Sloops | 18–22 guns | 6 | 1 | 7 | | | | |
| Luggers | 16 guns | 1 | 0 | 1 | | | | |
| Packets | 16 guns | 2 | 0 | 2 | | | | |
| Brigs | 8–24 guns | 21 | 0 | 21 | | | | |
| Bilanders | 12–18 guns | 2 | 0 | 2 | | | | |
| Galleys | 3 guns | 0 | 7 | 7 | | | | |
| | | 39 | 13 | 52 | | | | |
| Total warships | | 144 | 40 | 184 | | | | |

Sources: Archivo General de Indias, (General Archive of the Indies) Sevilla in papers of the Consulados (Tribunals) Legajo (Bundle) No 53. This table first appeared in Dr Jacques Barbier, 'Indies Revenue and Naval Spending: Cost of Colonialism for the Spanish Bourbons, 1763–1805' in *Jahrbuch für Geschichte von Staat Wirtschaft und Gesellschaft Latinamerikas*, Köln (Cologne) Vol 21, 1984.

rates called for similar hulls, structure and sail patterns, although to different sizes. The result was a dramatic increase in the efficiency of the shipyard at a time when Spain needed a quickly expanding fleet of new ships to defend a vast empire in its protracted sea wars against Britain.

The rate classification was based primarily on the number of gun decks in a ship and the number of guns on board. The First Rate *navíos* with three decks were the largest warships and carried the most artillery – from 100 to 120 guns. However, *Santísima Trinidad*, originally of 120 guns, had a fourth gun deck added near the end of her career, allowing her to mount 136–144 guns and making her the largest *navío* in history.

Second Rates carried 80 to 98 guns on three gun decks, although some two-decker 80s were built. Third rates usually carried 74 guns on two gun decks. Fourth Rates carried between 50 and 60 guns on two decks. Indeed at the beginning of the eighteenth century, the 60-gun ship was the standard *navío* in the emerging Spanish Navy. Spain's first three-decker, the 114-gun *Real Felipe*, was built in 1732. Fifth Rates carried between 32 and 44 guns originally on two but later on a single gun deck, and Sixth Rates between 20 and 28 guns on one deck.[5]

Central to the hull design and stability of the wooden warship was the number of guns it carried and where they were placed. The heavier and more numerous the guns and the higher in the ship they were carried, the greater the detriment to stability. Hence, all the navies always placed the largest guns on the lower deck. This kept the centre of gravity as low as possible in relation to the metacentre (centre of buoyancy). The distance between the centre of gravity and the metacentre was the righting arm that makes for a ship's stability. As a further aid to stability, an accepted international practice from the sixteenth century onward required the building of 'tumblehome' into the ship's hull. Tumblehome meant narrowing the topsides above the normal beam (or width), thus building relatively narrow upper decks. This produced a superstructure with a reasonably low centre of gravity.

Since the standard cannon ball was solid iron and not explosive, a great number of hits had to be made to overwhelm an enemy ship of equal force. Therefore, an enormous number of guns had to be carried, most of them made of cast iron. The largest gun in an eighteenth century three-decker was one of the most effective killing and wrecking weapons in the history of sea warfare. The lowest gun deck of the largest Spanish three-deckers such as *Santísima Trinidad*, *San José* and *Santa Ana* carried 30 guns, 15 on either side, each capable of firing a 32-pound shot. A 32-pound cannon ball could penetrate two feet of oak at 3300 feet and occasionally hit a target a mile and a half away. A single broadside from an eighteenth century three-decker could send as much as half a ton of metal into an enemy ship.

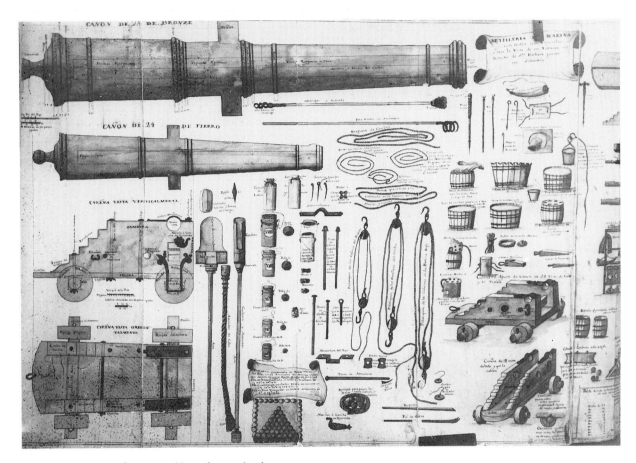

Spanish 24-pounders of bronze and iron, the associated gun carriage, and equipment for loading, firing, and swabbing out the guns. (*Museo Naval, Madrid*)

The firepower of the eighteenth century warship was most effective at point-blank range. When a ship of the line fired its 32-pounders in sequence from bow to stern as it manoeuvred into position ahead or astern of an enemy ship, the first gun facing the enemy bore on the target, following which all the gun crews on one side were ordered by the lieutenant on the deck to 'fire as you bear'. One gun after another was aimed at the same angle through each gunport. The shot could clear the opposing deck of gunners, unseat the heavy cannon and send thousands of wood splinters flying around the deck, each splinter a lethal weapon in its own right. Often because of so much smoke let loose in the gun deck, the gunlayer had to be quick to get the elevation before he no longer could see the target through the smoke. At such close quarters in actions of this kind and with gun decks only six feet high, the compressed roar of the firing caused permanent deafness among the ships' crews. Gun crew members were often badly mangled or killed when they were caught under a recoiling gun which they could not see through the dense fumes.

Despite such formidable firepower in all the European navies of the day, the ships of the line themselves were able to withstand hours of battle at close range. *Santísima Trinidad*, for example, served as a Spanish flagship during the long Spanish blockade of Gibraltar between 1779 and 1782, and fought at Cape St Vincent in 1797 and Trafalgar eight years later, where she survived considerable damage only to be lost in the storm which followed the battle.

Ballast in the largest ships, chiefly in the First Rates, made up a proportionately greater part of the weight of a ship than in a Sixth Rate. The book *El Buque en la Armada Española* (*The Ship in the Spanish Navy*) breaks down the *navío*'s 'distribution of weight elements' into the following percentages:

| | | | |
|---|---|---|---|
| Hull | 61.3 | Provisions, 3 months | 10.2 |
| Masts and rigging | 3.0 | Officers and crew | 1.8 |
| Guns | 8.9 | Ballast | 11.2 |
| Ship's boats, cutter | 3.6 | *Total* | *100.0*[6] |

To this day, the exact tonnages and lengths of eighteenth century Spanish warships remain in dispute. This is because at that time tonnages were not based on a ship's displacement in the water but on measurement of length between perpendiculars, beam and depth of hold. One of the official guidebooks on the *Victory* sold at HM Naval Base Portsmouth, lists her displacement tonnage at 3500. On this basis, *Santísima Trinidad* with a fourth full deck, probably had a displacement of over 4000 tons.

The key words in Spanish for assessment of tonnage and length are *eslora* (length on the deck from stem to sternpost), *manga* (extreme breadth of a ship) and *puntal* (depth of the hold). The Spanish usually measured a *navío*'s overall length from stem to stern at the level of the first deck (*eslora*). The French, on the other hand, made the same measurement from both the *eslora* and the waterline or often from the first battery. Since the Spanish were to borrow heavily from French warship design at certain periods during the century, a *navío*'s length could be determined from either the Spanish or French definitions of shipbuilding. There also was a period of English influence on the design of the Spanish *navío*. Vessels built in the 'English era' probably conformed to the more rigid British Admiralty instructions called 'Establishments' that set fixed dimensions for all naval vessels. McNeill says 'no fewer than five systems of proportions were used between 1722 and 1797, and since many [Spanish] warships were built in private yards or purchased abroad, the recommended dimensions did not always apply.' According to Gaztañeta's *Ordenanza* (Ordinance) of 1720, Fourth Rates were to measure 990 tons by calculation.[7] However, the *San Fernando*, launched in 1727 with 62 guns (the first *navío* built at Guarnizo), actually displaced 1560 tons. Although the arrival and later expansion of the Bourbon bureaucracy meant heavily-regulated Spanish shipyards, the Spanish, with typical indifference to the rules, often discarded their own guidelines or experimented with individual ship designs.[8]

From keel to upper deck a Spanish three-decker *navío* was as tall as an amply built five-

SPANISH LANGUAGE VOCABULARY FOR THE EQUIPMENT OF THE EIGHTEENTH CENTURY
*NAVÍO* OR SHIP OF THE LINE.

A – flying jib – foque volante o patifoque
B – jib – foque
C – fore topmast staysail – contra foque o trinquetilla
D – spritsail topsail – sobre cebadera
E – spritsail – cebadera
F – fore royal – sobre juanete e proa
G – fore topgallant sail – vela de juanete
H – fore topsail – vela de velacho
I – fore course or fore sail – vela de trinquete
J – main topgallant staysail – vela de juanete mayor
K – middle staysail – estay mayor
L – main topmast staysail – vela de estay y gavia
M – main staysail – vela de estay mayor
N – main royal – sobre juanete mayor
O – main topgallant sail – vela el penguito
P – main topsail – gavia
Q – main course or main sail – vela mayor
R – mizzen topgallant staysail – vela el penguito
S – mizzen topmast staysail – vela de estay de mastelero mesana
T – mizzen staysail – estay e mesana
U – mizzen topgallant sail – juanete de sobre mesana
V – mizzen topsail – sobre mesana
W – mizzen sail – mesana cangreja

1 – jib – foque
2 – bowsprit – bauprés
3 – fore mast – palo del trinquete
4 – main mast – palo mayor
5 – mizzen mast – palo de mesana
6 – topmast – mastelero
7 – topgallant mast – juanete
8 – stern – popa
9 – sheets – escotas
10 – hull – casco
11 – figurehead – figura

12 – yard – verga
13 – stem – proa
14 – waist – combés
15 – rudder – timón

Ship's Measurements
*eslora* – length on the deck from stem to sternpost
*manga* – extreme breadth of ship
*puntal* – depth of the hold

storey building. Hence, the now timeless expression for its English contemporaries as 'wooden walls' applied equally to the Spanish ones. Above the bilge in the typical First Rate of the day was the main hold, and above that was the orlop (or the overlap) deck. The three main gun decks, simply designated as lower, middle and upper were built above the orlop. In battle the orlop was the safest deck in the *navío*. Consequently it housed the surgeon's facilities for treating wounds and performing the many crude amputations necessary during bloody sea battles. The orlop also could house a charging magazine that stored pre-measured and ready-to-use powder charges for the guns.

In addition to the guns, the middle and upper gun decks included most of the truly meagre living quarters allotted to the crew. Eighteenth century warships were appallingly overcrowded because of the number of hands needed to man the many guns, work the miles of rigging, and handle the sails. Spanish *navíos* often were more overcrowded than English warships because Spanish naval tactics called for a large number of marines on board. This gave rise to a frequently unmanageable mix of landlubbers and professional sailors. At Trafalgar *Santísima Trinidad* was heavily overmanned with more than 1000 sailors and marines; *Victory* was crowded enough with more than 800 aboard. About a fifth of these were Royal Marines and the remainder aboard *Victory* were – in theory at least – professional sailors.

[ *27* ]

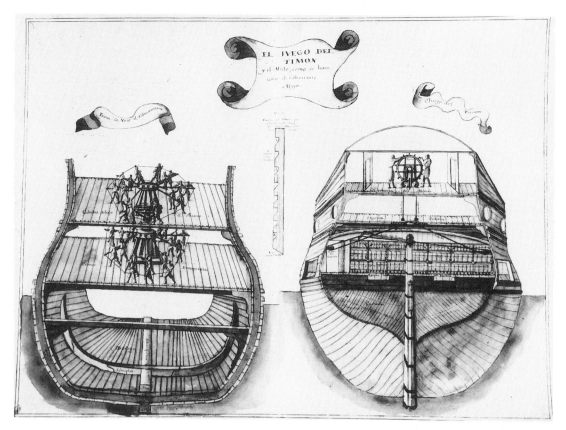

Capstan and rudder arrangements in the eighteenth century
*navío.* (*Marqués de la Victoria's Notebook*)

Large crews were necessary even in peacetime since almost all the work of running a ship was performed by hand. Before the start of a voyage everything on board, including the ship's stores, provisions, ammunition and even the heaviest cannon, had to be manhandled into position. When the ship was under way, sailors were constantly sent aloft to unfurl, furl or (in stormy weather) reef the many sails. Pumps mounted on the middle gun deck (in the larger *navíos*) to keep the water in the bilges at a safe level were operated by hand. During battle, additional pumps were kept running to put out fires and to wash blood and detached limbs off the decks.

Arrangements of blocks and tackles lightened the load somewhat, and manually-operated capstans weighed the anchors and handled the ship's boats. That the Spanish built sound, seaworthy and even beautiful ships there is no doubt. Vice Admiral Lord Collingwood called the three-decker *Santa Ana* that he fought at Trafalgar 'a Spanish perfection'. The preference shown by Royal Navy captains to command Spanish prizes before English-built ships is well-documented during the century.

The Spanish did not rebuild their eighteenth century navy in limbo nor without liberal amounts of what we today call 'transfers of technology'. The role of British artisans, master carpenters and shipwrights – in two cases the contributions of a father and son – was an important aspect of Spanish naval renewal in the middle of the century. How such artisans worked within a bureaucratic system largely borrowed from the French model but with senior Spanish administrators in charge, is a revealing part of the naval rejuvenation in Spain.

Despite the many British calumnies directed against Spanish maritime institutions over the centuries, her naval and maritime needs were never lost on appropriate English commercial interests. Michael Lewis has revealed to us in his definitive study, *The Guns of the Spanish Armada*, that about ten per cent of the Armada's cannon were English-made.

## PHASE I: GAZTAÑETA AND PATIÑO, 1710–1736

Admiral Antonio Gaztañeta y de Iturribálzaga was the father of scientific naval construction in Spain. His designs influenced Spanish naval shipbuilding until well past the middle of the century. The so-called 'Gaztañeta school' produced some of Spain's best warships of the age of sail. As we have noticed earlier, Gaztañeta came to his new assignment – literally to build a new Spanish Navy – with much previous experience both as a seagoing ship and fleet commander and naval architect. Although he did not hold the title, he was in modern bureaucratic parlance, Spain's first 'Director of Naval Construction'.

As such, Gaztañeta not only broke with prescribed warship design as developed by Captain Francisco Antonio Garrote, a late seventeenth century naval designer, but proposed a new *navío* to meet specific Spanish imperial needs. Garrote, in his design study of 1691 *Summary for the New Construction of Spanish Vessels* (*Recopilación Para la Nueva Fábrica de Vaxeles Españoles*), expounded the concept that a warship basically was an armed merchantman and the key design element must be the *manga*, or width at the waterline. By emphasizing width, Garrote was thinking of cargo-carrying capacity in terms of the maximum displaced cubic volume in the hull. Understandably Garrote's ships were also stable gun platforms, but they were slow and lacked manoeuvrability.

Gaztañeta, on the other hand, in his later naval architectural work of 1720 *Proportions for the Most Essential Measures for the Construction of Navíos and Frigates of War* (*Proporciones de Las Medidas más Esenciales . . . Para la Fábrica de los Navíos y Fragatas de Guerra*) proposed a new type of warship. This was his 60-gun *navío* of the *San Fernando* class. In the design of the *San Fernandos*, Gaztañeta determined that speed, manoeuvrability and gunnery were much better served by concentrating on the *eslora* or length of the first full deck, usually the lowest gun deck. In his superb study of eighteenth century shipbuilding at the *astillero real* (royal shipyard) in Havana, G Douglas Inglis goes so far as to say: 'Gaztañeta drew plans for slimmer, more streamlined hulls, plans whose influence was evident in [Spanish] warship construction until the advent of the screw for propulsion.'[9]

At the same time, the 60-gun *navío* was not built to fight in traditional fleet battles. Rather, it was designed and built for those ongoing needs peculiar to Spain, such as convoy protection for *La Flota* and the Cartagena Galleons of cargo and treasure ships that moved between Spain and the major Spanish American trading ports, as well as for the mercury fleets whose valuable cargoes were needed to refine the huge amounts of silver coming from the mines of Mexico and Peru. Indeed, *La Flota* had been temporarily terminated sixty years earlier, in part because Spain did not have warships of this type to protect it during the long passages back and forth across the Atlantic Ocean and into a pirate-infested Caribbean. Spain also needed fast warships for regular patrol duties in the New World as well as to carry messages and documents between the motherland and the senior administrators in the Hispanic-American viceroyalties.

Gaztañeta's 60-gun ships were more lightly armed than most English and French ships under construction and in service at the same time, a development that, unfortunately and unfairly, proved disastrous for Spain. A standard Gaztañeta 60-gun *navío* measured about 1000

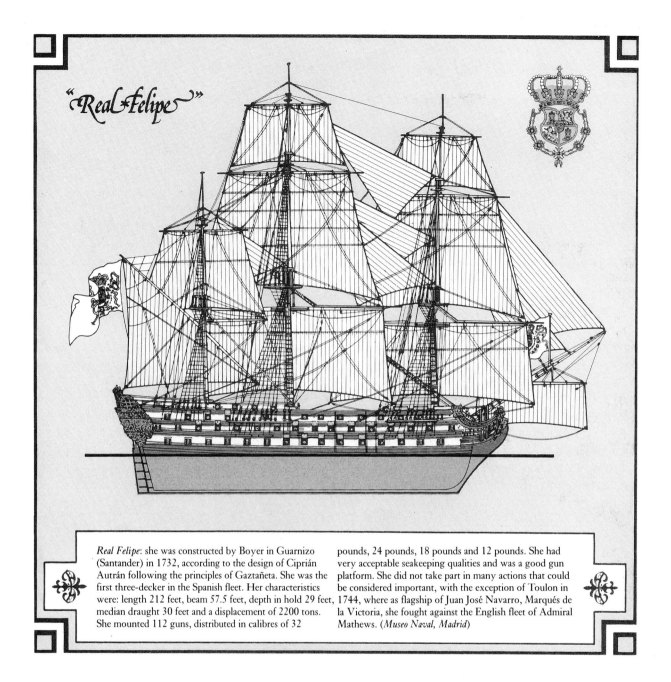

"Real Felipe"

Real Felipe: she was constructed by Boyer in Guarnizo (Santander) in 1732, according to the design of Ciprián Autrán following the principles of Gaztañeta. She was the first three-decker in the Spanish fleet. Her characteristics were: length 212 feet, beam 57.5 feet, depth in hold 29 feet, median draught 30 feet and a displacement of 2200 tons. She mounted 112 guns, distributed in calibres of 32 pounds, 24 pounds, 18 pounds and 12 pounds. She had very acceptable seakeeping qualities and was a good gun platform. She did not take part in many actions that could be considered important, with the exception of Toulon in 1744, where as flagship of Juan José Navarro, Marqués de la Victoria, she fought against the English fleet of Admiral Mathews. (*Museo Naval, Madrid*)

tons and carried twenty-four 18-pounders on the first gun deck, twenty-six 12-pounders on the second gun deck, and ten small 6-pounders positioned on the forecastle and quarterdeck. Such lightly-armed *navíos* clearly were not meant to engage in a major naval battle with the more powerful 70- to 90-gun British ships of the line. Yet the fate of Gaztañeta's new and promising navy was to be wiped out by a superior British fleet before the ship's crews had time to work up their new ships. It was a fate that Spain's navy would endure more than once during the eighteenth century, when yet another European dynastic war involved the Spanish Navy undergoing expansion and before it was ready to fight.

Gaztañeta experienced an even grimmer fate, one that was unique in modern naval history. He both commanded and lost the fleet he had designed and built, in a conclusive naval action

A profile of the *Real Felipe*, from a large manuscript original in the Library of the Ministry of the Navy. (*Museo Naval, Madrid*)

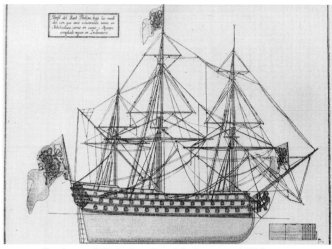

that took place before war had been declared between Spain and Britain. On 11 August 1718 most of the twenty-two ships in the Spanish fleet were destroyed or captured by a British fleet of the same number of ships under the command of Admiral George Byng, Lord Torrington, off Cape Passaro on the south-east coast of Sicily. Naval historians of the English-speaking world usually give short shrift to the Cape Passaro action by writing off the calamitous Spanish defeat as one to be expected from a country in a long decay. For example, in his classic work *The Influence of Sea Power upon History*, Alfred Thayer Mahan calls the Cape Passaro battle 'the engagement which can scarcely be called a battle'.[10] A comparison of the total firepower of both fleets follows:

*Fleet of Gaztañeta*

| | |
|---|---|
| 2 *navíos* of 70 guns each | 3 frigates of 40 guns |
| 7 *navíos* of 60 guns | 2 frigates of 30 guns |
| 4 *navíos* of 50 guns | 3 frigates of 26 guns |

The remaining ships were 1 smaller *embarcación* of 14 guns, 7 galleys, 4 *balandras* (small single-masted arsenal guard ships), and two fireships.

*Fleet of Admiral Byng*

| | |
|---|---|
| 1 ship of the line of 90 guns | 7 ships of the line of 60 guns |
| 2 ships of the line of 80 guns | 2 ships of the line of 50 guns |
| 8 ships of the line of 70 guns | 2 frigates of 24 guns [11] |

The Spanish scholar Pablo Emilio Pérez-Mallaina Bueno, in a study for the School of Hispanic-American Studies at Seville, commented on the result of Cape Passaro:

> Nevertheless, the principal defect of the Spanish Navy was that the unique nucleus of its forces was not conceived to confront a squadron of ships of the line, but to protect the merchant vessels of the *Carrera de las Indias* (the Indies run).[12]

The number of ships available to defend the empire's trade and lifelines was severely reduced after Cape Passaro. A document in the Simancas archives dated 19 December 1719 entitled

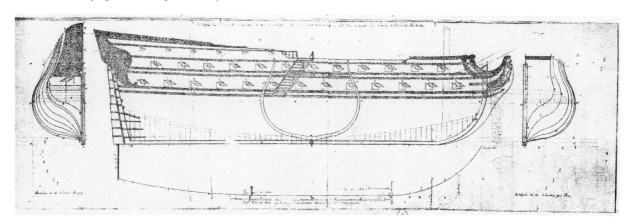

'The Status of *Navíos* in the King's Possession, Guns on Board and their Disposition', lists the locations of the remaining ships. This included one ship at Cádiz, the 60-gun *Cambí*, a Gaztañeta-designed *navío*; four at Santander in the north '... with orders to proceed to Cadiz...'; a 52-gun *navío* at Barcelona 'bought from Venice'; six at Sicily; four at Vera Cruz in Mexico, including the Gaztañeta-designed 60-gun *San Luís* that had survived the Cape Passaro battle. Other remaining *navíos* allocated included the *San Jorge* at Vera Cruz assigned to anti-pirate activities; three at Havana committed to 'transporting tobacco'; six at Callao, the port of Lima in Peru; for a slim total of twenty-six ships of the line to defend what still was the world's largest colonial empire.

From the viewpoint of Spanish history, however, the appearance in August 1718 of Gaztañeta's fleet plus 340 transports with 33,000 troops on board that re-captured Sicily for the Spanish crown, was part of an unexpected burst of military power that Spain exercised after the end of the War of the Spanish Succession in 1713. Where Gaztañeta had built a fleet to meet the defensive needs of Spain in the New World, the dynamic Cardinal Julio Alberoni, chief minister to Felipe V, used Spain's new military power, including the fledgling fleet, for the offensive policy of recovering Spain's lost Italian territories. Alberoni, a gardener's son born in the Duchy of Parma in 1664, came almost too late in time to be called a Renaissance man. Yet he was a priest, scholar, administrator, superb politician, and chef, the latter talent winning him the support of the powerful French Maréchal Vendôme, himself a great gastronome. Of Alberoni, who also was fluent in French, Vendôme once said that he prepared the best macaroni he had ever tasted in his life! When Vendôme died in 1712, the very old Louis XIV shipped off Alberoni to Madrid as an adviser to Felipe V.

Initially Alberoni met with great success in his Italian policy. In the fall of 1717, an earlier but smaller Spanish squadron of warships and 9000 troops completed the conquest of Sardinia. In the end, after a British declaration of war against Spain on 27 December 1719, Alberoni was not able to hold on to these conquests. A European alliance against Spain and the British naval intervention brought about a Spanish withdrawal from the two large Mediterranean islands of Sardinia and Sicily and Alberoni's dismissal.

In 1733, Spain did conquer Naples and Sicily during another dynastic war against the Austrian empire. Carlos, the second son of the Spanish King Ferdinand VI, was proclaimed King of the Bourbon Kingdom of the Two Sicilies. He returned to Spain in 1759 to succeed his father. As Carlos III (1759–1788) he initiated the Spanish eighteenth century Age of

Original body plan (with stem and stern profiles) of the 60-gun ships designed by Gaztañeta as the first *navíos* built in series in Spain. They formed the basis of Spain's first eighteenth century fleet under Bernardo de Tinajero, the first Spanish Minister of the Navy. The sheer plan is the original draught for the *San Luis*, one of this class built at Cantabria in 1717: she mounted twenty-six 28-pounders on the first deck, twenty-six 12-pounders on the second deck and eight 6-pounders on the quarterdeck. Her characteristics were: length 141 feet, beam 37 feet, depth in hold 18 feet. She measured 832 tons and carried a crew of 380. She was one of the many of her class that fought at Cape Passaro in 1718 where most of them were lost in that disastrous defeat. Though she survived that battle, her end came when wrecked in Spanish America in 1720. (*General Archive of the Indies, Sevilla*)

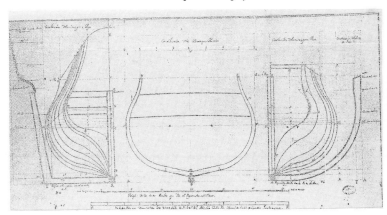

Enlightenment, which included the expansion of Spanish sea power and continued modernization of the Spanish Navy.

The disaster off Cape Passaro did not lead to another naval decline but rather to a fresh surge of building a new navy and in effect the continuation of Gaztañeta's basic designs until the emergence of Jorge Juan in the 1740s. The impetus for rebuilding the navy for a second time so early in the century lies with Jorge Patiño, Intendant of the Navy. Like Alberoni who appointed him to that post in 1717, Patiño was of humble origin, Italian-born like Alberoni but of Spanish parents from Galicia. Born in Milan in 1666, Patiño planned to become a Jesuit but abandoned the novitiate to enter government service. As early as 1711 he was superintendent of the army in Extramadura province. Vigour as an administrator and competence as an organizer marked Patiño's career until his death in 1736, when he was appointed posthumously a marqués of the realm.

If Gaztañeta was the father of modern naval shipbuilding method in Spain, Patiño was the father of the modern Spanish Navy. During his first two years as intendant of the fleet, Patiño founded the Spanish Marine Infantry (Royal Company of Marine Guards) in 1717 as well as schools for marines at Cádiz and for engineers and artillery at Barcelona. Patiño's choices for shipyard expansion by-passed the older Basque shipyards on the coasts of Vizcaya and Guipúzcoa provinces because of their vulnerability to enemy attack in the wars between 1701 and 1720. More than once, such yards had been occupied by Spain's enemies, who burned ships under construction on the stocks. Such attacks had taken place in 1712 during the War of the Spanish Succession and again in 1719. Patiño chose Guarnizo as the leading shipyard in the Basque region because its location at the mouth of the river at Santander could easily be defended. In 1722 he recalled Gaztañeta from sea duty to take charge of Guarnizo as well as to function as director of his new shipbuilding programme on the understanding that Patiño would accept the admiral's designs.

In the twenty years of his administration Patiño was in charge of the construction of 58 *navíos* and 9 frigates. Most of this construction took place at Guarnizo (22 *navíos* and 2 frigates) and at Havana (36 *navíos* and 7 frigates). On the orders of Alberoni, Patiño in 1717 had organized, supplied and despatched the two fleets and sizable armies that captured Sardinia that year and Sicily the following year. Given the devastating loss of *navíos* at Cape Passaro, Patiño's main task for the navy during the 1720s and early 1730s was to build another new fleet; in this he succeeded. Spain had a mere 22 ships of the line in 1722, but over 50 in the water by 1736, the year of his death. Many of these were of the 60-gun class initiated by Gaztañeta, since the basic defence needs of the empire had not changed. These were to protect the commercial fleets moving across the Atlantic and to defend the sea entrances to the Spanish Caribbean as naval units assigned to the *Armada de Barlovento*.

Building *navíos* solely for the needs in the New World was not enough. Two grievances from the wars of 1700–1719 rankled with Spanish leaders. These were the losses of Gibraltar and the Port Mahón naval base and shipyard, both captured by the British; and the growing contraband trade carried out in Spanish Caribbean and Pacific waters by British and French merchant ships. Patiño therefore built some heavier-gunned and larger *navíos* in addition to new 60-gun ships. These included one *navío* of 100 guns, two of 90 guns, nine of 80 guns, and two of 70 guns.

The final product of the Gaztañeta-Patiño period was the 114-gun three-decker *Real Felipe*, considered to be one of the best ships of the age of sail and as important in the history of European naval architecture as England's *Sovereign of the Seas* a century earlier or France's *Ville de Paris* of the 1770s. The *Real Felipe* was launched at Guarnizo in 1732. She was the first Spanish-built three-decker, and the third Spanish warship to carry the name. She had thirty bronze 32-pounders on the lower gun deck, thirty-two 24-pounders on the middle gun deck and thirty 12-pounders on the upper deck. A further twenty-two 8-pounders were positioned on the forecastle and quarterdeck. Although built according to the specifications of Gaztañeta that emphasized the long upper deck, the actual designer of *Real Felipe* was Cipriano de Autrán, one of the many new naval architects who were to emerge between 1730 and 1760. 'Her firepower and robust construction were clearly demonstrated in the Battle of Cape Sicié (in 1744) when she twice resisted the assault by four English ships which she forced to withdraw with severe damage. At the end of the battle she remained mauled and dismasted and was towed to Cartagena by a frigate' says the author of *The Ship in the Spanish Navy*. *Real Felipe*, Spain's first three-decker, did not fight in a sea battle again; she was broken up in 1750.

Patiño was able to carry out his extensive and lengthy programme of new shipbuilding over a period of twenty years for several important reasons. Not the least of these was Patiño's own considerable competence; enough, in fact, that he survived Alberoni's downfall. In addition, a receptive and growing Spanish Bourbon bureaucracy assured the navy and its senior administrators increased independence of action. In May 1726 Patiño was made Minister of the Navy and the Indies. In the same year he began the construction and expansion of naval shipbuilding facilities at El Ferrol, Cádiz, Cartagena and Havana. Patiño's role in Spanish public life during the period 1715–1736 was central to Spanish national recovery. This is because his career spanned so much more than naval activities. He was a superb bureaucrat of great organizational skill and persuasive power who restructured the economy of his country during his era. In the 1730s, Patiño took part in the incessant diplomatic manoeuvres continuing during most of the century between Spain and the courts of Europe.

Loyal to the protectionist mercantile system of his day, Patiño strengthened such key industries as the cloth works of Guadalajara, the Olmedo glass industries and the tapestry weavers of Madrid. Patiño created two overseas state trading companies in the Philippines and Cuba. From the latter, known as the *Compañía de la Habana* (The Havana Company), emerged a workable formula from which the Spanish state and the rising class of Cuban entrepreneurs co-operated in the economic development of sugar, tobacco and naval construction, that island's three main industries during the second half of the eighteenth century. However, the *Compañía de la Habana* did not actually commence operations until 1740, four years after Patiño's death.

[ *34* ]

The results of Patiño's many labours to advance Spanish sea power can be seen in the course of events in the two decades following his death, especially during the War of the Austrian Succession (1740–1748). These included the successes at sea of leading Spanish *navíos* of the Gaztañeta design and the elevation of the Havana shipyard to one of the best and most economical naval yards in the maritime world of the day. According to Commander González-Aller,

> the behaviour of the *Real Felipe ... Princesa ... Glorioso* constitutes the palpable truth of the soundness of [Gaztañeta's] naval construction ... and made very evident to the British Admiralty the inferiority of design and comparative size of the English warship. Gaztañeta produced the ultimate system ... genuinely and purely Spanish and in some aspects of naval construction, such as the extension of the deck length, he was an authentic precursor of his time.[13]

In the broader context of Spain's preparedness for the new wars against Britain that were to come after 1748 Douglas Inglis writes, 'by the time of Patiño's death in 1736 Spain possessed a professional navy of considerable strength, with its own independent system of construction, supply and maintenance.' Professor W N Hargreaves-Mawdsley, a British scholar of eighteenth century Bourbon Spain, sums up Patiño's overall place in rebuilding Spanish institutions: 'Thanks to him, Spain could sustain with honour a war against that colossus, Great Britain.'

## PHASE II: JORGE JUAN AND ENSENADA, 1736–1754

During the remainder of the eighteenth century Spain was fortunate to have officials in charge of its naval shipbuilding programmes who were both naval architects and professional naval officers. This good fortune was more than enhanced by the presence of strong pro-navy ministers in charge of the Spanish domestic economy, armed forces and the Indies. Where Gaztañeta had Alberoni, Jorge Juan had the even more impressive and effective Marqués de Ensenada who, by May 1743 had become at one and the same time, the Minister of War, Navy, Finance and the Indies. King's ministers such as Alberoni, José del Campillo y Cosío (also a mercantilist economist), and Ensenada were able to place the role and need for an ever-stronger fleet in the broader context of their imperial planning. It was a time of common causes between the senior Bourbon technocrats and the naval builders.

On account of the excellent work of Jorge Juan, followed by Francisco Gautier, José Romero y Landa, and finally Julián de Retamosa at the end of the 1790s, Spanish naval architecture continued to be of high quality. Many of the *navíos* built in the sixty-five years between the arrival of Jorge Juan and Trafalgar long outlasted their builders and in many famous instances, the naval battles in which they fought. It is both a calumny and a distortion of history to insist that Spain remained a second or third rate naval power during the eighteenth century because so many of her warships were taken by the Royal Navy. From the 227 ships of the line built or bought by Spain between 1701 and 1797, 55 vessels were lost in storms or wrecked, 35 were captured by the British and only 15 were actually sunk in sea battles.

The increased output of the Havana royal shipyard during the period of Jorge Juan meant that more Spanish *navíos* and frigates were built out of the sturdier and longer-lasting Cuban cedar and mahogany hardwoods. The authors of *The Ship in The Spanish Navy* say the following about Spanish *navío* longevity:

The two *navíos* of 80 guns, the *Fénix* and the *Rayo* that were constructed in Havana, proved to be very strong ships; the latter at the end of the century was converted into a three-decked vessel and fought with success at Trafalgar, being saved from enemy fire to run aground at the Gordas beach [near Rota] in the storm from the south-east that followed the battle ... It is to be noted how well these ships lasted, especially those built in Havana. The *Rayo* for example, achieved a life of 57 years ... this longevity was due to the magnificent tropical woods with which she was made.[14]

The *Fénix*, captured by the British during the battle of Cape Santa Maria in 1780 (Rodney's 'Moonlight battle'), served in the Royal Navy as the ship of the line *Gibraltar* until she was converted into a powder hulk in 1813; then to a lazaretto in 1824, not to be broken up until 1836. Accordingly she served 21 years in the Spanish Navy and 56 in the Royal Navy for a total of 77 years of service. The average increase in the life of the eighteenth century Spanish *navío* built between 1714 and 1800 was as follows:

| | | | |
|---|---|---|---|
| 1714–1724 | 12.6 years | 1750–1774 | 31.6 years |
| 1714–1749 | 14.7 years | 1775–1800 | 22.4 years |

Despite a record too often marred by inefficient ship-manning and maintenance, Spanish fleet commanders were more fastidious in docking their commands than were the English or the French. The reason was self-evident. Many Spanish naval vessels were committed to lengthy periods at sea in service between Spain and the New World as convoy support, as well as extensive service in Caribbean tropical waters, where wood rot and the actions of the teredo worm against ships' hulls were more pronounced. Because of strong prevailing winds on the return voyage across the Pacific Ocean, the Manila Galleon that serviced Manila and the Philippine economy from its long voyage out of Acapulco was often continuously at sea for as long as five months. Indeed, during the middle and late decades of the century, refitting of Spanish naval ships was often required less frequently than in other European fleets, given the longevity of Cuban hardwoods in ships' hulls.

What is most memorable from Jorge Juan's successful efforts at importing outside naval shipbuilding technology was his unique visit to England of 1749, under orders from the Marqués de Ensenada. It was also a spying mission made possible by one of the few peaceful interludes during the many Anglo-Spanish wars. The mission was conducted by Jorge Juan who at thirty-eight was a brilliant young naval captain, already steeped in the theory and practice of shipbuilding and with much seagoing experience. Ensenada's explicit instructions to Juan as preserved in the Spanish archives directed him to search out the following:

> You will make and remit plans of a *navío* of each class that makes up the English fleet ... including those [plans] of masts, rigging and hulls [*arboladuras*] ... all the secret plans for the colonies and the fortifications that the English have in the Americas ... the number of *navíos* that the English have armed for the defence of the seas, colonies and arsenals and of those that they likewise may have sent to America and other places in the world.[15]

Ensenada also gave Juan instructions to send back as many 'nautical books and instruments' as he could.

An essay on Juan's valuable English visit written by Capitán de navío José Luís Morales Hernández in the June 1973 edition of the *Revista General de la Marina* reports that 'During his long presence in London, giving good proof of the universality of his acquaintances, he supplied information about the most heterogeneous matters, remitting drawings and plans of ships and equipment whenever he judged it necessary.' Juan's full name in Spanish was Jorge Juan y Santacilla. Nevertheless, Capitán de navío Jorge Juan in translation is Captain George John, a most English of names. Perhaps he ingratiated himself with the English experts he met. He certainly persuaded some of them (including Richard Rooth and his family) to live and work in Spain. They changed their place of employment from the royal shipyards of His Most Britannic Majesty George II to those of The Most Catholic of Kings Ferdinand VI. Or as Juan put it in his report of 3 April 1749 to Ensenada, they were 'moving to another kingdom'. Juan directly recruited 'three constructors [ Barth, Rooth and Bryant], a master rigger, a master sailmaker, labourers [numbers not defined] and families.' Of Barth he said, '… without contradiction, the best England has', yet Barth appeared to have had a small role in Spanish shipbuilding, in contrast with Rooth, two Bryants and two Mullans.

The leading English and Irish *constructores* hired by Jorge Juan from 1749 to 1770 were not 'naval architects' as we understand the term today. However, the Spanish experts they worked for, such outstanding ship designers as Juan de Acosta and Cipriano de Autrán, were professionally trained in a manner that was not available in England at that time. In August 1730 Juan de Acosta, already the 'captain of the royal shipyard' in Havana in 1729, was appointed its 'master shipwright' under instructions from Patiño to Rodrigo de Torres y Morales, the commanding general of the American squadrons. Acosta also had considerable accounting skills and is identified as the senior Havana shipyard official who was able to quote lower construction prices and then build *navíos* at lower cost than those constructed in Guarnizo, Cádiz or El Ferrol. Autrán and Juan Pedro Boyer designed the famous *Princesa* of 70 guns.

Clearly, such senior naval constructors as Richard (Ricardo) Rooth, Matthew (Mateo) Mullán and his son Ignacio, as well as Edward (Eduardo) Bryant and his son Thomas (Tomás) in the employ of the Spanish, were much more than *meros carpinteros*, 'carpenters of merit', as the imported artisans were called in the Spanish records of the day. On the other hand, a valuable list of the 55 English artisans who worked in Spain at this time with their job classifications and salaries as published by Merino, includes 6 construction foremen, 3 woodcarvers, 7 armourers, 2 augurers, 29 carpenters of various types and 8 wood sawyers among the group.[16]

The Jorge Juan period has been over-identified as the one of *la construcción inglesa*. This does not mean that English *constructores* took over Spanish naval shipbuilding from 1750 to 1770, but that they held senior shipyard positions working with already distinguished and experienced Spanish ship designers. Few of the imported English naval constructors were appointed to the most senior bureacratic posts in the navy's administration, which were always held by Spaniards. For example in April 1770, Autrán was promoted colonel and director of refitting operations from his previous position as 'director of construction'. Shortly after, he was appointed the founding head of the new School of Naval Engineers.

The two Mulláns, father Mateo (Matthew) and son Ignacio (Ignatius), did obtain quite senior dockyard positions in Havana. Mateo Mullán, who had come to Spain in 1749, was first assigned to Cádiz where he married a Spanish lady in 1754. He is generally accredited as the designer of the famous *Santísima Trinidad* even though he died in 1767, two years before she was launched, in March 1769. His son Ignacio (presumably from an earlier marriage) completed his father's work and was present at her launching in 1769. Ignacio Mullán later served as a lieutenant in the Spanish Navy. Some historians contend that Pedro de Acosta, son of Juan de Acosta, was the designer of *Santísima Trinidad*, and that Acosta senior placed Ignacio Mullán in charge of construction of the three-deckers built at Havana. However, the younger Acosta also died before the big ship was finished. This left the younger Mullán as the only one in charge of completing the giant three-decker *navíos*.[17]

Though Eduardo Bryant's considerable correspondence with Jorge Juan revealed him to be an expert who understood ship construction, his usefulness to Spain ended when he was accidentally killed at Cartagena on 27 April 1768. One of the tackles hauling up the Moroccan frigate *Mahoma* unexpectedly parted and killed him. Eduardo Bryant, whose son Thomas (Tomás) was more famous in Spain than his father, was largely responsible for the design of the

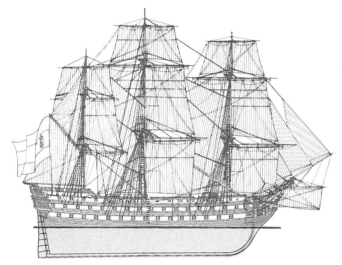

Like her sister ship the *Fénix*, *Rayo* was constructed at Havana in 1749 as a two-decked *navío* of 80 guns. Her builder was Pedro de Torres who followed the directions of Gaztañeta. She was a good example of her era. The initial characteristics for both were the following: length 198 feet, keel 165 feet, beam 57 feet, depth in hold 28.3 feet, draught 27 feet, for a measurement of 1889 tons. In the year 1803, the *Rayo* was enlarged by Engineer Bouyon in the Cartagena shipyard, increasing the number of her guns to a total of 100 pieces and increasing their calibres. This rebuilding involved adding a third complete gun deck. The drawing shows her as rebuilt and the model represents her original appearance. She was at Trafalgar under the command of Commodore Enrique MacDonnell and two days later she was lost on the beach at Rota, the result of a storm when she was trying to reach Cadiz. (*Museo Naval, Madrid*)

first *navío* named *Velasco*, one of the new 74-gun ships. It was launched at Cartagena in 1764, served in the fleet for almost half a century and was broken up in 1801.

Why the demand at this time in Spain for English artisans and naval specialists? A reason given is that the Marqués de Ensenada and Jorge Juan, the gifted naval captain and director of naval construction, were impressed with the performance of Royal Navy ships that won so many naval battles against Spanish warships. If this was the main rationale behind the arrival in Spain of so many British shipbuilding artisans, then both Juan and Ensenada were wrong. It was the well-trained British crews as much as their ships that often outdid the Spanish crews. In fact, the period was marked by the signal success of a Spanish-designed ship (where no British constructors had been involved) in impressing the Royal Navy rather than English-designed vessels setting a standard for Spanish *navíos*.

The Spanish ship referred to was the first *navío* named *Princesa*, completed at the Guarnizo yard in 1730, a large ship for a 70-gunner. This was because she served as a prototype for the still-larger 1925-ton *Real Felipe*, completed at Guarnizo in 1732 as Spain's first three-decker. Though designed by Acosta and Autrán as indicated earlier, the *Princesa* was built according to the Gaztañeta principle that meant a long gun deck (in her case 165 feet in length) but also given her greater size, a wider breadth of 50 feet than Gaztañeta's earlier 60-gun *San Fernandos* of the 1720s. The *Princesa*'s qualities of stability and greater hull strength for a 70-gun ship

came to the attention of the Royal Navy during an unexpected action off Cape Finisterre on 8 April 1740. Three English 70-gun ships, each smaller in size than the *Princesa* (the *Kent, Lennox* and *Orford*) required six hours of hard fighting to capture her even though she previously had lost one of her topmasts in an accident.

Brian Lavery, a specialist on the eighteenth century English ship of the line, writes that 'her extra size gave her stability which the British ships lacked.' This relatively large hull and consequent stability was a dominant feature in fact of both French and Spanish *navíos* of the period, and one which many English ships of the line sought to achieve in their hull designs throughout the rest of the century. This important *navío* in the history of Spanish naval shipbuilding also lived up to the Spanish reputation for warship longevity. She served as the *Princessa*, a Royal Navy ship of the line for the next twenty years, was hulked in 1760 and finally sold in 1784.

By the time of the golden age of naval shipbuilding in Spain, many of the design features from the earlier 'English construction method' of the mid-century, and the later *método francés* (French method) had been synthesized into ship design that remained essentially Spanish.

## PHASE 3: FRANCISCO GAUTIER, 1773–1782

Jorge Juan's legacy to his successor as director of naval construction (engineering) was Spain's first major study of naval architecture since Gaztañeta and Garrote. Juan's book *Examen Marítimo Teórico-Práctico* (*A Maritime Inquiry into Theory and Practice*) was published in July 1773. As a summation of a lifetime of experience in navigation, naval engineering and structural research, it was one of the leading studies on naval architecture in the age of sail. Most of Juan's studies took place during a ten-year period of sea service for the Viceroy of Peru, prior to his call to Madrid in 1745.

Unfortunately, both Gautier, a French Navy commodore and naval engineer, and the ministers of the anglophobe Carlos III who invited him to Spain in 1769, ignored Jorge Juan's warnings against making a shift in warship design. Weeks before his death, Juan wrote an impassioned letter to Carlos III warning against the dire results for Spanish sea power by shifting to French-style warship design. Juan's letter to the king dated 21 June 1773 was to the point: 'I can bring to your knowledge the serious damages that would have to follow for the country...' Such a change meant a shift from the proven heavier, well-balanced and dependable sailers perfected since the 1720s under the Spanish-English design systems, to the French style of lighter-hulled and faster-sailing *navíos*.[18]

Gautier's first three *navíos*, the 74-gun *San Pedro, San Pablo* and *San Gabriel* built between 1769 and 1771, were inadequate sailers suffering from severe pitching. Gautier was compelled to re-study his models for future ships to avoid the bad sailing features of the above three. But once again in the historic Spanish tradition of ship longevity, these three ships had long, useful lives. *San Pablo*, built at El Ferrol in 1771 and renamed *Soberano* in 1814, was broken up in 1854, having served 83 years. *San Pedro* and *San Gabriel* built at El Ferrol in 1770 and 1772, served 31 and 36 years respectively.

*San Nicolás*, an 80-gun ship built at Cartagena in 1769, was one Gautier-designed ship to achieve fame in British naval history. *San Nicolás* was the Spanish *navío* boarded and taken by Nelson at Cape St Vincent on 14 February 1797 between his engagement and mauling of the 130-gun *Santísima Trinidad* and final boarding of the 112-gun *San José*. This was the breathtaking manoeuvre made by Nelson against the greatest odds – three Spanish *navíos* totalling 322 guns – in his single ship, the 74-gun *Captain*, that won him rear admiral's rank and his knighthood. The captured *San Nicolás* served as a prison ship from 1800 until sold in 1814.

Gautier's brief period as 'director of engineering' produced two three-deckers, *Purísima Concepción* and *San José*, both of 112 guns and both built at El Ferrol and launched in 1779 and 1783 respectively. Although designed in the previous Spanish-English style, Gautier modified their hull design. The *Purísima Concepción* served for 31 years, until she was wrecked in Cadiz Bay in 1810. After her capture by Nelson at Cape St Vincent, *San Josef* became the most famous Spanish prize in the history of the Royal Navy in her capacity as Nelson's first and favoured flagship in 1800–1801. Made into a hulk in 1836, *San Josef* was not broken up until 1849, for a total of 66 years in service.

Gautier and the Spanish naval administrators in general were plagued with crises of raw material supplies and shortage of manpower, which had begun with the record expansion of the fleet under Patiño. These critical shortages of wood and personnel continued unresolved to the end of the century. By the time of Trafalgar, Spain found it difficult to meet the large manpower needs of the fine ships she was putting into the water.

Parallel to the manpower shortage was the one in timber for ships. As early as the 1750s

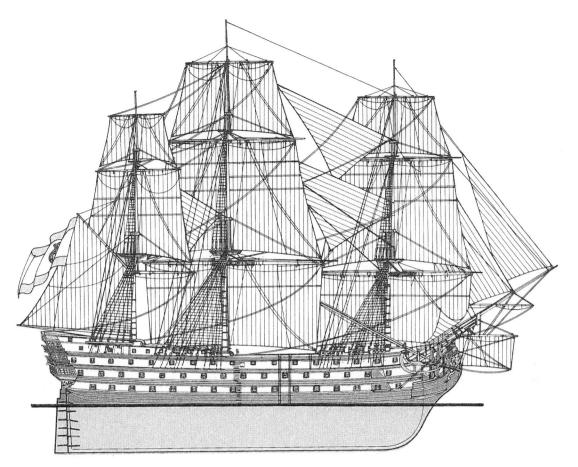

Sister ship of the *San José* (later the British *San Josef*), *Concepción* was built at El Ferrol in 1779. These were the only three-deckers built to Gautier's principles. Her measurements were: length 213.8 feet, keel 186.9 feet, beam 58 feet, draught at stern 29 feet, depth in hold 28.3 feet, and measured 2163 tons. Her armament was made up of thirty-two 36-pounders, thirty 24-pounders, thirty-two 12-pounders, eighteen 8-pounders and six mortars (for firing grapeshot) of 24 pounds. She had acceptable seakeeping qualities but was not a good gun platform in heavy seas. In 1810 she was lost at Cadiz during a storm partly because of the poor condition of her hull. She took part in many actions, among them Cape St Vincent and carried the flag of Mazarredo when in the Brest Squadron. (*Museo Naval, Madrid*)

the growing shortages of oak for hulls and pine for masts were becoming critical. As Minister of the Navy and the Indies, the Marqués de Ensenada emulated Colbert a century earlier in France by planting new oak forests, two million new trees in all. This activity was to replace what had previously been cut for the construction of 70 *navíos* and 25 frigates. As indicated earlier, building a single 74-gun *navío* consumed 3000 trees and its standing and running rigging about 12 miles of rope.

Added to these crises was the climb in the rate of inflation between 1760 and 1800. This was a development over which naval administrators had little control. In terms of naval needs, the inflation increase is immediately noticeable in the mounting cost of building *navíos* in the half-century from 1740 to 1790. In 1749 it cost 143,000 pesos to build the 80-gun *Rayo*, compared with 328,500 pesos to build the admittedly larger 112-gun three-decker *Mejicano* in 1784. However, the latter *navío* was constructed in Havana, which since the 1760s built *navíos* at a lower cost per ship than all the other royal shipyards of Spain.

*San Eugenio*, a Gautier-designed 80-gun two-decker built at El Ferrol in 1775. (*Museo Naval, Madrid*)

These various crises of supply, adequate manpower and inflation were not unique to Spain. They were experienced by all the major European naval states. Spiralling inflation could be traced to the chronic wars they fought among themselves, from the War of the Spanish Succession in 1701 to the end of the Napoleonic Wars in 1815. Merino observes that by 1815, *Victory*'s many refits and overhauls from her launching in 1765 cost £371,922 compared with her original building outlay of £63,174.

### PHASE 4: JOSÉ ROMERO Y LANDA, 1782–1794

The score of years (1780–1800) prior to Trafalgar marked the apogee and not the nadir of the Spanish Navy. Some of the best *navíos* built in Spain during the entire century, were built at this time. These included the *San Ildefonso*, the first in her class of 74-gun ships, launched at Cartagena in 1785, and a decade later the 74-gun *Montañés* (also first of her class), launched at El Ferrol in 1794. Others built during these final two shipbuilding phases of the century included the *Bahama* and *San Leandro*, both 74 guns, of the *San Ildefonso* class, and the *Neptuno* (80 guns) and *Monarca* (74 guns) of the *Montañés* class. Of the 15 Spanish *navíos* that fought at Trafalgar, 9 were built during the periods when José Romero y Landa and Julián de Retamosa were directors of engineering between 1782 and 1805, including the giant three-decked 112-gun *Santa Ana* that put up such a stout resistance at Trafalgar.

Paradoxically, in the decades close to the end of the great Spanish colonial experience in the New World in the 1820s, Spanish sea power reached a peak not seen since the far-off era of the

Spanish Armada. In 1790, the navy possessed 76 *navíos* and the shipyards had achieved a level of operating efficiency never seen earlier, despite the constant raw material and manpower shortages which were never completely solved. Alejandro Malaspina's famous circumnavigation of the world had begun the previous year in two 24-gun ships, the *Atrevida* and *Descubierta*. They were custom-designed and built in the Carraca yard as special exploration and discovery vessels. Merino, who was generally pessimistic about the course of his country's fleet throughout the century, was buoyant about the general state of Spain in the year 1790. He wrote:

> In 1790, the panorama was relatively optimistic ... things appeared firm ... free trade [introduced in 1778 by Carlos III throughout the empire] had increased enormously [the] interchange of commerce. As for three centuries past, money continued to arrive from the American mines. Spain was controlling almost for the first time all of the Gulf of Mexico, which gave a certain security and affirmed the occupation of other ample zones. The economy appeared to have handled well the paper money, and the government though short of resources was solvent ... public works and new construction gave an air of work in the country ... and despite the alarming signs that evidently existed, the Spanish of 1790 were able to look at the future with optimism.[19]

In this positive atmosphere, and like Gaztañeta and Jorge before him, with a supportive bureaucrat in charge of the Ministry of the Navy, Romero y Landa designed the *San Ildefonso* class, which was to be one of the best of the 74-gun ships built in European navies of the time. Before succeeding as director of engineering for the navy upon Gautier's death in 1782, Romero had worked in the shipyards of Guarnizo, El Ferrol and Cartagena between 1765 and 1776. He returned to El Ferrol in April 1777 as its director of engineering, a title as we have seen synonymous with director of construction.

Antonio Valdés, the son of an aristocratic family, was appointed Navy Minister by Carlos III in 1787, and reaffirmed in that position on the accession of Carlos IV the next year. Valdés was a competent and effective minister, who understood not only the naval service which he had joined as a 13-year-old cadet in the Royal Marine Corps, but the worlds of politics and of the court. As a young officer, he was taken prisoner by the British during their capture of Havana in 1762 and later fought against the Barbary pirates of Algeria in 1769. By the early 1780s, after several senior administrative posts, he had reached the rank of commodore.

The correspondence between Romero and Valdés on ship design and sea trials after launching, indicates a clear understanding by Valdés of shipbuilding activities. In June 1784 Romero wrote to him for permission to build a *navío* of 74 guns, to be called *San Ildefonso*. On 4 November 1789, four years after *San Ildefonso*'s launching at Cartagena, Romero wrote again to Valdés about the performance of *San Ildefonso* and her sister ships. On that occasion Romero submitted his analysis of information provided by the commanding officers and builders about their qualities. Accompanying Romero's report is a 'comparative plan' of the cost of the *navíos Principe* and *San Ildefonso*.

In 1785, Vice Admiral José de Mazarredo one of Spain's best admirals of the century, was in charge of the sea trials of the new *San Ildefonso* and the 74-gun *San Juan Nepomuceno*, built earlier at Guarnizo in 1766. Of the *San Ildefonso*'s sea-keeping qualities, Mazarredo commented positively that 'she sailed to windward like the frigates; she managed and tacked like a boat; she has a spacious battery ... stable in all positions, instances and circumstances.'[20]

No wonder José de Córdoba, the doomed Spanish commander-in-chief at Cape St

Vincent, was so severely dealt with at his court martial for losing a battle he easily could have won with ships of this quality. Though the *San Ildefonsos* were products of the best of Spanish design over the years, they were not perfect ships. Other critics note that despite their many good qualities they were inclined to pitch in heavy seas, a trend remedied by Romero's successor in the early 1790s. The Romero period also saw the construction of seven of Spain's twelve giant three-deckers. The first three, all built at El Ferrol, were *Santa Ana, Salvador del Mundo* and *Reina Luisa* finished in 1784, 1787 and 1791 respectively. The remaining four were built in Havana, the largest shipbuilding facility in the Spanish empire. They were *Mejicano, Real Carlos, San Hermenegildo* and *Principe de Asturias*, built in 1786, 1787, 1789 and 1794 respectively. Along with the *Montañés* 74-gun class that were constructed in the ensuing Retamosa period, these three-deckers represented the epitome of Spanish naval building, and

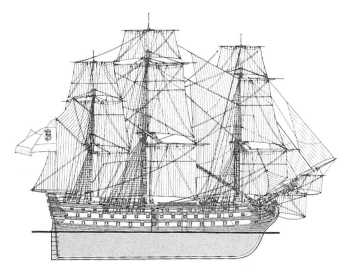

*Santa Ana* was constructed at El Ferrol to the plans of Romero y Landa in the year 1784 and with her the three-decker of the eighteenth century reached its technical apogee. There were seven sister ships to the *Santa Ana* along the same general lines, all constructed in the two shipyards of El Ferrol and Havana. Her characteristics were: length 210 feet, keel 185.8 feet, beam 58 feet, depth in hold 27.5 feet, draught 29 feet, and a measurement of 2308 tons. She mounted thirty 36-pounders, thirty-two 24-pounders, thirty 12-pounders, and twenty 8-pounders. From her entry into service, she was present at all the naval actions in which the Spanish Navy was involved. Her performance at Trafalgar was especially brilliant, where under the command of Capitán de navío Gardoquí and flying the flag of Vice Admiral Alava, she not only fought with success but later collaborated in the recovery of some of the Spanish prizes taken by the English and after this act of rescue was towed into Cádiz. She foundered at Havana in 1812. (*Model and drawing: Museo Naval, Madrid*)

incorporated many of the best features of Spanish hull design of the century. Despite some modifications, they were generally similar to the *Real Felipe*, the first three-decker built by Spain more than half a century before the *Santa Ana* class. They all displayed good sea-keeping qualities during their lifetime, with *Santa Ana* identified in the record as a better performer than the *Principe de Asturias*, the Spanish flagship at Trafalgar.

With the exception of the earlier *Santísima Trinidad* which carried a crew of 1100, the *Santa Anas* were the most labour-intensive *navíos* in the Spanish Navy. Each had a crew of approximately 850 men and 40 officers. This was a huge complement to be housed and closeted in wooden ships, each of no more than 2200 tons. Larger ships meant bigger and often more of the standard equipment to be manhandled. For example, during heavy weather 150 men were needed to man the ship's pumps in the *Santa Ana*; it took 250 men to move her five large anchors of 3.5 tons each, and three smaller kedge anchors of 1.2 tons each. The *Santa Anas* also carried three different sizes of ship's boats or launches which required ample manpower for peace or wartime duties. The largest launch, 11.5 metres (37¾ feet) long and 2.8 metres (9 feet) wide was used to move the anchors, bring fresh water and provisions on board and transport visitors. In wartime it was fitted with a single 24-pounder. Two smaller boats, each 10 metres (32¾ feet) long, were secured by davits from the poop. Usually constructed from hardwoods, they were

heavy and difficult to manoeuvre. Most of the manpower, however, was needed to man the sails and operate the cumbersome iron and bronze guns in the sailing ship of the line.

Despite the constant crises in obtaining wood for construction and vital ships' supplies such as resin, tar and pitch, iron and rope, by the end of the century the Spanish royal shipyards had mastered logistics well enough to build some of the largest ships of the day. The Havana shipyard which managed to build the smaller *navíos* at lower cost than the mainland Spanish shipyards, also reduced the cost of building the three-deckers. The 120-gun *Santísima Trinidad* cost 400,000 pesetas to build at Havana in 1769, compared with 328,449 pesetas to construct the 112-gun *Mejicano*, launched from the same yard only seventeen years later.

Pine for masts built in the metropolitan shipyards of Spain was often imported from the Baltic region and Russia and, for the Havana shipyard, from the coastal pine forests of Mexico. When these were depleted after about 1760, even the distant Havana yard often had to rely on Baltic pine for masts. Some of the pitch and *alquitrán* (an anti-fouling mixture of resin, grease and oil to cover the ship's bottom) were supplied by Britain, Holland and Sweden. The forests of Asturias could still supply much of the oak for the hulls – except for the four three-deckers built in Havana from Cuban hardwoods. Iron for the ship's parts, as well as coal, came from Vizcaya and Asturias.

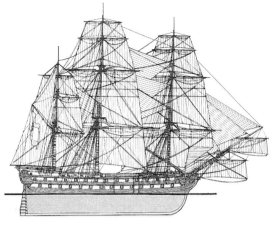

The plans of *Montañés* (1794) reproduced here are the original building draughts, currently kept at El Ferrol dockyard. They show that the ship was designed as a 74-gun ship, but the armament was later increased to 80 guns. (*Museo Naval, Madrid*)

## PHASE 5: JULIÁN DE RETAMOSA, 1794–1805

In the decade remaining prior to Trafalgar, the Spanish Navy experienced a final phase of shipbuilding excellence, before defeat in that battle and the Napoleonic invasion of Spain in 1808–1812 obliterated Spanish sea power in the age of sail. Julián de Retamosa, who was appointed 'secretary in charge of arsenals, shipyards and construction of ships' in 1793, was not a naval constructor like his predecessors. It is true that he shared with them a long career as a naval officer prior to entering the bureaucracy. But he did not apparently write major treatises on ship design, as did Gaztañeta and Jorge Juan.

Where Jorge Juan achieved only the rank of capitán de navio, Retamosa was promoted commodore in 1794, vice admiral in 1802 and commandant of the corps of naval engineers prior to Trafalgar. During 1794 he was overseer for the design and construction of the *Montañés* class of 74- and 80-gun *navíos*. It was the last, and in the opinion of some experts, the best of the many classes of Spanish Navy ships built since Gaztañeta's *San Fernandos* at the start of the century. Retamosa made important changes in the *Montañés, Neptuno* and *Argonauta* from the *San Ildefonso* design. He modified the arrangement for ballast weight, reduced the tendency to excessive pitching that the *San Ildefonsos* experienced in heavy seas, and reinforced the sterns. Commander González-Aller, the modern Spanish naval historian, says of the *Montañés* class: '... the result of this fifth and ultimate system that the Spanish Navy knew, was the maximum perfection achieved by Spain in the naval construction of wooden ships ... they were comparable ... to the best of the foreigners.'

This chapter has concentrated on the design and construction of the Spanish *navío* with only a

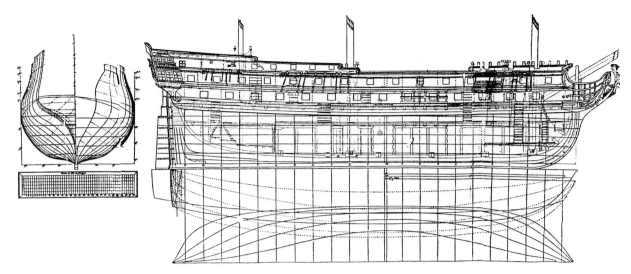

few references to the design and production of frigates that had continued at the same time and at much the same pace as the production of the larger ships of the line. At the same time, the smaller naval vessels, including the Fourth to Sixth Rates, should not be ignored. Smaller vessels in the Spanish Navy often carried out quite different functions from similar ships in other European navies.

The Spanish versions are best identified by their admittedly quite unfamiliar Spanish names. These include the *aviso, bergantín, jabeque, goleta, urca, balandra*, and *lombarda*. The 16-gun two-masted *bergantín* and *aviso* (a good Spanish word for 'notice') were, in effect, the eyes and ears of the empire, its equivalent of a telegraph system in the pre-electronic era. They were the small, fast vessels that carried messages and official correspondence back and forth between Spain and the viceroys overseas who governed the vast land masses of Spain's viceroyalties in Hispanic America. As their Spanish name *virrey* indicates, these powerful officials were literally 'vice-the-king', the stand-ins appointed by the distant Spanish monarchs in Madrid to represent them overseas. These were monarchs who, despite Spain's protracted role in the New World, never crossed the seas to visit their American or Pacific possessions, so a developed system of advice boats was a real necessity.

The 200-ton *bergantín* also functioned as a speedy communication link between both naval squadrons at sea and the shore bases, or as a watchdog for the central maritime traffic routes. The 250-ton eighteenth century *jabeque* (usually known as the xebec in English), a small three-masted vessel with three large lateen sails – fore, main and mizzen – had remained almost unchanged in structure over the centuries. Columbus would have recognized the eighteenth century Spanish Navy *jabeque* although it had become much larger and could carry as many as 30 guns. On his first voyage to the New World, Columbus' tiny ship the *Niña*, although two-masted and called a *carabela*, was in rig a late fifteenth century version of the *jabeque*.

Spanish shipyards continued to build this classic type of vessel as late as the 1770s. In the eighteenth century the Spanish also built a so-called *jabeque-bergantín* with a combination of lateen and fore-and-aft sails. A large jib was secured to a lateen mast, set at its familiar rakish angle forward in place of the upright fore mast, followed by a main mast with standard main topsail and topgallant sails. This was followed in turn by another lateen mast with a single lateen sail in lieu of the later mizzen. A lovely reproduction of a *jabeque-bergantín* on a coloured ceramic plate dated 1779 can be seen in Barcelona's Maritime Museum. It came from the Oratory of the Sailors' Guild in Palma de Mallorca.

[ *47* ]

◁An early eighteenth century scene reveals the stern of a 34-gun frigate, a *bombarda* of 10 guns flying an early eighteenth century version of the Bourbon Monarchy's flag, a lateen-rigged galley flying the Maltese flag and, in the distance, a *bergantín* of unknown nationality. Museo Naval Christmas Card, 1985 from the painting by Rafael Monleón in the Museo Naval (*Museo Naval, Madrid*)

▽Building plans for what must have been among the last of the *jabeques* constructed in Cartagena in 1749 for Mediterranean service. (*Museo Naval, Madrid*)

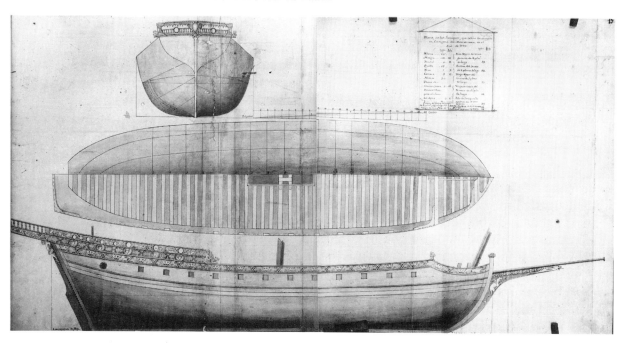

The *goleta* or schooner must have been as familiar in Spanish, Hispanic American or Philippine coastal waters as were her English, French, Dutch and Scandinavian counterparts. Like the much-larger *registro*, licensed by the Spanish crown for a single voyage to a specified Hispanic American port, the *goleta* was usually a commercial vessel.

The lumbering and ungainly *urca*, also called the *fragata de carga* or 'cargo frigate', was widely used by the Spanish and probably first designed by the Dutch. It is believed that the high-pooped, lumbering and ungainly Spanish ships that the English naval leaders, including Sir Francis Drake, identified wrongly as large Spanish galleons, were *urca* transports positioned in the centre of a Spanish Armada that had to transport food supplies for sailors and the thousands of troops on board. There was another sound reasoning for the English misunderstanding. Juan Martínez Recalde, second-in-command of the Spanish Armada and one of the great European navigators of his day, already knew the English coasts close to which the Armada was sailing. Recalde ordered many of the *urcas* to precede the fleet so they would be out of the way when hostilities commenced.

Unnamed *navío* of 80 guns, from a large Berlinguero painting. (*Museo Naval, Madrid*)

The ungainly and tiny *balandra* was a single-masted vessel used as a guard ship to protect a naval shipyard and arsenal. The *lombarda* bomb vessel, named for the Lombardy gun (incidentally the name for a Spanish red cabbage), was an awkward but essential vessel used to lob mortar shells into fortifications under siege. Its mortars – usually three of them – were placed in the waist, stern and in the position usually reserved for the fore mast. Accordingly, the *lombarda* usually had only a small main and mizzen mast. Finally, the all-important *azogue* (mercury) squadrons of two to three vessels that carried quicksilver or mercury from Spain to the New World for the vital refining of gold would consist of *goletas* and *bergantíns* with a navy frigate attached for its protection.

All these smaller but important vessels, some of them based on Mediterranean designs originating in the Middle Ages, continued to play key roles in the Spanish Navy of the eighteenth century, alongside the big three-deckers and the sophisticated 74- and 80-gun ships, even as the age of the wooden warship was coming to its inevitable end.

PLATE I

The 74-gun *San Telmo* with fore topsail backed to let go the second anchor. The *San Telmo*, built at El Ferrol in 1788, was lost off Cape Horn with all hands in 1819. One of a collection of water colours in the Naval Museum in Madrid by Don Alejo Berlinguero de la Marca y Gallego (1759–1810), Lieutenant in the Spanish Navy and a professor in the Pilots' School at Cartagena. (*Museo Naval, Madrid*)

PLATE II

*Montañés* was constructed at El Ferrol in 1794 by Retamosa, improving on the design of Romero y Landa for *navíos* of 74 guns and two decks. Her characteristics were: length 190 feet, keel 169.5 feet, depth in hold 25 feet, draught 28 feet, and a measurement of 1499 tons. Her armament was twenty-eight 24-pounders, thirty 18-pounders, sixteen 12-pounders and six 8-pounders. She was the most perfect example of Spanish naval technology of her time and one of the best ships built during the eighteenth century. During an overseas commission in the Philippines, she had the chance to demonstrate this, achieving speeds greater than 14 knots. She was involved in a very limited way in the Battle of Trafalgar under the command of Capitán de navío Francisco Alcedo. (*Museo Naval, Madrid*)

PLATE III

The 64-gun *Asia* in a storm, from an 1824 oil by Angel Cortellini in the Naval Museum, Madrid. The *Asia* was the only eighteenth century Spanish *navío* to mutiny. In a bizarre episode in 1825 her crew seized the ship in the remote Spanish Marianas, put their officers ashore then sailed the ship to Mexico and turned her over to the new Mexican Navy. (*Revista General de la Marina, Madrid*)

PLATE IV

*Santísima Trinidad* was constructed in the royal dockyard in Havana by Mateo Mullán in 1769, and underwent refits in the years 1771, 1778, 1797 and 1803. After the last refit she carried an armament of thirty-two 36-pounders, thirty-four 24-pounders, thirty-six 12-pounders, eighteen 8-pounders and ten mortars (for firing grapeshot) of 24 pounds. Her characteristics were: length 220.5 feet, keel 186 feet, beam 58.4 feet, depth in hold 28.2 feet, draught at the stern 30 feet, and a measurement of 2879 tons. Along with the *Victory*, she was the most famous ship of her time but was superior to the British ship in number of guns. She took part in nearly all of the naval actions between 1775 and 1805, among them Cape Spartel, Cape St Vincent and Trafalgar and flew the flags of admirals Lángara, Don Luís de Cordova, Don Antonio de Córdoba, Mazarredo and Uriarte. She was lost as a result of damage received at Trafalgar, where she resisted the attack of three British ships of the line, losing more than a third of her crew dead and wounded. (*Museo Naval, Madrid*)

PLATE V

*Navío Catalán* in a single-ship action in 1729 against a British warship, commanded by Captain Vernon. (*An oil by R Monleón*)

PLATE VI

Action of the *Glorioso* under the command of the Marqués de Vega Araujo against a British ship of the line, 1747. (*An oil by A Cortellini*)

PLATE VII

The Spanish text reads as follows: 'View of the position of the *navío Real Felipe* under the command of the Spanish commander, Rear Admiral Don Juan José Navarro, when the *Namur*, commanded by Admiral Mathews, directed a fireship to set on fire the *Real Felipe* [but failed to do so] in the naval battle of 22 February 1744 in the waters off Toulon [Battle of Cape Sicié] on the coast of Provence in which the Spanish maintained control of the sea.' (*Oil by Moraleda, 1783*)

PLATE VIII

Selected flags of the eighteenth century Spanish Navy from *Banderas de la Marina de España – Flags from the Navy of Spain.*
A
1700: Flag of the Spanish Hapsburgs who died out in 1701 – flown from the stern of Spanish Navy ships mainly in the previous seventeenth century.
B
1760: Flag of the Spanish Bourbons who came to the throne in 1701 – flown by all *navíos, fragatas* and other ships of the *Armada Española* as it emerged early in the eighteenth century until the new red–gold–red flag both as the naval ensign and state flag first came into use in 1785.
C
1785: The new red–gold–red naval ensign which persists to this day with coats-of-arms changes as various national regimes changed (see the last flag in this group). Also flown by coastal defence units.
D
1748: Flown by *buques mercantes*, or merchant ships, from 1748 to 1762.
E
1762: Flown by *buques mercantes*, or merchant ships, from 1762 to 1785.
F
1785: The merchant marine version of the new red–gold–red flag flown since 1785 by Spanish merchant ships who do not fly *escudos* or house flags of their own.
G
1732–1760: Flag of the naval Department of El Ferrol between those years.
H
1732–1760: Flag of the naval Department of Cartagena between those years.
I
1700–1760: Flag of the naval Department of Cádiz during those years.
J
1748: Flag flown by the Spanish privateers (*corsos*) that flourished in the Caribbean at mid-eighteenth century.
K
1732–1760: Flag of the *Apostaderos* (Naval Stations) of the Americas – naval bases in the Spanish New World.
L
1981: The naval ensign of Spain's modern *Armada Española* (Spanish Navy) is the same as the 1785 flag, but including the modern coat-of-arms of the Spanish Bourbons, who were restored to the throne in 1976 with Juan Carlos I as the first King of Spain since 1931.

II

III

IV

VI

VII

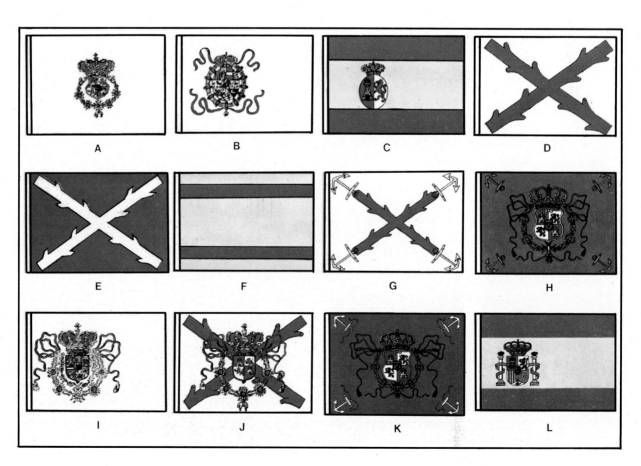

VIII

## CHAPTER THREE

# Cuba and the New Navy

*Cuba was the best of Spain and America.*

Curtis Wilgus, late professor of Latin American
history, University of Florida at Gainesville.

CUBA'S ROLE as an outpost of Spanish imperial power in the Caribbean has a
contemporary ring. Whether ruled by Spanish captains-general, its own presidents too often
captive to US interests, or at present by Fidel Castro in fief to the Soviet Union, control of
Cuba's geographic position as the regional gateway is the prerequisite for any nation planning
to hold power in the Caribbean.

There is much that is modern about Spain's eighteenth century needs for a major naval
shipyard, large fortifications and permanent military and naval forces in Havana. In the late
twentieth century the Soviet-built and equipped *Puerto Pesquero* (Fishing Port) that was
constructed on the site of Havana's old city dump is heir to Havana's *astillero real*, the royal
shipyard built long ago on wasteland. Both facilities are seen as outreaches of maritime power
from the distant yet controlling European metropolitan state. The Fishing Port plays only an
auxiliary role as the centre for Marxist Cuba's expanding deep-sea fishing fleet. But, as the
largest terminus outside of the USSR itself for Soviet fishing fleets, the Fishing Port also serves
the intelligence-gathering activities that Soviet fish factory trawlers and mother ships carry out,
alongside their world-wide fishing activities.

In the eighteenth century, the great royal shipyard of Havana played an even more
important naval role because it built ships of the line for the fleet of the imperial motherland.
Four of the fifteen ships of the line in the Spanish Navy at Trafalgar were constructed in
Havana, including the 112-gun *Principe de Asturias*, the Spanish flagship. The others were the
giant 120-gun *Santísima Trinidad* (1769) the 100-gun *Rayo* (1749) and the 74-gun *Bahama*
(1784). Since Spain lost Cuba in 1898 – her richest and most dynamic colony in 350 years of
world empire – the warships and merchant vessels, first of the United States and then of the
Soviet Union, have steamed into Havana harbour on missions of strategic and economic
interest.

All of these ships have sailed past the two sites of the great naval shipyard that built so
many of Spain's biggest and best *navíos* in the age of sail. Hordes of sailors suddenly on shore
leave when 'the fleet's in', are far from being a phenomenon of the twentieth century. The
jaunty 'gobs' of the US Navy who eagerly headed for Havana's fleshpots from the 1920s to the
1950s, were heirs to the Havana Squadron of ships from both *La Flota* and the Spanish Navy
who did the same 200 years before them. Under Castro, Havana is no longer the uncontrolled
Caribbean centre for gambling and sexual pleasures that it had been before he came and
conquered in 1959. The Soviet sailors seen on shore leave in Havana from the warships and big

## SHIPS CONSTRUCTED IN THE ROYAL SHIPYARD OF HAVANA, 1700–1800

| Year | Rate | Type | Name (*Alias*) | Year | Rate | Type | Name (*Alias*) |
|------|------|------|----------------|------|------|------|----------------|
| 1700 | 50 | Navío | Santa Rosa | 1748 | 70 | Navío | *San Lorenzo (Tigre) |
| 1701 | 50 | Navío | Rubí | 1749 | 80 | Navío | *San Alejandro (Fénix) |
| 1714 | 50 | Navío | San Francisco | 1750 | 74 | Navío | *San Luis Gonzaga |
| 1718 | 60 | Navío | San Juan Bautista | | | | (Infante) |
| 1718 | 60 | Navío | Victoria | 1750 | 74 | Navío | *Santiago el Mayor |
| 1720 | 64 | Navío | Principe de Asturias | | | | (Galicia) |
| 1723 | 60 | Navío | Conquistador | 1753 | 30 | Fragata | *Triunfo |
| 1724 | 60 | Navío | San Juan Bautista | 1754 | 20 | Fragata | Volante |
| 1725 | 60 | Navío | San Antonio | 1755 | 44 | Fragata | Tetis 2° |
| 1725 | 50 | Navío | San Lorenzo | 1755 | 22 | Fragata | Tetis |
| 1726 | 58 | Navío | Incendio | 1757 | 74 | Navío | *Princesa |
| 1726 | 16 | Paquebot | San Antonio (Triunfo) | 1757 | 16 | Bergantín | Santa Teresa (Triunfo) |
| 1727 | 54 | Navío | San Jerónimo (el Retiro) | 1758 | 18 | Fragata/Chata | Santa Bárbara (Fénix) |
| 1727 | 56 | Navío | Santa Rosa | 1758 | 18 | Fragata/Chata | San Carlos (Cazador) |
| 1727 | 22 | Fragata/Chata | Santa Bárbara | 1759 | 64 | Navío | Asia |
| 1728 | 60 | Navío | N S de Guadalupe (el | 1759 | 60 | Navío | San Eustaquio (Astuto) |
| | | | Fuerte) | 1760 | 18 | Paquebot | San Blas (Volante) |
| 1728 | 60 | Navío | San Dionisio (el | 1761 | 70 | Navío | San Genaro |
| | | | Constante) | 1761 | 64 | Navío | San Antonio |
| 1729 | 70 | Navío | Conquistador | 1761 | 22 | Fragata | N S de Guadalupe (Fénix) |
| 1730 | 66 | Navío | Gallo Indiano | 1761 | 14 | Goleta | San Isidro |
| 1730 | 64 | Navío | N S del Carmen | 1761 | 14 | Bergantín | San José |
| 1730 | 52 | Navío | Volante | 1762 | 30 | Jabeque | Caiman (San Fransisco) |
| 1730 | 16 | Paquebot | el Marta | 1765 | 98 | Navío | San Carlos |
| 1730 | 16 | Paquebot | el Jupiter | 1765 | 94 | Navío | San Fernando |
| 1731 | 66 | Navío | San Cristóbal (Constante) | 1765 | 16 | Goleta | San Julián |
| 1732 | 70 | Navío | San Jose (Africa) | 1766 | 60 | Navío | Santiago (América) |
| 1734 | 64 | Navío | N S del Pilar (Europa) | 1766 | 16 | Goleta | San Joaquin |
| 1734 | 64 | Navío | N S de Loreto (Asia) | 1766 | 17 | Goleta | San Lorenzo |
| 1734 | 58 | Navío | Santo Cristo de Burgos | 1767 | 94 | Navío | San Luís |
| | | | (Castilla) | 1767 | 16 | Goleta | San Lorenzo 2° |
| 1735 | 50 | Navío | Santísima Trinidad | 1767 | 16 | Goleta | San Antonio de Padua |
| | | | (Esperanza) | 1767 | 16 | Goleta | Santa Rosalia |
| 1735 | 24 | Fragata | San Cristobal (Triunfo) | 1767 | 10 | Goleta | Santa Clara |
| 1736 | 64 | Navío | N S de Belén (America) | 1767 | 10 | Goleta | Santa Isabel |
| 1737 | 64 | Navío | Santa Rosa de Lima | 1768 | 34 | Fragata | Cecilia |
| | | | (Dragón) | 1768 | 18 | Paquebot | San Francisco de Paula |
| 1737 | 24 | Fragata/Chata | Santa Bárbara (Astrea) | 1769 | 130 | Navío | Santísima Trinidad |
| 1738 | 70 | Navío | N S de Belén (Glorioso) | 1769 | 70 | Navío | San Francisco de Paula |
| 1739 | 70 | Navío | San Ignacio (Invencible) | 1769 | 70 | Navío | San José |
| 1739 | 50 | Navío | N S de Guadalupe | 1769 | 12 | Goleta | San José |
| | | | (Bizarro) | 1770 | 30 | Jabeque | Caimán |
| 1740 | 66 | Navío | Soberbio | 1770 | 12 | Goleta | N S de Loreto |
| 1743 | 64 | Navío | N S del Rosario (Nueva | 1771 | 80 | Navío | San Rafael |
| | | | España) | 1771 | 68 | Navío | San Pedro Alcántara |
| 1744 | 70 | Navío | *San Jose (Invencible) | 1771 | 34 | Fragata | Santa Lucia |
| 1744 | 70 | Navío | *Reina | 1772 | 26 | Fragata | Santa Ana |
| 1745 | 70 | Navío | *Jesús, María y José | 1772 | 18 | Paquebot | San Carlos |
| | | | (Conquistador) | 1772 | 12 | Bergantín | San Juan Bautista |
| 1745 | 64 | Navío | *Santa Teresa de Jesús | 1772 | 12 | Bergantín | San Francisco Javier |
| | | | (Dragón) | 1772 | 12 | Goleta | Santa Elena |
| 1746 | 74 | Navío | *Santo Tomás (Vencedor) | 1773 | 74 | Navío | San Miguel |
| 1746 | 70 | Navío | *San Francisco de Asís | 1775 | 68 | Navío | San Ramón |
| | | | (Africa) | 1775 | | Ganguil | San Julián |
| 1747 | 60 | Navío | Castilla | 1775 | | Ganguil | San Salvador de Orta |
| 1747 | 24 | Fragata/Chata | *Santa Rosalia (la Flora) | 1776 | 64 | Navío | San Leandro |
| 1748 | 80 | Navío | *San Pedro (Rayo) | 1776 | 64 | Navío | San Isidoro |

*Santísima Trinidad*, a scale model in the Smithsonian Institution, Washington, DC, USA. (*Author*)

| Year | Rate | Type | Name (Alias) |
|---|---|---|---|
| 1776 | 10 | Bergantín | Santa Catalina Martir |
| 1777 | 46 | Fragata | Santa Cecilia |
| 1778 | 46 | Fragata | Santa Matilde |
| 1778 | 34 | Fragata | N S de la O |
| 1778 | 31 | Fragata | Santa Agueda |
| 1778 | 12 | Goleta | Santa Teresa |
| 1780 | 74 | Navío | San Cristóbal (Bahama) |
| 1780 | 40 | Fragata | Santa Clara |
| 1780 | 34 | Fragata | Santa María de la Cabeza |
| 1780 | 30 | Jabeque | Santo Cristo |
| 1780 | 16 | Bergantín | el Pájaro |
| 1780 | 14 | Goleta | el Viento |
| 1781 | | Goleta | |
| 1782 | 14 | Paquebot | Borja |
| 1782 | | Pontón | San Pedro |
| 1782 | | Pontón | San Pablo |
| 1786 | 112 | Navío | San Hipolito (Mejicano) |
| 1786 | 112 | Navío | Conde de Regla |
| 1786 | 36 | Fragata | N S de Guadalupe |
| 1786 | 36 | Fragata | N S de las Mercedes |
| 1787 | 112 | Navío | Real San Carlos |
| 1787 | 34 | Fragata | Catalina |
| 1788 | 64 | Navío | San Pedro Alcántara |
| 1788 | 34 | Fragata | Santa Matilde |

| Year | Rate | Type | Name (Alias) |
|---|---|---|---|
| 1789 | 112 | Navío | San Hermenegildo |
| 1789 | 64 | Navío | San Jerónimo (Asia) |
| 1789 | 40 | Fragata | N S de Atocha |
| 1789 | 40 | Fragata | Minerva |
| 1790 | 74 | Navío | Soberano |
| 1790 | 18 | Bergantín | San Carlos (Volador) |
| 1790 | 18 | Bergantín | el Saeta |
| 1791 | 74 | Navío | Infante Don Pelayo |
| 1791 | 40 | Fragata | Ceres |
| 1791 | 12 | Bergantín | el Saeta |
| 1791 | | Pontón | Number 1 |
| 1791 | | Pontón | Number 2 |
| 1791 | | Ganguil | Number 1 |
| 1791 | | Ganguil | Number 2 |
| 1791 | | Ganguil | Number 3 |
| 1791 | | Ganguil | Number 4 |
| 1792 | 44 | Fragata | Gloria (Santa Monica) |
| 1794 | 112 | Navío | Los Santos Reyes (Principe de Asturias) |
| 1794 | 50 | Navío | San Carlos |
| 1794 | 18 | Bergantín | San Antonio |
| 1795 | 74 | Navío | Asia |
| 1797 | 40 | Fragata | Anfitrite (Santa Ursula) |

NOTES:

In no one place are the records of ship launchings to be found, thus the dates given represent an approximate launch date. Where launch dates are unknown, the date of incorporation into the Spanish Navy has been used.

'Rate' represents the number of guns the ship usually served with, rather than the number she carried at launch. An example was the *Santísima Trinidad*, launched in 1769 as a 112-gun vessel but later received an additional gun deck and the staggering total of 144 cannon. This proved too great a strain, however, so she was relieved of 14 guns bringing her rate down to 130, the *number* of guns she carried through most of her career.

The Spanish were not very original when it came to naming their vessels – the same names appear over and over. It was not uncommon to have a *navío*, a *fragata*, a *paquebot*, etc, all with the same name, at the same time. Usually, however no two vessels of the same type possessed the same name at the same time. The aliases were official names given at the time of construction and usually were the names most often used in correspondence, orders, etc. *Navíos* tended to have saints names with secular aliases, while *fragatas* usually possessed the inverse, secular names and saint aliases.

N S = *Nuestra Señora* (Our Lady of...).

Havana Company constructed ships are denoted by an asterisk (*) preceeding the name.

(SOURCE: 'The Spanish Naval Shipyard at Havana in the Eighteenth Century' by G Douglas Inglis, former archivist, Texas State Archives, Austin, Texas, 1983, pages 31–34, unpublished.)

tankers are more discreet, because they have to be. At the start of his social revolution, Castro closed down and destroyed the brothels and gambling dens of capitalist Havana.

The strategic and economic lines of communication between Cuba and the Soviet Union are even longer than were those between that island and imperial Spain. Without the steady arrival of Soviet oil tankers from Odessa to Havana to supply a Communist Caribbean satellite economy that has no oil, the Cuban economy would come to a complete standstill within a week. In the heyday of Spanish rule, Cuba was less captive to the European imperial power than that imperial power was to Cuba. One hundred years ago without the earnings from Cuba's sugar exports, Spain would have faced a sharp decline in her external revenues. Cuban economic historian Levi Marrero reveals the considerable extent of this Spanish dependence on Cuba:

> Between 1823 and 1866, the Cubans contributed more than 82 million pesos to the Spanish treasury, the amounts varying from a little less than 6 per cent to a little more than 37 per cent of the total public receipts in Spain. In this way, the metropolis came to be highly dependent on economic development in the colony.[1]

Before the sugar industry expanded in the middle of the eighteenth century to become Cuba's major export to this day, the Havana shipyard was the largest consumer of local supplies, and the biggest single employer in the island. So much was this the case that both the

Details of sailmaking techniques for a large sail (the *vela de trinquete* or fore sail) and attaching of lines. (*Marqués de la Victoria's Notebook*)

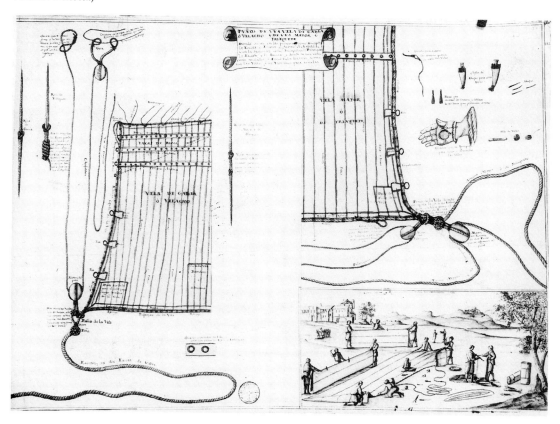

Lorenzo Montalvo Ruíz de Alarcón y Montalvo (1710–1778), Intendant of the Havana Shipyard. (*Courtesy of José Ordóñez y Montalvo, Concord, NH*)

yard and the sugar barons competed fiercely for the country's dwindling wood resources, the former to build ships, and the latter to use wood as fuel for boiling the sugar liquor from cane stalks. Spanish Cuba in the eighteenth century produced not only some of the world's best wooden warships as well as sugar, tobacco and rice, but the beginnings of an emerging class of entrepreneurs unique to the Caribbean. Their present descendants, exiles from Castro's Marxist Cuba, created one of Hispanic America's truly dynamic business classes. Its aggressiveness in exile has produced new Cuban business communities in Miami, South Florida and Puerto Rico. Other exiled Cuban businessmen also have enlivened moribund industrial societies in those Latin American republics – Venezuela, Colombia, Panamá and the Dominican Republic – where they have settled in large numbers and prospered greatly.

The Cuban *criollo*, or native entrepreneur, was unique for another major reason. Though his ancestors came from Spain as *peninsulares*, they stayed to prosper on the island. In time, many of them created huge fortunes entirely in Cuba and were ennobled by successive Spanish monarchs for their work in Cuban economic development to create a genuine and indigenous Cuban-born aristocracy. Such local aristocracy was the only one of its kind in Caribbean colonial history. Unlike many of those British fortune-hunters and sugar barons who returned from such Caribbean colonies as Jamaica and Barbados to build some of Britain's great country houses, the Cuban *criollo* entrepreneurs built their great estates in Cuba and remained permanently on the island with their fortunes and families.

Lord Hugh Thomas in his book *Cuba, or The Pursuit of Freedom*, emphasizes that the large British expedition that captured Havana in 1762 was made as much to enrich three of its cash-shy land and sea commanders (all brothers) as it was to reduce this most strategic of the Spanish Caribbean ports. The brothers were George, third Earl of Albemarle, the English

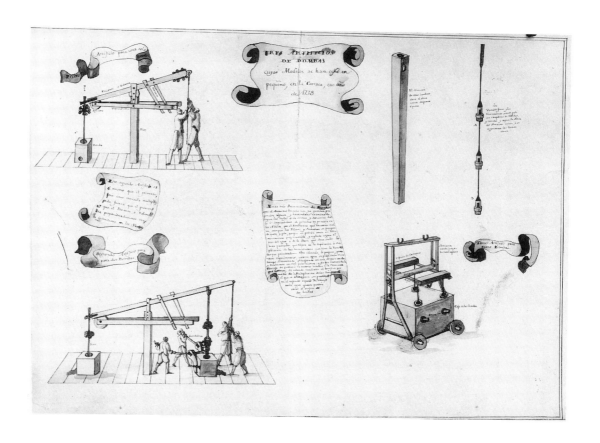

commander-in-chief, Commodore (later Admiral) Viscount Augustus Keppel, and Major General William Keppel, respectively second-in-command of the naval forces and one of that expedition's two divisional commanders. Where their father, described as 'plump, fair and unimaginative' had squandered his £90,000 inheritance during his lifetime, his sons did very well out of the Havana enterprise. Their success was made possible in part because the Spanish military commander of Havana before he surrendered, tried but failed to hide the city's bullion. After the end of the Seven Years' War, Albemarle bought the estate of Quidenham in Norfolk for £63,000.[2]

Some English histories inaccurately portray an inefficiently-run Spanish Cuba, rescued from ruin in 1762 by the British conquest. This took place, they say, because the temporary introduction of free trade to the colony made possible its subsequent economic prosperity. Not included in the so-called 'new era' was shipbuilding because the English occupiers had both sacked and dismantled the already expanding royal shipyard. Little of this is accurate. Albemarle did not conquer all of Cuba, only the city of Havana. Before 1762, the new Cuban class of entrepreneurs already was engaged in much illicit free trade, through the massive smuggling of slaves and sugar that took place between them and the nearby British and French island sugar colonies.

After the English left, the Havana shipyard was fully restored and expanded. It then entered into its greatest period of shipbuilding, made memorable both by the design and launching in March 1769 of the *Santísima Trinidad* as well as by the construction of 74 of the 227 *navíos* that served in the Spanish Navy during the eighteenth century. The shipyard's post-1762 renewal, as well as its activities immediately before the arrival of the English, was the work of one of Cuba's first entrepreneurs. He was Lorenzo Montalvo, the first of a succession

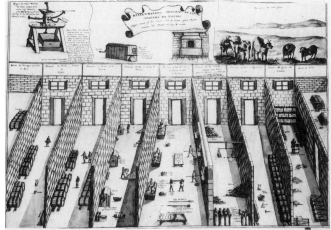

Division of dockyard warehouses for provisions including ▷ meats, corn, beans, wines. (*Marqués de la Victoria's Notebook*)

◁ Three different kinds of hand-operated pumps for shipyard use made in the Carraca (Cádiz) shipyard in 1738. (*Marqués de la Victoria's Notebook*)

Shipyard anchor production showing forges and fabricated ▷ sections. (*Marqués de la Victoria's Notebook*)

of Condes of Macuriges and the only shipyard intendant appointed by a Spanish king (Carlos III) outside of Spain itself. In fact, Lorenzo Montalvo Avellaneda y Ruíz Alarcón, first Count of Macuriges (named for his vast estate outside of Havana) had been in Cuba since his arrival in 1734 as navy commissary, and where he lived for the rest of his life. At the time of his death in 1778, Montalvo had spent forty-four years on the island, initially as the senior official behind the shipyard's growth but later in life, as one of the island's major investors in rich tobacco and sugar plantations.

The story of the Montalvos through Cuban and Spanish history indicates the great staying power of these once-influential families of the old Cuban oligarchy. Though Montalvo was born in Spain at Medina del Campo near Valladolid in 1710 and hence was a *peninsular*, the numerous Montalvo descendants who followed to this day, were Cubans and flourished in Cuban society as part of that country's oligarchy, until the Castro revolution ended it all for them in 1959.

A few examples from a succession of Montalvo family roles and functions will give some idea of its longevity and service. There were eight Counts of Macurigues ending with José María Montalvo y Orovio, executed in 1936 by the Spanish republicans during the Spanish Civil War. The son of the original Lorenzo Montalvo served as a lieutenant in the Spanish

Navy, married in Havana into another family of the Cuban commercial oligarchy and died there in 1794. Many of the descendants of the first Montalvo filled Cuban government posts and began private businesses during the nineteenth and twentieth centuries. These included senior cabinet posts in the ministries of Cuban presidents after independence in 1902, founders of railway companies in nineteenth century Cuba, and marriage into the families of the Hispanic rich and famous in Cuba and Spain. Carlos Saladrigas, a direct descendant of Lorenzo Montalvo, was Cuban prime minister and a candidate in 1944 for the Cuban presidency. José A García Ordóñez Montalvo, nephew of Saladrigas and a direct descendant of Lorenzo

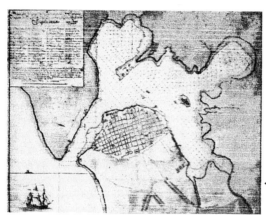

City and Bay of Havana, 1773. City has reached northern ▷ boundary of the shipyard that itself has expanded since 1749. (*Archivo General de Indias, Sevilla*)

◁ City and Bay of Havana, 1749. Shipyard still is far removed from City of Havana boundary. (*Archivo General de Simancas, Valladolid*)

Montalvo, retired in June 1987 from his post as history master at St Paul's School in Concord, New Hampshire. As his family's historian, he records with gallows humour the end of this long period of dominance by the *criollo* aristocracy in pre-Castro Cuba:

> A Cuban count (not named) who did not leave to go into exile and who I think died in Cuba, had a post in the National Museum where he was called 'Comrade Count'. If the tale has a telling truth (*veridico*) to it the *criollo* sense of humour has not been totally lost.[3]

The long Cuban-Spanish shipbuilding connection has lasted to the present. During the 1960s and 1970s, instead of Cuba building *navíos* for the Spanish Navy as it did two centuries ago, Spain built factory trawlers for the new state fishing fleet of Castro's Cuba.

The relationship was more than commercial but has lasted so long because of the unbroken familial relations between Spaniards and Cubans. The families of both Castro and Franco – the former a Marxist dictator and the latter an anti-Communist military one – came from Galicia. This is the rugged north-west maritime region of Spain that not only supplied the old Spanish Cuba with many of its entrepreneurial families, but was a major recipient of the profits that long ago accrued to the mother country from Cuba's once profitable sugar and tobacco industries. The former elite *Centro Gallego* (Galician Centre) in Havana which before the Cuban revolution was a private social club for wealthy Cuban families of Galician origin, is still in business, but as the major centre in Havana offering state marriages to all Cubans.

This Cuba-Spanish connection has not ended with Juan Carlos I, a Bourbon and a constitutional monarch who is the direct descendant of Carlos III. During a 1985 in-transit stopover in Madrid by Fidel Castro, returning from the USSR in his Soviet Il-62 jumbo jet, the Cuban leader wept when for the first time he stepped onto Spanish soil. Castro's father was a Gallego immigrant to eastern Cuba, where he owned profitable sugar planations. In the

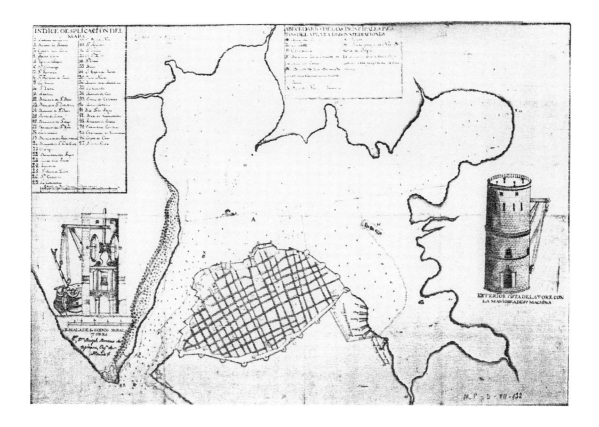

Hispanic world, as in the Anglo-Saxon, blood continues to run thicker than water.

Throughout the eighteenth century the *astillero real* at Havana remained central to Spanish naval shipbuilding policy, with its high point in output and efficiency coincident with the long stewardship of Lorenzo Montalvo. Why did this distant colonial shipyard so far from the motherland become the single most important shipyard of the Spanish empire in the eighteenth century, and one of the major producing ones of any European navy of the same era? Before the British captured Havana in 1762, the city's naval shipyard built 46 ships for the Spanish Navy, and 50 more after the English withdrawal. In the pre-1762 construction period going back to the launching of the 50-gun *Santa Rosa* in 1700, 32 of the Havana-built *navíos* carried 50 or more guns, while 14 carried 24 or fewer guns. The size of ships and the number of guns increased substantially after 1762, with four 112-gun ships built there between 1786 and 1794, three with more than 94 guns, five 74-gun ships, and seven more of between 60 and 68 guns. McNeill writes that:

> Havana not only built more ships than any port in Spain, it also built larger and more durable ones. Since accessible large timbers had become scarce in Spain, Havana built a disproportionate number of large ships. Of nine vessels of more than 80 guns in the Spanish Navy of 1778, six had been built in Havana, all before 1770. In 1771, six of the eight largest ships in the Spanish navy were Havana-built.[4]

The reasons for Havana's predominance as naval shipbuilder were all practical ones. Cuban tropical hardwoods – mahogany and cedar – lasted much longer in wooden ships than did Spanish and other European timbers. Cuban timbers were cheaper than Spanish ones, as was the partly slave Cuban work force. Skilled labour in the Havana shipyard appeared to be more

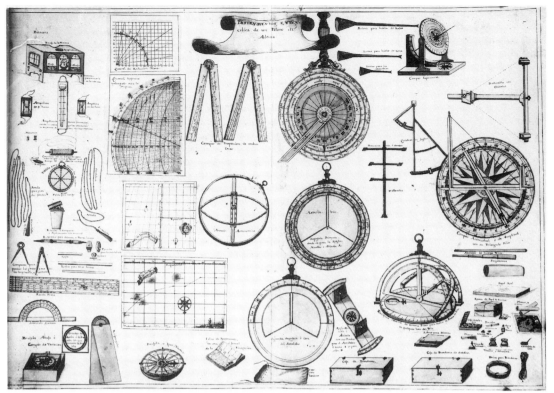

Many navigational instruments used by senior pilots, including an astrolabe (the sextant's predecessor), plain and azimuth compass, binnacle box, quadrant. Spanish ship captains and their most experienced pilots on board – especially those on the many very long voyages of exploration between 1770 and 1800 – were constantly perfecting such instruments. Churruca, himself no mean mathematician, perfected the chronometer late in the eighteenth century (around 1796). (*Museo Naval, Madrid*)

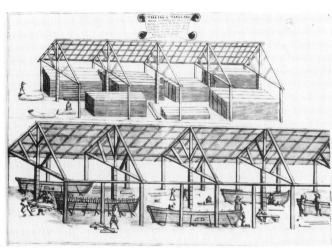

◁ Sheds for storing cut timber and construction of the ship's boats for a mid-eighteenth century *navío* (*Museo Naval, Madrid*)

efficient than in similar yards in Spain. This may indicate the emergence of craftsmen who displayed at another level the Cuban propensity to be competitive and entrepreneurial.

McNeill comments further that the operations of the Havana *astillero real* had lower materials and labour costs than the Spanish royal shipyards:

The availability of cheap lumber and labour accounted for the low shipbuilding costs of Havana. Together, these costs amounted to 86 per cent of the total construction costs of two 70-gun ships, the same proportion on two 60-gun ships and 69 per cent on an 80-gun ship. Fitting out (sails, cordage and pitch) came to no more than 30–32 per cent of the total cost of building these warships in Havana, less than in Europe. Labour and lumber costs on these three vessels were almost equal,

Shipyard anchor and buoy storage shed. (*Marqués de la* ▷
*Victoria's Notebook*)

▽ Workshops for making and storing various ship's parts such
as masts, cordage, cables, ship's weights for measuring both
food and gunpowder portions. On the right is the workshop
forge. (*Marqués de la Victoria's Notebook*)

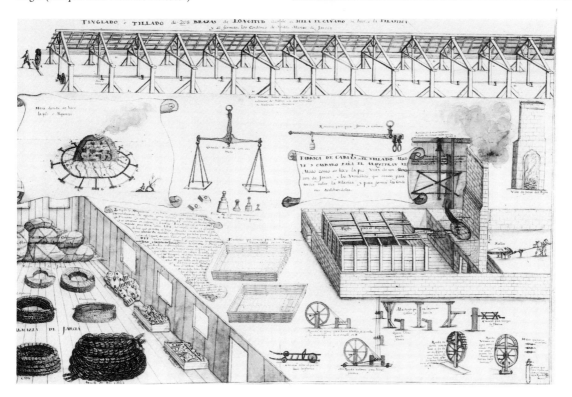

but this accounting included only wages paid to craftsmen, and not the cost and maintenance of
slaves of whom the arsenal employed 230.[5]

Undoubtedly, a factor in keeping unskilled labour costs in Havana below those in metropolitan
Spanish shipyards, was ready access to slave labour in Cuba. Studies on this aspect of labour
costs at the Havana *astillero* during the century are spotty. Yet in the early 1770s, both unskilled
and semi-skilled slave labour in the shipyard accounted for 25 per cent of the yard's total
estimated work force of 600.

Warship construction operations of the size and calibre produced in the Havana shipyard
played a major role in the expansion of the Cuban colonial economy two decades before the

Working drawing from around 1740 for the construction of ▷
a drydock (*dique*), which indicates that the wooden crane
(top left) for stepping and unstepping masts and yardarms is
of English origin. (*Museo Naval, Madrid*)

▽ The top right shows a method of stowing one of a *navío*'s
main anchors on the ship's hull, aft of the beakhead. The
main view shows a careened warship being graved. The old
anti-fouling is being burned off before a new solution is
added in an attempt to deter the teredo worm and prevent the
growth of weed on the ship's bottom. (*Museo Naval, Madrid*)

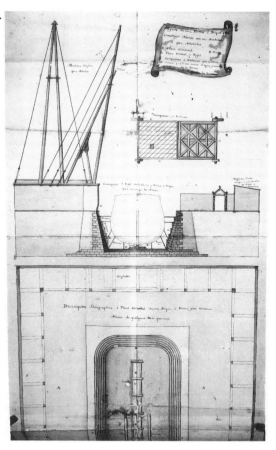

British occupation of the city in 1762 was supposed to have opened it up to 'free trade'. As
early as 1749, the Spanish Crown took measures to conserve and replant cedars in forest areas at
an increasingly greater distance from Havana, which yard managers had to exploit as material
needs accelerated. By the 1760s, the increasing timber needs for building some of the largest
*navíos* in the world were competing with the quickly-growing sugar industry. In 1760, the
boiling of sugar syrup from cane consumed 15 million cubic feet of wood annually, the same
quantity required for building a dozen ships of the line. Cuba's sugar barons did not long have
the Spanish Navy as a competitor. Its last Havana-built ship, the 40-gun frigate *Santa Ursula*,
was launched in 1797.

The central role of Havana as a principal shipbuilder for the Spanish Navy spanned the
eighteenth century. The first ship was launched in 1700 and the last, as noted above, in 1797. In
total, the Havana royal shipyard built 160 ships ranging from the giant 120-gun *Santísima
Trinidad* to tiny *goletas*, *ganguiles* and *bergantíns* of between 12 and 18 tons. The shipyard took
part in every major programme to rebuild the Spanish Navy from the report for modernization
of Bernardo de Tinajero in 1714 to the construction of the 112-gun *Principe de Asturias* in
1794, one of the *navíos* designed by Romero y Landa. Indeed, Havana's early inclusion in naval
shipbuilding plans reflected the bias that Tinajero demonstrated against the King's French
advisers who had come to Spain with Felipe V and who wanted Spain revived as a European
naval power. By contrast, Tinajero emphasized the strategic importance of the Atlantic, beyond

which lay the vast empire that supplied Spain with specie and raw materials.

To renew the Atlantic role meant rejuvenating the *Flota* to Vera Cruz that had languished since the middle of the seventeenth century, as well as the creation of a major regional and easily accessible shipbuilding capability at Havana. Cuba was recommended by Tinajero because its timber supply could reduce Spain's dependence on foreign wood imports. Three other Caribbean sites, two in Mexico and one in Venezuela, were considered along with Havana. But the others had neither Havana's fortified protection, nor its adequate manpower and raw materials facilities. Tinajero also subscribed to the naval design ideas of Admiral Antonio Gaztañeta for building *navíos* in standardized series rather than based on the whims of individual designers. Unfortunately, Tinajero's American naval redevelopment plans had to be shelved after the arrival of French businessman Jean Orry from the court of Louis XIV, to be the chief minister to Felipe V, in charge of Spain's finances.

Orry was instructed to strengthen Spain's economy in preparation for new wars against the European enemies of the two Bourbon kingdoms. Orry also reinstated the unsatisfactory policy of the late King Carlos II and bought naval ships from abroad, rather than building them at home. His overseas purchases included warships from France and Genoa. Tinajero remained the first secretary of navy affairs independent of the Council of the Indies. Nevertheless, he had to implement Orry's ideas for the navy, although they ran counter to his own. Orry did not last long. He was soon replaced as first minister by Cardinal Julio Alberoni, a favourite of the dominant Isabel Farnese. Though Italian-born like the queen, Alberoni was loyal to Spanish bureaucratic needs and abolished the navy secretariat as an unwanted French-inspired reform structure.

Tinajero's sound and workable ideas later were reinforced by Jorge Patiño whose impetus for taking charge was Spain's significant ship losses at Cape Passaro. According to G Douglas Inglis in his essay, 'The Spanish Naval Shipyard at Havana in the Eighteenth Century',

> By the time of Patiño's death in 1736, Spain possessed a professional navy of considerable strength with its own independent systems of construction, supply and maintenance. Patiño had made Tinajero's ideas a reality.[6]

The escalation of the existing Havana shipyard took place as a result of important local fleet and senior naval administrative changes. The New World merchant convoys made increasing use of Havana. At sea, the new post of commanding general of the American squadrons was created with the redoubtable Vice Admiral Rodrigo de Torres y Morales in the post. During his tenure, Torres both coordinated and increased Spanish Navy activities in the Caribbean, Gulf of Mexico and the western Atlantic. Torres also worked closely with Montalvo, the naval commissioner, on land after they had received instructions from the king to build new *navíos* in the Havana *astillero* or, as often happened, when ships' refits and repairs were needed for convoy naval escorts. These needs escalated considerably during the 1730s and 1740 as the *Flota*'s trans-Atlantic voyages were increased with the concomitant requirement of having to sail during the murderous Caribbean hurricane seasons.

In an eighteenth century navy too often criticized for having little or no administrative competence, Torres at sea and Montalvo on land were superb administrators who 'got things done' and, as the documents reveal, were free of inter-personal conflicts. Both men came from impoverished *hidalguía*, families with titles and usually a coat of arms, but little money. After long and hard years of service, the king elevated them to *títulos* or nobles of the realm. Montalvo already has been introduced: Torres now commands our attention.

Born at León in Spain in 1690, Torres began his career in the famous Manila Galleon that made its regular and usually lucrative return voyages every two or three years between Acapulco and Manila, as permitted by weather conditions at sea and political events on land. Like his naval contemporary, Blas de Lezo, he early came to attention because of his gallantry during the siege and recapture of Barcelona in 1714 from the Hapsburg forces that resisted Felipe V during the War of the Spanish Succession. Torres continued to fight in the Mediterranean theatre and to help win battles that resulted in the restoration of the islands of Mallorca and Sardinia to Spain. As early as 1719 when he was only twenty-nine Torres was promoted commodore because he saved his *navío* during the battle off Cape Passaro.

In his essay on Torres in the January-June 1982 issue of the *Revista de Historia de America*, Lowell W Newton has written one of the few studies in depth on the career of a prominent eighteenth century senior Spanish naval officer. At this mid-point in Torres' career when he was still under thirty-five years of age, Newton says of him:

> In the early 1720s, Commodore Torres joined a growing elite company of officers, such as the brilliant engineer Admiral Gaztañeta, Blas de Lezo, Manuel López Pintado [who developed, but did not carry out the first building programme at Havana for 60-gun *navíos*]. All [of them] would command *azogues* as well as treasure fleets. In the sense of professional dedication, Torres was now one of the 'new' Bourbon naval commanders of the *Carrera*.[7]

During the late 1720s and much of the 1730s, Torres continued in the 'Atlantic Trade' as commander of the all-important *azogue* fleets often operating in unseaworthy and dangerous ships. The naval documents in the General Archives at Simancas contain correspondence between Patiño and Juan de Acosta, about the constantly grim state of Torres' naval ships.[7] At one point, Juan de Acosta referred in particular to the *Santa Rosa* of 64 guns which he said was '… one of the worst vessels to sail the seas' and 'needs hurricanes of wind to be sailed'. This correspondence is confusing. *Santa Rosa* appears at the top of the definitive list of Spanish ships of the line prepared by Christian de St Hubert (see Appendix), who identifies her as a late-seventeenth century leftover from the almost non-existent navy of Carlos II. According to St Hubert, the *Santa Rosa* never saw service in the Caribbean or at Havana, but was captured by the British at Cape Passaro and laid up at Minorca. St Hubert further indicates that 'Britain offered to return the ships captured at Passaro [almost all of them new ones built by Gaztañeta], but they were found to be rotten and (were) broken up.' The answer could be that although in the documents Acosta referred to the *Santa Rosa*, he must have meant the *Rosa*, a 56-gun *navío* launched at Pasajes in 1727 and wrecked off Vera Cruz in 1736.

In any case, worse befell Torres, namely the dismasting of two ships under his command in a tremendous Caribbean hurricane in 1731 and his later loss of the complete fleet under his command in July 1733 when it was caught in one of the worst recorded storms of the period. A replacement of rescue ships was sent out from Havana after 500 sailors in Torres' fleet had been lost. Salvage efforts were successfully attempted since his ships went down in shallow waters. Torres was not blamed or punished for these losses. In the latter instance, the king in far-off Madrid wrote of his relief that Torres had been spared from death in the storm.[9]

These disasters reflected the urgency of moving to Spain the valuable specie that was contained in the vessels of *La Flota*. Too often during seasonally bad weather, the Spanish commanders and their superiors in Havana took chances with the fleet, hoping thereby to outrun it, in the rush to reach the broad Atlantic. Torres' mainly successful voyages with the *Flota* during the late 1720s and early 1730s remind us that, despite war and bad weather, most

Concept only (the Spanish word used is *Idea*) for a floating ▷
'machine' to step or raise up (*arbolar*) or unstep and lower
masts (*desarbolar*) in larger ships such as frigates and *navíos*
and built on a *chata*, a flat-bottomed barge used in shipyards.
(*Museo Naval, Madrid*)

▽ Chief types of anchors and buoys used by mid-eighteenth
century warships. (*Museo Naval, Madrid*)

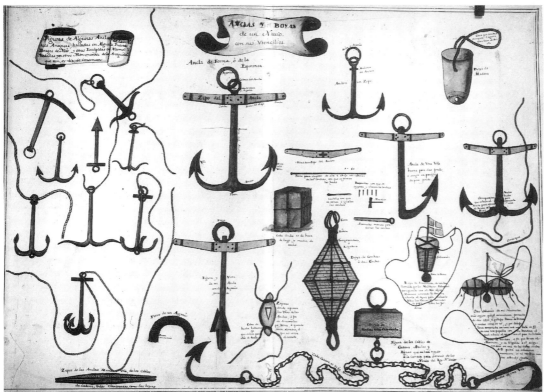

of the *Flota*'s convoys reached Spain successfully.

    Throughout the history of the operations of the *Flota*, more ships were lost in the
devastating Caribbean hurricanes, or because crews were decimated from yellow fever picked
up at Vera Cruz and Havana, than were captured or sunk by the English. The fleet that sailed
under Torres from Havana in the spring of 1731 reached Cádiz safely in July 1731 with
1,700,000 pesos in bullion, coins, gems and precious herbs on board. On the other hand, the
fleet that Torres lost in the summer hurricane of 1733 in the deadly, narrow passage between

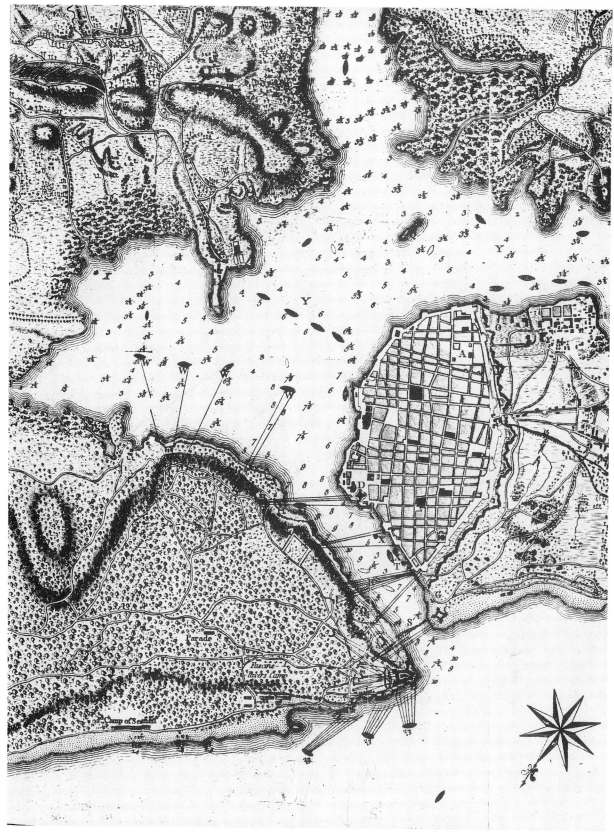

Havana and its environs, 1762. The map depicts the position of ships during the British attack. The dockyard, marked 'O', is south-east of the city, immediately outside the city walls. (*From a contemporary work by Thomas Mante*)

south Florida and the northern coast of Cuba contained cargo worth 12.5 million pesos. Professor Newton comments on why such skilled fleet commanders as Torres took such great risks, although the New Summation of the Laws of the Indies expressly prohibited fleet departures during the hurricane season: '... Fleets sailed regularly during the hurricane seasons with breath-taking high-handedness. Despite the laws or Patiño's Ordinances ... the needs of empire came first, caution and precaution second.' In history, therefore, it is manifestly untrue to repeat that the major cause of inaction or loss at sea of the Spanish Caribbean bullion fleets was English attacks. On one spectacular occasion, the British took the same chance with the weather as did the Spanish. This was in the route chosen by Lord Albemarle's large fleet and army on his way to attack Havana. On this occasion, the stakes were much larger since the forces taking the more dangerous passage around Cuba to Havana were greater in number than those of any *Flota* that sailed.

Lord Albemarle's fleet, under the command of Sir George Pocock, included 22 ships of the line, 30 transports and 11,351 troops from England, North America, South Carolina, Dominica, Guadeloupe, Antigua and Newfoundland. Albemarle knew of the other great menace that faced them at Havana, the prospect of major troop and crew losses from yellow fever and malaria. Already, no fewer than 4308 sick and dying troops of the original English force of 15,659 had been left behind in the Caribbean islands of Martinique, St Lucia, Grenada, Dominica and the Grenadines. A most revealing account of Albemarles's choice of his expedition's passage to Havana is the contemporary one written by Major Thomas Mante, a brigade major in the Havana expedition. In his book *The History of the Late War in North America and the Islands of the West Indies*, published in London in 1772, he writes:

> With his fleet the Admiral had the choice of two routes to the [sic] Havanna: the first and the most obvious was the common one, along the south-side of Cuba, and so into the track of the galleons. But this, though by much the fastest, could not but prove equally tedious, and delays above all things were to be avoided, as the success of the whole enterprise depended, to all appearance, on its being in forwardness before the hurricane season came on. He therefore resolved to run along the north shores of that island through that very intricate and almost unknown passage of the old Bahama Straits, in length nearly fifty leagues; and this though in great want of pilots for such a course ... scarce any one of them had the least satisfactory knowledge of these straits, or was able to take the charge of a single ship through them, much less to conduct so large a fleet.[10]

Major Mante then continued with the identical observation without doubt made many times both by *Flota* and Spanish Navy ship captains and commanders, who had to beat against the prevailing trade winds around the western end of Cuba to bring them into Havana harbour on the north coast:

> The first reason that induced him [Sir George Pocock] to risk this passage ... was, that if he endeavoured to go round the island of Cuba ... many of the transports and heavy-laden store ships would not, perhaps, have been able to beat up in again in time from the west-end of Cuba to the [sic] Havanna, against the trade-winds and currents.[11]

Albemarle's successful decision to reach Havana via the more dangerous Bahamas* Passage route was not unlike Lord Nelson's even more successful attack in 1798 against the French

---

*The very name of the Bahamas is an abbreviation of the Spanish name assigned to the waters around that archipelago as long ago as the voyages of Columbus. In its unabridged form *baja mar* in Spanish, Bahamas means 'low water'.

Navy from the landward side in the Battle of the Nile. On the decision of his expedition's course to Havana, Albemarle displayed what later in the same century was to be called 'the Nelson touch' – nerve and taking a chance to win not anticipated by the enemy.

Such actions do not take away from the many daring sailing decisions made by Spanish commanders over the years. Some of the most dangerous of these were carried out in the same Cuban waters. Nevertheless, the British propensity to go one step further to win – even at great risk to substantial naval forces – was the basic reason they so often discomfited the Spanish in an

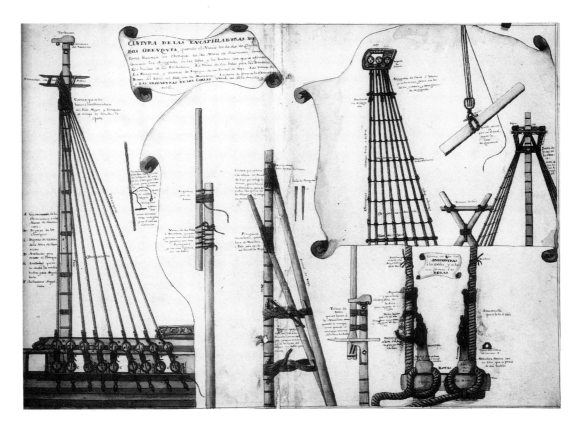

action the latter could have won, or at worst, could have forestalled.

Torres was not the only eighteenth century Spanish fleet or ship commander whose long life at sea in this particular service was marked both by great bravery and the practice of the best of seamanship through the most perilous weather conditions. The professionalism of other officers and men who sailed in the Windward Fleet – or for that matter, in the Manila Galleons, which usually were at sea for months – also gives the lie to Nelson's arrogant and unfounded remark following his brief Cádiz visit in 1793 that 'the Spanish do not make men'.[12]

The Havana *astillero* with which Torres was associated both for the construction of new ships and the repair of others under his command that were badly damaged in Caribbean hurricanes, experienced two major phases of growth during the eighteenth century. Before 1735, the first rudimentary yard was small, inefficient and highly labour-intensive even for such a facility in the pre-industrial era. Launchings in the old yard often took days to complete, for the lack of proper launching equipment. A contemporary map in the General Archive of the

Indies in Seville, dated 1733 by its anonymous maker, shows only bare land at the then-remote bay outside the city limits where Montalvo built the new *astillero real* in 1736. A later map of the 'City and Bay of La Habana' dated 1749 by José Montero de Espinos and preserved in the General Archives of Simancas, shows five slipways and an integrated shipyard.

A 1794 map of the city by José del Río toward the end of the Havana *astillero*'s era of growth – and held by the Naval Museum in Madrid – indicates how the city had expanded beyond the *astillero*'s boundaries. A nineteenth century map dated 1817 in the Military

Deck plan of all beams and supporting pieces, including the ▷ many hatchways of the main deck of a *navío*. (*Museo Naval, Madrid*)

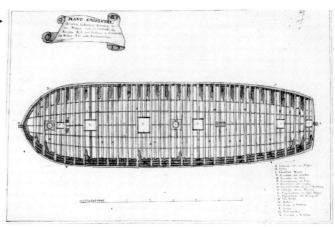

◁ Shrouds and their fittings for the mid-eighteenth century *navío* (*Museo Naval, Madrid*)

▽ Views through the decks from the bow and stern of a mid-eighteenth century *navío*, displaying the main pieces and shapes of wood used in a *navío*'s construction. (*Museo Naval, Madrid*)

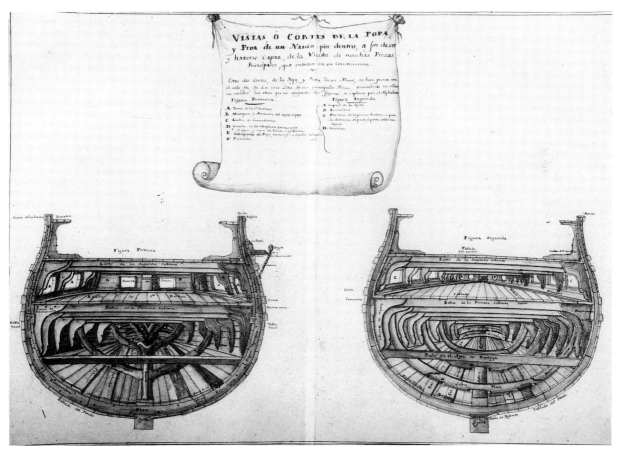

Historica Service of the Ministry of the Army in Madrid, indicates a fully-integrated facility to serve a much-reduced Spanish Navy that continued, nevertheless, to operate in the defence of Spanish Cuba. On 12 August 1730 Patiño wrote to Rodrigo de Torres y Morales, directing him to construct one *navío* a year in Havana and to employ Juan de Acosta as 'captain of the royal shipyard'. In April 1731 Torres was in a high-level meeting with four senior officials, including the captain general of the island and the navy commissioner, to plan an expanded shipyard.

The organizational and financial structures of the new yard were one of the first manifestations of Cuban entrepreneurism. Montalvo and his staff helped to develop the two methods of royal shipbuilding used at Havana. In neither case was the Spanish state the sole builder. The first method was the *asiento*, or contract-letting process. The second method, and in the long run the less successful of the two, was the creation of a separate private trading company with royal orders to build warships.

Under the *asiento*, the Spanish state let out a contract to a private person prepared to invest his funds in naval ship construction. After the ship was built, it was purchased by the navy for an agreed price. The master shipwright – Juan de Acosta at the start – was in charge of all phases of ship construction, as well as the dispersal of funds for shipbuilding. Inglis describes how the Havana Company functioned:

> Martín de Aróstegui as the president of the company, received a monopoly of the island's export agricultural production and trans-Atlantic imports. Campillo [First Minister José de Campillo y Cosío] garnered five per cent of the company's stock for the royal family, free transportation in the company's ships of munitions and naval stores bound for Havana and an open clause that Aróstegui would contract separately with the Admiralty for future naval construction in Cuba.[13]

In the long run the Havana Company was not a success. Though it built twelve *navíos* and two frigates, none of them was constructed at a profit. The three 70-gun ships *Vencedor*, *Africa* and *Tigre* each cost 167,000 pesos to build, but the purchase price paid by the crown was only 75,000 pesos each. Campillo instructed the company directors that they would have to meet the continued costs of the new shipyard's equipment and installations over the years. These included new slipways and administrative buildings as well as smaller sheds for the manufacture of rope and the storage of pitch.

Normally, ship repair and maintenance are lucrative shipyard activities, especially those conducted on a cost-plus basis. Yet, the Havana Company did not seem to do well with these activities even though according to the records, it docked and resheathed the bottoms of no fewer than 42 ships. Winding up the naval shipbuilding activities of the Havana Company was tedious and required the approval of Ferdinand VI. The king agreed to close down the company only after it completed the last five ships of the line and two frigates already contracted. Among these were the two 80-gun ships *Rayo* and *Fénix*. Despite its financing difficulties with the crown, the Havana Company certainly built *navíos* to last. The *Rayo* lasted 56 years, survived Trafalgar as one of Admiral Gravina's *navíos*, only to be stranded and lost on the shoreline at Rota in the devastating storm on the day after the battle. The *Rayo* was one of the last ships of the line built by Juan de Acosta who, for more than twenty years, had been the master shipwright in the Havana *astillero*.

Following the departure of the English from Havana in 1762, the Spanish were able to recover the five *navíos* taken after the capture of that city. These included the three ships sunk as block ships at the entrance to Havana harbour but which failed to stop the English fleet from entering the port, and two uncompleted *navíos* on the stocks. These were the 94-gun *San Carlos* (the third of that name) and the 60-gun *América*. Like *Rayo*, *San Carlos* and *América* were Havana-built to last. The former was completed as a two-decker, converted to a three-decker at the Cartagena yard in 1801 and was not broken up until 1819. The *América* surrendered to the British in the capitulation agreement of 1762 but was not finished by them. Indeed, she was not completed until 1766 and survived even longer than *San Carlos*, before being broken up in 1823.

After the Havana Company's withdrawal from naval shipbuilding, the crown reverted to

Nails for the construction of *navíos* and frigates were categorised by weight and number in the inventories of eighteenth century Spanish shipyards (*astilleros*). (*Museo Naval, Madrid*)

the *asiento* method of financing and building vessels at Havana but with recurring difficulties in securing private investors. The year following the British withdrawal from the city, the first navy treasury was opened in Havana (in July 1763) for the full state financing of new *navíos* and frigates. This development terminated the navy's reliance on the uncertain *asiento* contractual system. In any case, Cuban entrepreneurs had set their sights on other investment projects in post-invasion Spanish Cuba which were more lucrative than building warships, namely, sugar, tobacco, rum and the slave trade.

On 17 December 1763 Carlos III created a naval intendancy at Havana similar to those in the shipyards of peninsular Spain, and appointed Montalvo as Spain's first naval intendant overseas. The expanding roles of the intendant included his control over the declining forest reserves of Cuba with the sugar industry demanding ever more timber, both for processing cane juice and as staves for the barrels and boxes for shipping sugar and molasses abroad. Montalvo also had to find a non-Cuban substitute for the tall pines required for the lower masts of *navíos* and frigates. Such pines did not grow in Cuba but were found in abundance in central Florida. Unfortunately, Spain had to cede that territory to England under the terms of the Treaty of Paris in 1763. Florida was not re-conquered until 1780.

In the meantime, pine cutting areas were opened up at Cuatzacoalcos on the Mexican coast,

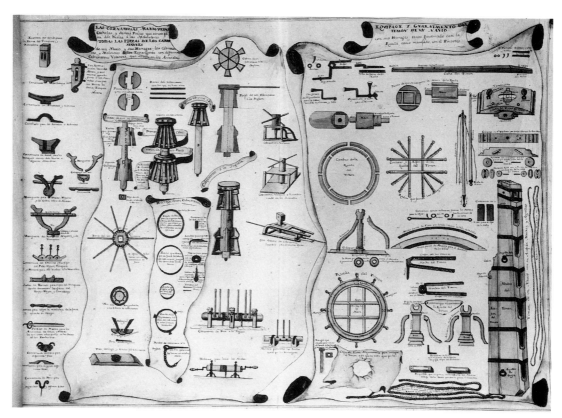

On left, parts of an eighteenth century *navío*'s capstan (*cabrestante*) and deck fittings; on right, parts of the rudder (*timón*) and steering gear. (*Museo Naval, Madrid*)

a low-lying and unhealthy Caribbean site if ever there was one. Prior to the Havana shipyard's expansion after 1735, Torres under direction from Patiño in Madrid, had investigated Cuatzacoalcos as a place to expand Spain's Caribbean shipbuilding activities. Although some construction had taken place there, he recommended that it should not be expanded. In the long run, Cuatzacoalcos became mainly a source of supply of pine for the big yard in Havana. Even with the small amount of shipbuilding at San Blas on its west coast for the north Pacific explorers of the 1770s, the territory of the Viceroyalty of New Spain never amounted to much as naval shipbuilder for the Spanish crown. Limited colonial shipyards were in existence at Guayaquil in modern Ecuador and on Nicaragua's Pacific coast, with further limited repair and careening facilities at Buenos Aires. However, none of these approached Havana as a major naval shipbuilding centre.

Meantime, during the 1760s and into the 1770s, almost to the year of his death in 1778 aged sixty-eight, Montalvo expanded and integrated an increasingly busy Havana shipyard. Such expansion included new offices for both the naval treasury and the naval intendant, a graving facility (careenage) for the smaller fast trans-Atlantic packet-boats and a forge to fashion iron from Spain into ships' fittings. At the same time, the city was steadily expanding westwards from its pre-1762 dimensions with the growing shipyard pressing on such key edifices as the Royal Tobacco Factory. The earlier Havana Company also had lost its

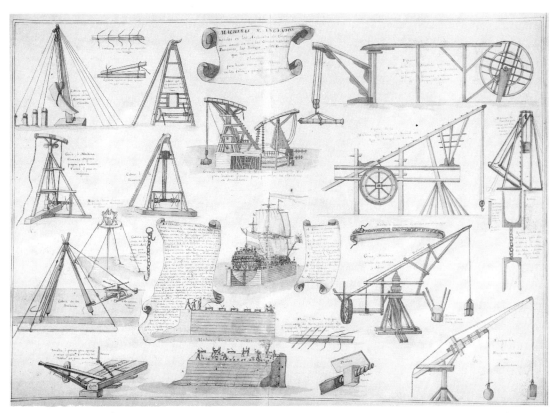

Various kinds of *machinas y ingenios* (machines and mechanical devices) used in ship construction and repair in the eighteenth century Spanish shipyard. (*Museo Naval, Madrid*)

monopoly on tobacco export which then reverted to this factory, one of the many crown corporations to be found in the economy of Spanish America. These space limitations forced Montalvo to place the essential cordage and rope warehouses across the harbour from the *astillero real* and the powder magazine at the harbour's end, close to or on the site of the present Soviet-built Fishing Port.

Both before and after 1762, the Havana *astillero* was known for building *navíos* at lower costs than the metropolitan yards in Spain. Academics give many reasons for this, including Cuba's cheaper and more accessible timber supplies. A contract dated April 1731 indicates that the self-same master shipwright, Juan de Acosta, who built some of Havana's best *navíos* of his era, also received 120,000 pesos annually as a private wood contractor for the crown. It would seem that Acosta too had caught the spirit of Cuban entrepreneurship.

As observed earlier, Cuban cedar had a much longer life than Spanish oak; it was more resistant to tropical wood-rot organisms and less likely to splinter from hits by cannon balls than European oak. Such long-lived *navíos* as the Havana-built *Rayo* were in active service for as long as twenty years before their first major refit. On the other hand, wounds from Cuban hardwood splinters festered sooner than those inflicted by oak. Cuba's reliance on slave labour also kept costs down in the shipyard. Many of the great Cuban impresarios during the eighteenth and nineteenth centuries made their fortunes not out of sugar, rum and tobacco, but

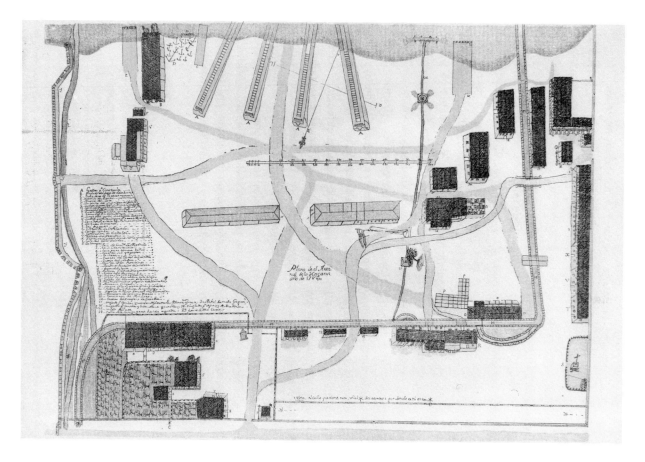

from the slave trade. Day labourers in the yard and on the logging teams were largely slave labour, with only 100 out of 900 workers identified as 'skilled craftsmen'.

Despite the growing presence of the sugar industry as early as the 1770s, the Havana shipyard continued to play a major role in Cuba's economy. The vital role of the Spanish Navy and Caribbean-based ships supporting the rebels in the American Revolutionary War, particularly in the successful Spanish campaign against English Florida, resulted in a record annual expenditure of 6 million pesos on the Havana shipyard. It is inaccurate to say that the Havana *astillero* went into a steady decline after the British left. Rebuilt, expanded and properly funded, the yard entered its golden era, one of quality ship production. Many of the post-1762 warships were produced there using unexcelled naval shipbuilding methods until the end of the century.

Even after Spain ceased to be a great naval power in the age of sail following the crippling disasters of Trafalgar, the Napoleonic invasion of the motherland between 1808 and 1812 and the loss of most of her American empire in the early 1820s, the Spanish Navy's *astillero real* at Havana was enlarged and prospered, as the Havana city map of 1817 clearly indicates. Cuba, 'the Pearl of the Antilles', along with neighbouring Puerto Rico, remained as Spanish imperial territories until they were lost in the Spanish–American War of 1898, a century after the last big Havana-built *navío* was launched in 1797. As the nineteenth century progressed, these two rich sugar-producing islands became even richer from their ever-expanding sugar exports. By the 1860s, even the personal fortune of the Spanish royal family included ownership of Cuban sugar plantations.

Among the other great Cuban sugar-producing families, with their strong familial and business connections at the highest level in the Spanish court, the centres of business and industry were the O'Farrills, owners of eleven sugar mills and an immense 19,000 producing acres of sugar. With the O'Farrills we come full circle. The Montalvo descendants who

In 1980, a set of stamps from Marxist Cuba honoured ▷ eighteenth century Spanish naval shipbuilding in the Havana royal shipyard.
- 3 centavos: *navío Rayo* under construction, 1749.
- 7 centavos: *navío Santísima Trinidad* under construction, 1769.
- 10 centavos: *navío Santísima Trinidad* under full sail.

◁ Detailed plan of Havana Shipyard in 1788 following the period of greatest production. (*Museo Naval, Madrid*)

inherited the substantial sugar estates acquired by the original Lorenzo Montalvo, remained influential and powerful for other reasons.[14] Not the least of these was inter-marriage with other powerful Cuban-Spanish families with the best connections, including the O'Farrills. The mid-nineteenth century marriage of a Montalvo descendant of the first generation of Cuba's sugar barons, to an O'Farrill from the even-richer second generation of the same, linked through the altar those families whose wealth and aggressiveness continued to make Spanish Cuba the richest European Caribbean colony well into the nineteenth century.[15]

To defend and protect this rich colony, it is understandable why the *astillero real* was still necessary during the later age of steam and iron ships, and why a Havana naval squadron now composed of armoured cruisers, sloops and gunboats was needed as were the *navíos* and frigates at the height of Spain's power in the Caribbean. Without carrying the analogy too far, it is true to say that the entrepreneurship in eighteenth century Cuban naval shipbuilding, both during the years of the Havana Company, and more especially in the long tenure of Lorenzo Montalvo, helped to fashion Cuban military and economic history. Small wonder then, that as recently as 1980, Castro's Marxist anti-capitalist regime – the one that sent Cuba's business class into permanent exile – glorified the activities of the *astillero real* in a series of special stamps featuring the *Rayo* and *Santísima Trinidad* under construction.

The 112-gun *Real Carlos* built in Havana, which blew up
accidentally in the 1801 night action off Gibraltar. From the
Alejo de Berlinguero painting. (*Museo Naval, Madrid*)

## CHAPTER FOUR

# Spaniards at Sea: Officers and Men

*Thence we sailed against the Spaniard*
*With his hordes of plate and gold*
*Which he wrung with cruel tortures*
    *from Indian folk of old*
*Likewise the merchant captains*
    *with hearts as hard as stone*
*Who flogged men and keelhauled them*
*And starved them to the bone.*

    Charles Kingsley, 'The Last Buccaneer'

*I cannot praise enough the forebearing virtue of*
*the Spanish. Rarely or never is it given to us to*
*encounter a nation that has suffered so many adverse*
*calamities as they suffered in their discoveries of*
*the Indies – persisting nevertheless in their*
*enterprise with unconquerable perseverance and*
*succeeding in enticing to their country such*
*marvellous regions that one loses the memory of past*
*dangers.*

    Sir Walter Raleigh in his *History of the World*

WHO ARE WE TO BELIEVE in assessing the true character and real purposes of the Spanish in history? Is it to be Charles Kingsley, the Victorian socialist and hispanophobe who perpetuates in his harsh verses the all-too-familiar English view that the Spanish in history were fundamentalist purveyors of cruelty, corruption and fierce Catholic bigotry? Or, do we accept the laudatory remarks of Sir Walter Raleigh, one of the Elizabethan 'seadogs' who, unlike Kingsley and the rest of the Anglo-Saxon detractors of Spain, was sought by the Spanish as a detested pirate and so had a reason to hate Spaniards?

In searching for the true nature of Spain, the Spanish do not help with their mystical and fatalistic view of themselves. We forget that whatever they accomplished in a century that bordered on the industrial revolution and the emergence of contemporary institutions of government, was done within a devout Catholic society where the grim Inquisition could call a wayward believer to account. Jorge Ortega y Gasset, the great liberal Spanish philosopher of our own time, once wrote that 'Spain is a cloud of dust on the road of history.' H V Morton, in his book with the honest title *A Stranger in Spain*, wrote of Philip II, the creator of the great, doomed Spanish Armada: '... he was the junior partner of Spain, the senior being the deity.' Both illusive and fatalistic, the Spanish continue to confuse, to elude, and at times, to anger the more pragmatic English. The latter would have ignored their eccentricities if history's many religious and dynastic wars had not placed these maritime states on opposite sides.

The eighteenth century Spanish ship captain, dockyard manager, and Madrid bureaucrat, inherited the religious fatalism of their ancestors. At the same time, they had little in common with the proselytizing, rampaging sixteenth century *conquistador*. For the Spanish naval leaders of the 1700s, the religious zeal of the Catholic Counter-Reformation was replaced by the excitement of the eighteenth century's intellectual and scientific enlightenment. New methods of navigation, innovative ship designs and technocratic style in government did not mean the abandonment of Catholic values. These functions were seen as God's will and purpose. This

FATES OF LINE OF BATTLE SHIPS IN THE EIGHTEENTH CENTURY ARMADA ESPAÑOLA

| | | | |
|---|---|---|---|
| Wrecked, burned, sunk in storms | 55 | Broken up, stricken or hulked | 91 |
| Sunk in battle | 15 | Captured from the British | 2 |
| Captured by the British | 35 | Captured from the French | 14 |
| Sold | 20 | Assigned to the French Navy (after 1796) | 6 |
| Mutiny | 1 | | |

may explain the Spanish fatalism that was especially noticeable after a defeat at sea. It also emerged in such statements about Trafalgar as in the mid-nineteenth century study on that battle by Manuel Marliani that '... there are disasters that may be honoured as victory.'[1] Spain throughout the eighteenth century remained a most Catholic of countries in which saints' and religious names were used in abundance. Of the 227 *navíos* built in Spain during the eighteenth century, 75 bore the names of church saints. Some of them carried the names for Our Lady the Holy Mother and of Catholic doctrine. Ships so named included the famous 136-gun *Santísima Trinidad* (The Most Holy Trinity) and the 30-gun *Nuestra Señora de Atocha* (Our Lady of Atocha). The latter was the first frigate built at Guarnizo in 1723, a namesake of the earlier famous treasure ship that sank in a hurricane off Florida a hundred years earlier. Others with religious names included the two 112-gun three-deckers, *Purísima Concepción* (Most Pure Conception) and the *Salvador del Mundo* (Saviour of the World).

Yet, the Church did not reject bureaucratic method. The mediaeval Saint Teresa of Avila operated her religious houses with the executive skills of a modern hotel chain president. Her impatience with others was sometimes expressed in secular terms. 'God save me from sullen saints,' she once blurted out. The Spanish Jesuits in particular, before they were expelled from Spain and her dominions by Carlos III, were thoroughly bureaucratized in the modern sense. Jesuit reports to Rome on all kinds of state activities within Hispanic America, had all the marks of contemporary briefs sent to CIA or MI5 headquarters from their operators in the field.

Despite all this, many of the English state papers and memoranda written from overseas between the demise of the Armada and the Anglo-Spanish Wars of the 1700s, constantly referred to Spanish naval captains and fleet commanders as Catholic zealots who were losers and incompetents at sea. The considerable bureaucratic reforms of Carlos III that marked the highlight of Spanish national revival in the 1700s were introduced by a devout Catholic monarch for whom his daily ritual of morning mass remained as important as the secular duties of ruling his vast empire. Yet, he was no Philip II. That most Catholic of Spanish kings considered himself an instrument of God while he choked imperial decision-making by single-handedly processing his government's paperwork. Where Philip II was said to have 'ruled the world with two inches of paper,' Carlos III delegated authority and perfected the many state ministries begun at the start of the century, including those associated with the navy and the Indies.

Nor was Carlos III a gloomy religionist like Philip II, his Spanish Habsburg predecessor. Carlos III remained a widower who loved the hunt – excessively so – and the quiet pleasures of country palaces constructed by his Bourbon ancestors. Aranjuez Palace, 25 miles removed from Madrid and built by the French Bourbon Felipe V to remind him of Versailles, was far removed from Philip II's ominous pile of the Escorial, the repository for the remains of Spanish kings. Today, the visitor to Aranjuez can relax in the gardens and sylvan delights of his palace as did Carlos III. Added to by Carlos III and his son Carlos IV, Aranjuez is laid out as a miniature Spanish Versailles with a profusion of long gardens, rows of boxwood hedges,

CHRONOLOGY OF SPAIN'S EIGHTEENTH CENTURY WARS AGAINST BRITAIN

WAR OF THE SPANISH SUCCESSION, 1701–1713
English capture Gibraltar, 23–24 July 1704.
First and second unsuccessful Spanish attempts to recapture Gibraltar, 1704–5.

WAR OF THE QUADRUPLE ALLIANCE, 1718–1720
Spanish naval defeat off Cape Passaro, 1718.

ANGLO–SPANISH–FRENCH WAR, 1727–1729
Third unsuccessful Spanish attempt to recapture Gibraltar, 1727.

'WAR OF JENKIN'S EAR' AND WAR OF THE AUSTRIAN SUCCESSION, 1739–1748
Actually a single war that began for England in 1739 in the Caribbean following the incident of 'Jenkin's ear' but which in effect was another European dynastic war that began in 1740.
The English captured Portobelo in 1739 but the Spanish repulsed the major English land/sea attack against Cartagena de Indias in 1741 and fought a drawn naval battle against an English fleet off Cape Sicié near Toulon in 1744.
Commodore George Anson's wartime circumnavigation of the world 1740–1744 and capture of Spanish Manila Galleon *Nuestra Señora de Covadonga* filled with treasure.

THE SEVEN YEARS WAR, 1756–1763
(Spain did not declare war against England until 1762, but quickly lost Manila, Havana and Florida).

AMERICAN REVOLUTIONARY WAR, 1776–1783
Spain declared war against England in 1779, captured east Florida and the Bahamas from the English in 1780 and 1781 – and won naval successes against a Royal Navy that had been in a state of disrepair since the end of the Seven Years War.
Fourth unsuccessful Spanish attempt to recapture Gibraltar during the three-year siege of The Rock, 1779–1782.
Peace of Paris in 1783 assigned Florida, Louisiana and Majorca to Spain, returned the Bahamas to England and confirmed the creation of the United States of America.

NAPOLEONIC WARS (1) 1796–1802
Spain at war with England by the Treaty of San Ildefonso signed with France in August 1796 and continued until the Peace of Amiens, 1802.
Spanish naval defeat at Cape St Vincent, 14 February 1797.

NAPOLEONIC WARS (2) 1803–1808
Resumption of war against England until the Napoleonic invasion of Spain in 1808 that made Spanish Loyalist forces allies of the invading British armies during the Peninsular War 1808–1814.
Battle of Trafalgar, 21 October 1805 and destruction of the Combined Squadron of the French and Spanish fleets.

NOTE: Spain and Britain were wartime allies only once during the eighteenth century. In 1793, Spain joined the European monarchies – including England – who declared war during 1793 against the new revolutionary and anti-monarchist regime in France. However in 1795 under the Treaty of Basel, Spain withdrew from the monarchist alliance to ally itself once again with France in a new war against England that broke out in 1796.

straight pines, birches and sycamores. Much of the naval correspondence addressed to Carlos III from commanders at sea and the shipyard managers (including that of Jorge Juan) went to the king in residence at Aranjuez.

The many reforms of Carlos III were not necessarily a measure of a 'new Catholicism' in Spain any more than improved ways of governing the British nation and managing the Royal Navy were part of a 'new Protestantism' in Georgian Britain. And yet, the Spanish remain in British history more villainous, treacherous and cruel than Britain's other enemies. Kingsley's bitter little verses are a mid-Victorian version of the calumnies about the Spanish race and character that have continued to the present.

Despite these sharp differences, other factors suggest that Spain and England were not 'natural enemies'. After all, Anglo-Spanish enmity originated during the years of the European Reformation when English Protestants and Spanish Catholics fought each other in 'holy wars'. As great sea powers, the English and Spanish had to employ their navies in similar ways in the business of empire. For both countries, large navies were needed to defend the commerce that moved between their colonial empires and the European motherlands. This was a naval role carried out first by Spain because in history, Spanish imperial expansion preceded that of the English.

Many English and Spanish definitions of the meaning of sea power are identical. 'To speak of the empire is to speak of the navy of sailors, of the things of the sea'—familiar thoughts to generations of Englishmen about their Royal Navy, but uttered by a famous Spaniard about *La Armada Española.*[2] He was none other than Generalíssimo Francisco Franco, *Caudillo* or Leader of Spain from 1939 to 1975, whose many appearances in the uniform of a captain general of the navy were a reminder that Franco's military career began in the Spanish Navy, not in the army. The loss of two fleets in the Spanish–American War of 1898 resulted in the closing of the Spanish Naval Academy at El Ferrol. Therefore, naval cadet Francisco Franco, the son of a poorly paid naval paymaster, was compelled to enter the army. As a naval officer, he would have been lost to history. In nineteenth and twentieth century Spain, it was the army and not the navy that carried out military coups such as that of 18 July 1936 which resulted in the Civil War and brought Franco to power.

For both the Spanish and the English in the age of empire-building, more than trade followed the flag and the fleet. 'We wish to recall that until Trafalgar arrived in history the ... grandeur of the Spanish Navy is the same grandeur of many maritime nations, and this is and for always ... our language.' So wrote *Arriba* in June 1942, the now-defunct newspaper of Franco's Falange Party. Such statements of pride and place can be historically inaccurate. In late 1983 the Royal Canadian Mint announced the sale of $100 gold coins to commemorate the 400th anniversary of the landing in Newfoundland of Sir Humphrey Gilbert. In Canadian, British and American newspapers they were advertised as follows: 'How an unruly rabble of fishermen, musicians and adventurers founded the greatest empire the world has known.' The Royal Canadian Mint's 'unruly rabble' would be familiar to the Spanish, but as destitute sheep-herders, poor farmers and fortune-seekers from the hard, barren lands of Castile and Extramadura, not as down-and-outers from Elizabethan ports and rural towns. The advertisement's boast referred to the second 'greatest empire the world has ever known' because the first was Spanish.[3]

After their hard-fought naval battles during the Napoleonic Wars, English and Spanish naval commanders shared an immediate and curious camaraderie not often found after battles between the English and the French. In July 1797 the port commander at Tenerife offered the services of his Spanish surgeon to Nelson whose right arm was shattered during his unsuccessful attack on the capital of the Canary Islands. Not to be outdone, Nelson for once in defeat, replied in kind to Don Antonio Gutiérrez commandant general of the Spanish Canary Islands:

> Sir, I cannot take my departure from this island without returning to your Excellency my sincerest thanks for your attention towards me, by your humanity in favour of our wounded men ... under your care and for your generosity towards all our people who were disembarked ... Your most humble obedient servant.
>
> Horatio Nelson.[4]

The post-Trafalgar correspondence between the two seconds-in-command of the English and Spanish fleets is equally touching and honourable. The following letter of thanks was written from Cádiz on 23 December 1805 by Vice Admiral Ignacio María de Alava, taken prisoner after his 112-gun *Santa Ana* was captured. It was addressed to his English captor, Vice Admiral Cuthbert Collingwood:

Most excellent Sir ... I hasten to fulfil the duties of gratitude, by returning to your Excellency my warmest thanks for your great kindness to me which will ever be deeply engraven on my heart. I have ... the greatest satisfaction in acknowledging the generosity and politeness with which Lieutenant Maker and a Marine Officer of the *Thunderer* behaved to me on board the *Santa Ana*, and I have the honour of recommending these officers to your Excellency...[5]

In much of British history, what were acceptable actions if performed by the English

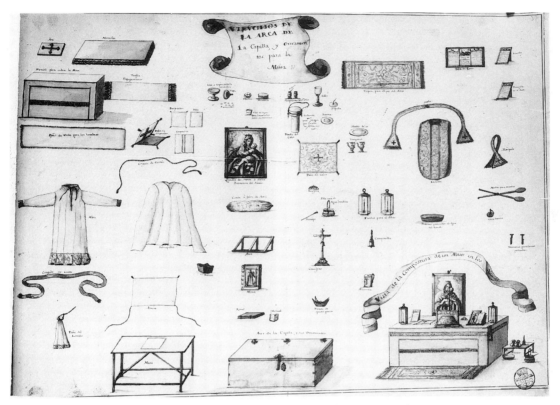

In the navy of 'The Most Catholic of Kings' practice of the Roman Catholic faith was compulsory. This drawing shows various elements for mass in a *navío*'s chapel – usually found on the orlop deck – and also priests' vestments, miniature paintings for adoration of the Holy Mother and Christ Child. From the *Marqués de la Victoria's Notebook*. (*Museo Naval, Madrid*)

against their enemies were branded crimes and brutalities when practised by the Spanish. The myths of Spanish 'misdeeds' in history included a lust for prize money and the gold of the Indies, maltreatment of heretics(hapless captive English Protestant sailors) and impressment of the unwary and unwilling into a naval life they abhorred.

It is difficult to determine why the Royal Navy's use of the press gang was more justified – or, in terms of the Spanish 'black legend' more humane – than the corresponding *la leva* in the *Armada Española*. The fact remains that during the latter half of the eighteenth century, neither navy was able to solve the chronic problem of insufficient manpower without resorting to the press gang. For the English, manpower shortages increased because of the growth of overseas trade and the ensuing need for more merchant ships and trained crews. For the Spanish, crew shortages in the navy resulted in part from epidemics that ravaged the port cities of southern Spain.

British popular histories continue to perpetuate *la leyenda negra* against Spain. In *The True Glory: the Story of the Royal Navy over a Thousand Years* (1984), Warren Tute declared that '... the Elizabethan sailor could slit a Spaniard's throat, capture his ship, throw the crew overboard, buy and sell negro slaves, and all with a prayer of thankfulness to God for his munificence.'[6] In the same book we read that at a time when the Spanish Navy was expanding and designing new ships of the line, it could not match the English for the following reasons: 'The Spaniards were paralysed by material greed and spiritually had turned in on themselves.' Writing in *The Hispanic American Historical Review* in August 1982 American historian Lawrence A Clayton of the University of Alabama asks the key questions about the character of the Spanish naval officer of the eighteenth century:

> How did the officers and men feel about their missions and themselves? Were they satisfied? Were they fulfilled? Did they accomplish their mission? These are not simple questions. They need to be answered if we are ever to explain clearly why Spain at sea was not as successful as England, or even France.

In terms of every maritime activity undertaken during the century, except for winning the big naval battles, the Spanish at sea were just as 'successful' as the English or the French. The fact that Spain lost most of the big naval engagements of the century does not mean that her fleet in its other activities – such as shipbuilding, exploration, innovative techniques in navigation and the ocean sciences – was in decay or always was found wanting. At the same time, Spain's navy ministers and naval commanders were slow to adjust to their navy's many deficiencies in manpower, morale and discipline. The British identified such matters accurately and corrected them early. In a few key instances, often crucial to the well-being of the navy, senior Spanish naval administrators did nothing.

During his visit to Portsmouth in 1793, Admiral Gravina was introduced to the miraculous function of citrus juice in the sailor's diet as a sure preventive against the dreaded scurvy that ravaged all the navies of the age. Yet, the regular issue of lemon juice, a routine procedure in the Royal Navy, never became general in the Spanish fleet. Dr Julian de Zulueta, to whom I am indebted for his fine essay, 'Trafalgar – The Spanish View', writes:

> many were the Spanish officers and doctors ... made prisoners in a naval engagement and ... taken on board an English man-of-war, who must have witnessed the daily issue of grog with lemon juice. Yet none of them seems to have realized that lemon juice was one of the main ingredients in the English recipe for success in naval warfare.[7]

Dr Zulueta emphasizes how other medical crises severely reduced the competence and fighting qualities of the Spanish ships' crews at Trafalgar. These included the devastating yellow fever epidemics that raged through the major recruiting regions of southern Spain between 1803 and 1805: 'The lack of seamen [for Gravina's fleet in early 1805] was extreme. The coasts of Spain had suffered during the last years the ravages of yellow fever, decimating an always scarce seafaring population...'[8] Spain's naval archives offer adequate proof of the yellow fever epidemics. On 30 October 1804 the 'chairman of the supreme committee of health' in Cadiz writes of the quarantine it established as a 'result of a declared epidemic...'[9]

Another document dated 20 February 1805 reveals that 9326 inhabitants in Málaga's population of 36,530 died of yellow fever. It should be remembered, too, that the Royal Navy

*Descubierta*: a photo of the scale model of Malaspina's ship
that was specially designed for his voyages of exploration.
(*Museo Naval, Madrid*)

delayed applying the curative properties of oranges, limes and lemons, even though these were identified by Dr James Lind in 1753 in his *Treatise of the Scurvy*. General use of citrus fruits in Royal Navy ships did not begin until almost half a century after Lind's discovery. Lind's efforts were encouraged by the worst recorded decimation of crews from scurvy in an eighteenth century European navy at sea, in the English fleet at that. This was the almost complete loss by scurvy of the crews of Commodore George Anson's eight ships, during his round-the-world voyage between 1740 and 1744. As detailed earlier Anson set sail with a total complement of 1955 men. Nearly 1300 of them were to die of scurvy.

If the Spanish failed to restore their navy during periods of peace because of a too long lay-up of their *navíos* in harbour, the more efficient Royal Navy also had its periods of decline and slump. In the early 1740s during the War of the Austrian Succession, and in the late 1770s during the American Revolutionary War, the Royal Navy performed badly because of peacetime neglect in training crews and building ships. Admiral Thomas Matthews, court-martialled in 1744 for negligence at sea, could have defeated the combined Spanish–French fleet off Cape Sicié if his ships' companies had been better trained.

British naval historians have relied on selective comparison to analyze the performance of the eighteenth century Spanish naval officer, usually restricting their comments to a criticism of his record in combat. Such stellar accomplishments of the Spanish Navy as Captain Alejandro Malaspina's circumnavigation of the world between 1789 and 1794 – a much longer period than any of Captain James Cook's three voyages – are overlooked or downgraded in English-language accounts of late eighteenth century European explorations. Like Cook, Malaspina carried specialists with him in the major marine and land sciences. Artists on board Malaspina's two ships etched and painted coastlines, animals, flora and fauna, and the activities of indigenous peoples. His ships, *Descubierta* and *Atrevida*, were custom-designed in Spain for his round-the-world voyage. Like Cook's ships, they faced the same great hazards from the actions of the sea. Among his hand-picked officers was Dionisio Alcalá Galiano, whose skill in navigation and cartography added greatly to the already considerable knowledge of the physical characteristics of the west coasts of South and North America. Galiano, who combined seamanship with scholarship as a Spaniard of the age of enlightenment, captured the imagination of Spanish writers and poets, one of them praising him after death as 'the honour of Spain, the honour of the sciences'.

Warren Tute in his eulogistic Royal Navy study, calls Cook 'without question, the most famous and successful sailor of his era and perhaps remains to this day the most competent and inspired navigator and cartographer that has ever been.'[10] Understandably, Spanish naval historians challenge such oft-repeated statements because of Spain's extensive maritime record which paralleled Cook's. Is the brilliant naval career of Dionisio Alcalá Galiano to be judged solely on his brave but not victorious command of the *navío Bahama* at Trafalgar, in which he was killed, and not on his earlier role as explorer and navigator of the west coasts of South and North America? Antonio Gaztañeta, founder of the eighteenth century Spanish Navy and one of the first European naval engineers to build ships of the line in series, is denigrated because the fleet he commanded and built was destroyed off Cape Passaro in 1718. It is true that Vice Admiral José de Córdoba y Ramos, commander of the Spanish fleet at Cape St Vincent in February 1797 (called 'not very bright' by a fellow admiral) was responsible for one of the worst Spanish defeats of the eighteenth century.

However, Admiral of the Fleet Luís Córdoba y Córdoba, one of Spain's most aggressive naval commanders of that century, is ignored by foreign naval historians. He inflicted the two worst convoy losses (a total of 79 merchant ships taken) experienced by the British in the eighteenth century. In August 1780 his combined French-Spanish fleet captured 55 English merchant ships from a convoy of 63 vessels. Paradoxically, the luckless José de Córdoba y Ramos was captain of the 74-gun *Arrogante* in the fleet of Luís Córdoba y Córdoba that captured the English convoy in August 1780. In 1781, in the midst of cruel storms in the English Channel, Córdoba y Córdoba repeated his exploit of the previous year by capturing another 24 English merchant ships without loss to his own squadron. For his successes, he was promoted to Captain General of the Fleet in 1783. He died in 1796, a year before his close namesake was defeated at Cape St Vincent in February 1797 and later court-martialled.

Spain never had enough commanders of the quality of Córdoba y Córdoba to take charge of its eighteenth century fighting fleets, and win the big battles. The Spanish must be faulted because of their unfortunate, even disastrous choices of fleet commanders, passing over more aggressive officers who should have been given key wartime fleet commands. Although they commanded some of the best ships of the line in Europe, the chronic plight of Spanish naval commanders was that they could not win fleet engagements. Two important Spanish documents among the few that openly and frankly criticize fleet performance, define that plight and explain why Spanish naval officers never surmounted it. The first is an excerpt from the report of proceedings by Admiral José Córdoba, the unfortunate commander-in-chief of the Spanish fleet.

Córdoba's dismal report published on 10 March 1797 in the *Gaceta de Madrid*, clearly shows that he was quite inexperienced in fleet manoeuvring for battle. Writing to Captain General Juan de Lángara y Huarte, himself a naval commander-in-chief with a fine record and appointed navy minister by Charles IV in the same year as the Battle of Cape St Vincent, he concluded in this manner:

> So it was that a mere seventeen of my squadron were in a position to take part in the action, one of which, the *Santo Domingo*, was shipping water fast and therefore of precious little use. Of the seventeen ... some joined in the fighting from time to time and many were never in a position to fire a single shot, leaving the whole enemy force to concentrate their fire on six Spanish ships... The resistance offered by these is all the more worthy of praise since there was not a single one of them that had enough hands on board to man her properly.

In the second account, the reasons why Royal Navy officers were more competent than the Spanish at Trafalgar are honestly set down by Lt Col José Cuevas Fernández of the Spanish Marine Infantry in his essay 'About Trafalgar' published in the *Revista General de la Marina* in September 1947:

> Although never inferior to our enemies in determination, audacity, self-denial, valour and patriotism, what the officer of the [Spanish] Navy needs [is] very remote in general from the aptitude, expertise [and] the consummate practical experience acquired by our enemies in lengthy voyages, in constant navigation, in the blockade of our very ports.

Why were the Spanish ships of the line under-manned at Cape St Vincent? Why did Spanish fleet commanders not engage their ships in much longer training exercises away from harbour, as did the English? Why were there fewer Spanish fleet exercises at sea than were practised in the Royal Navy?

Brian Lavery, the British specialist on the eighteenth century Royal Navy warship, cites three reasons why the British often surpassed the Spanish in performance – reasons that encompass both psychological and technical factors.[11] First, he says the Spanish 'will to win' dwindled away among the ships' crews because the English won more of the naval battles as the century wore on. For many Spanish naval historians, this is not a valid explanation. The British did not win all the wars of the century. As noted earlier, the Treaty of Paris of 1783 at the end of the American Revolutionary War was a disaster for Britain. At Paris, Britain accepted both the loss of its thirteen American colonies and the existence of the new United States of America as well as the surrender of Florida to Spain. Nor did the Royal Navy conduct itself as successfully between 1779 and 1783 as it did during the Seven Years' War of 1756–1763. In 1780, the capture of 55 ships (almost an entire English convoy) by Admiral Luís Córdoba y Córdoba resulted in the loss of 150 million reales' worth of weapons and supplies bound for Jamaica, plus the loss of 3000 British sailors captured by the Spanish. Although the Spanish did not succeed in recapturing Gibraltar during their long blockade and seige of 1779–1782, the English were not able to break it sooner. Still, in February of 1782, the Spanish did succeed in recapturing the Minorca naval base from the British garrison. Spanish historian Vicente Rodríquez Casado is even more positive. He writes:

In any case, the peace of 1783 [has] a clear Spanish indication and represents the largest political triumph of the [Spanish] Catholic Monarchy since the times of Philip II. It was possible [to say] in definitive terms that for the first time since the Invincible [Armada], our navy had control of the sea.[12]

The Spanish Navy did not always lack the 'will to win'. Rather, as Rodríquez says, '…the control of the sea that Carlos III succeeded in achieving in 1779 because it was not crowned with glaringly victorious deeds, could not be sustained since one is not able to break the legend of Britannic invincibility.'

The second reason given is that British ships' crews, before as well as during Nelson's time, were always trained longer and harder and spent lengthier periods at sea, than did Spanish crews. This was true. At the same time, it did not mean that the Spanish Navy never went to sea on exercises or, when it did, that these were always of short duration. Near the end of his reign, Carlos III ordered the navy to form so-called 'working-up squadrons', in which ships were to engage in extended nagivational exercises and naval tactics after concluding active service, instead of laying alongside. In December 1787 Admiral Juan de Lángara y Huarte reported to the navy minister, the former distinguished seaman and retired vice admiral, Antonio Valdés on his five months' long training cruise. Valdés was one of Spain's most effective navy ministers, and like many of his predecessors in that position, already had served as a senior naval officer, with a solid reputation at sea and in combat. A second 'working-up squadron' under Admiral Córdoba spent six months, mainly in the western Mediterranean. It included seven *navíos*, two frigates, a *balandra* and three brigantines. Between June and September 1785 Vice Admiral José de Mazarredo also was at sea testing the navigational systems, guns and signalling routines of *navíos* in the new *San Ildefonso* class.

The third reason, says Lavery, is that English ships' captains and fleet commanders sensed when discipline in a ship at sea was breaking down, or rather, when the breaking point was near for men constantly exposed to all the chronic hazards of life at sea mentioned earlier. 'The English, unlike the Spanish or the French, sensed when the will to win was changing to a dangerous mechanical process to obey,' says Lavery. The author cites Nelson's many admonitions to his crews that officers and men serving at sea or preparing for battle share what they are doing together. Compare this with the stern rebuke to his ship's company of Cosmé Damián Churruca, one of Spain's best naval captains of the century. On the one hand Churruca warned of the dire consequences of desertion, and on the other, of eternal reward in the world to come if killed in action. Lavery speculates that in all three navies – Spanish, English and French – individual ship mutinies took place more often than we know, and were dealt with quietly at sea without being given any publicity. 'The [Royal Navy] mutiny at the Nore in 1797 was the most publicized because it was the largest,' Lavery contends.

Since crew members in all three fleets were largely illiterate and could not write 'letters home' as do sailors in modern navies, we do not know from them directly if mutinies or 'incidents' close to mutiny were common. Indeed, we know very little from crew members of European navies about life on board during the century, even though in Britain in recent years, a small amount of eighteenth century seamen's correspondence has come to light. The long essay 'Trafalgar' written at the turn of the twentieth century by Spanish novelist Benito Pérez Galdós, may or may not have portrayed accurately the reactions and feelings of Spanish crew members both before and during that battle. After all, Pérez Galdós was a story-teller not a historian. Did sailors in the Spanish fleet in the fall of 1805 know that much about Nelson's short stature and his winning ways with men to describe him affectionately as *el almirante pequeño*, 'the little admiral'?

British historians make much of the belief that it was chiefly the men and the officers of their fleet, to the exclusion of the Spanish and French in the age of sail, who experienced Nelson's cementing of human relationships at sea that he called 'the band of brothers'. This theme comes through in Dr N A M Rodger's study of the Georgian navy at the mid-point of the eighteenth century. A reviewer comments:

> The organization of a sailing ship navy was such that an ambitious officer needed to have prime seamen in the tops and smart fellows running out the guns if he were to rise and prosper in his career … From top to bottom, everyone depended on everyone else – for those men stood to gain as well. The Georgian navy was thus held together by personal links … It was self-interest that made team work the lifeblood of the eighteenth century navy.[13]

Are we to believe that such gallant and (where their crews were concerned) sensitive Spanish naval commanders as Blas de Lezo, José de Mazarredo, Juan Francisco de la Bodega y Quadra, and the many captains of Manila Galleons that were at sea for months on end did not practise the Nelsonian formula of the 'band of brothers?' If 'self-interest' was the 'lifeblood of the eighteenth century' then the many enlightened Spanish ship commanders during the long age of sail in their many places of duty on the high seas, practised 'self-interest' as did their English counterparts at sea.

---

NUMBER OF OFFICERS IN THE ARMADA
ESPAÑOLA OF 1795

- 1     captain general (admiral of the fleet)
- 16    vice admirals
- 15    rear admirals
- 43    commodores
- 110   captains
- 143   commanders
- 221   lieutenant commanders
- 224   lieutenants
- 242   sub lieutenants
- 309   midshipmen

Grand Total:
- 1324 officers

---

(SOURCE: Legajo 2855, Estado, Archivo Histórico de la Nación, Madrid, 1795.)

Notwithstanding, the Spanish had problems with manning and efficiency of crews to an extent not shared by the Royal Navy. Throughout the century the uncertain quantity and uneven quality of seamen bedevilled Spanish naval commanders. The crisis accentuated towards the end of the century, as the warship build-up planned and executed in the final two decades supplied the navy with more new ships than it could properly man. Professor McNeill writes: '… It was the unavailability of skilled labour, rather than the lack of funds which effectively limited the size, and thus the power, of the Spanish Navy.' As early as 1751, the Marqués de Ensenada had informed King Ferdinand VI that without sufficient numbers of trained seamen, efforts to expand the fleet made little point. Still earlier, the new admiralty administration formed in 1737 was required by a royal ordinance to create the seamen's registry (*matrícula del mar*) as had been done prior to that date in the French Navy. The seamen's registry continued in force until the end of the 1700s, often confirming the constant manpower shortages by never showing enough available men on its lists to meet the navy's manpower requirements.

In 1759 there were 50,000 names on the seamen's registry, but only 26,000 were actually available for the navy's use. This was because the Spanish empire's many commercial activities at sea, in Europe and the New World were extensive and had to be performed by thousands of skilled sailors. These included cod fishing off Newfoundland's Grand Banks begun in the sixteenth century, the seasonal but large sardine catches off the coast of Galicia and the coasting

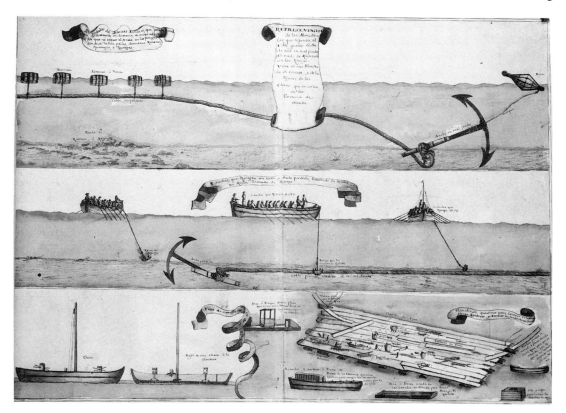

The use of empty wooden water or wine casks attached to the cable in effort to float a fouled anchor; use of grappling iron to recover a lost anchor and cable. (*Museo Naval, Madrid*)

trade between Spanish and Mediterranean ports. Internationally, still larger Spanish commercial shipping operations constantly needed substantial numbers of trained seamen. Half way through the century after it resumed service, the *Flota* of commercial galleons from Cádiz to Vera Cruz and Havana used up a significant percentage of trained sailors. Towards the end of the eighteenth century, *La Flota* was phased out for the last time. It was almost immediately replaced by the largest number of ships ever to visit Spanish American ports carrying mainly foreign cargo. This was the direct result of the declaration of free trade by Carlos III in 1778 for the nine major Spanish ports in the New World. Most of these assignments offered jobs at sea to Spanish sailors who continued to shun naval service.

A good part of the reason for the chronic shortage of naval manpower had to be the harsh discipline of the age. As in the Royal Navy, cruel lashings were meted out for minor offences. Desertion the first time could bring as many as 50 lashes to the miscreant, who was tied down over a cannon. Second and third efforts at desertion could result in a severe punishment never known in England, namely a lengthy consignment to the galleys, a holdover from mediaeval times. Even though the threat of the galleys was unique, the Spanish commanders did not have a monopoly of harsh punishments at sea. All the European naval administrations treated their men badly. Flogging, imprisonment and denial of food to seamen who broke the myriad rules on board were applied universally.

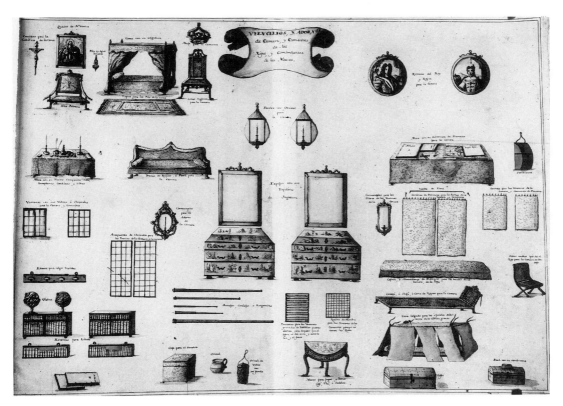

Sophisticated furniture and comforts for a *navío*'s commanding officer or admiral. Compare all this with the 14 inches of hammock space allowed the seamen below decks with no additional creature comforts for them whatsoever. Among the many items are two mirrors and two desks for two officers or in case the admiral's wife is also on board. Note that the desks underneath the mirrors are of English manufacture. Other items include cameo paintings of reigning king and queen, painting of Our Lady The Virgin, large and ornate crucifix, a bed with canopy not unlike Nelson's surviving in HMS *Victory*, with chamber pot and a commode standing next to it. All in all, these are similar to the commanding officer's accoutrements found in British ships of the line of the same period – again as one can see them in HMS *Victory*. (*Museo Naval, Madrid*)

Throughout the eighteenth century Spanish monarchs as well as their navy ministers failed to break the mediaeval tradition of utilizing the Spanish ship of the line as a floating fortress and fighting warship simultaneously, even though every navy or Indies minister of the same century complained about the chronic shortage of seamen. As a result officers, cadets and men of the shore-based corps of marine infantry, artillery and engineers often made up as much as twenty per cent of the manpower on board a *navío*. Hence, by the reign of Carlos III, two centuries after the demise of the Spanish Armada, which went to sea with thousands of troops on board and many *urcas* (supply ships) in train, the Spanish Navy continued to function in part, as an ocean-based military force. Its ships, as one Spanish historian has written, were 'castles in transit'.

Moreover, this 'militarization' was perpetuated in ships that, as in all other navies of the era, required hundreds of seamen on board to manipulate and handle sails, rigging and anchor cables. On 8 July 1787 Carlos III declared that 'a ship should be considered as a regiment' and further declared that 'each *navío* ought to have its own flag with a separate motto from the others, and distinct uniforms as in a regiment that would arouse the emulation of the others [crews].' Carlos III further suggested that 'the manner of establishing it in a working form in my fleets is to be examined by the great generals of the sea and of the land.' This was both a curious and paradoxical response from the monarch who did more than any other to restore Spanish sea

OFFICIAL COMPLEMENTS OF SPANISH WARSHIPS

SHIPS-OF-THE-LINE

| Rank | 112 guns | 94 guns | 80 guns | 74 guns | 68– 70 guns | 64 guns | 58– 60 guns | 50– 54 guns | 44 guns | 40 guns | 34 guns | 26– 30 guns | 18 guns |
|---|---|---|---|---|---|---|---|---|---|---|---|---|---|
| Officers | 23 | 23 | 22 | 21 | 21 | 21 | 21 | 21 | 19 | 19 | 19 | 18 | 11 |
| Master Gunners[1] | 30 | 20 | 15 | 15 | 12 | 12 | 12 | 12 | 10 | 10 | 10 | 10 | 6 |
| Gunners[2] | 100 | 100 | 80 | 80 | 70 | 70 | 60 | 60 | 55 | 55 | 55 | 30 | 15 |
| Seamen | 200 | 200 | 120 | 100 | 100 | 80 | 80 | 70 | 65 | 60 | 55 | 40 | 20 |
| Boys[3] | 230 | 200 | 150 | 120 | 100 | 100 | 90 | 80 | 65 | 60 | 60 | 40 | 20 |
| Officers' Servants[4] | 40 | 34 | 30 | 24 | 24 | 20 | 20 | 20 | 10 | 10 | 8 | 8 | 6 |
| | 623 | 577 | 417 | 360 | 327 | 303 | 283 | 263 | 224 | 214 | 207 | 146 | 78 |
| Marine Infantry | 168 | 168 | 168 | 112 | 112 | 112 | 112 | 84 | 56 | 56 | 56 | 56 | 40 |
| Artillerymen | 57 | 57 | 57 | 38 | 38 | 38 | 30 | 25 | 19 | 19 | 19 | 19 | 10 |
| | 225 | 225 | 225 | 150 | 150 | 150 | 142 | 110 | 75 | 75 | 75 | 75 | 50 |
| Total Naval Personnel | 623 | 577 | 417 | 360 | 327 | 303 | 283 | 263 | 224 | 214 | 207 | 146 | 78 |
| Total Military Personnel | 225 | 225 | 225 | 150 | 150 | 150 | 142 | 110 | 75 | 75 | 75 | 75 | 50 |
| Grand Total of Ship's Company | 848 | 802 | 642 | 510 | 477 | 453 | 425 | 373 | 299 | 289 | 282 | 221 | 128 |

power in the age of sail. One can only assume that the reason nothing was done in this regard is that Carlos III was dead within six months of making this proposal which, mercifully for his navy, did not appear as a royal ordinance.

Despite the many Anglo-Spanish wars which required a steady flow of lower deck manpower, that reality did not convince the navy to end the uneven mix of sailors and soldiers in the *navíos*. Rather, one of the most important developments in the first series of naval reforms in 1717 included the founding of the Royal Company of Marine Guards, plus later measures to strengthen its role in the fleet. Even more critical to Spanish performance at sea was the divisive nature of mixed command in a ship of the line with the ship's captain responsible for the soldier at sea, and the pilot – usually a junior naval officer under him – in charge of the ship's company. A navy will never win its battles when its warships go to sea with divided commands.

Was this mix of soldiers and sailors in the Spanish Navy's ship complements the main reason for Spanish failure? Down the years, the many Spanish and English critics of Spanish seamanship do not tell us. Like many other observers, Angel O'Dogherty, the contemporary Spanish naval historian, merely criticizes Spanish failures without defining the root causes. He writes '... at the end of the eighteenth century the problem of sound seamanship persisted. In the great battles, St Vincent and Trafalgar, that signify the sunset of our Armada, the superior skill of the British sailors remained evident.'[14]

Among his wide-sweeping naval administration reforms, Carlos III tried to eliminate the differences between the soldiers at sea and ships' crews, and ordered the former to undergo regular shore instruction in seamanship and navigation. His General Regulation for Garrisons and Crews of 1 January 1788 defined the manpower needed for a refurbished navy of 68 *navíos* and 42 frigates. As indicated earlier, the year 1790 marked the apogee of Spanish sea power in

| JABEQUES/JABEQUES WITH LATEEN FORE SAIL | | | | | | CORVETTES AND OTHER THREE-MASTED SHIPS BRIGANTINES AND OTHER TWO-MASTED SHIPS | | |
|---|---|---|---|---|---|---|---|---|
| *Rank* | *30– 34 guns* | *32 guns* | *26– 28 guns* | *18 guns* | *16– 20 guns* | *Rank* | *18–22 guns* | *12–16 guns* |
| Officers | 13 | 13 | 13 | 13 | 10 | Officers | 11 | 10 |
| Master Gunners[1] | 10 | 10 | 10 | 6 | 4 | Master Gunners[1] | 6 | 6 |
| Gunners[2] | 34 | 32 | 24 | 35 | 20 | Gunners[2] | 15 | 14 |
| Seamen | 105 | 100 | 90 | 35 | 30 | Seamen | 18 | 18 |
| Boys[3] | 42 | 42 | 44 | 40 | 40 | Boys[3] | 20 | 18 |
| Officers' Servants[4] | 8 | 8 | 6 | 4 | 4 | Officers' Servants[4] | 4 | 4 |
| | 212 | 205 | 187 | 133 | 108 | | 74 | 70 |
| Marine Infantry | 70 | 60 | 50 | 45 | 20 | Marine Infantry | 30 | 25 |
| Artillerymen | 17 | 15 | 14 | 10 | 6 | Artillerymen | 8 | 7 |
| | 87 | 75 | 64 | 55 | 26 | | 38 | 32 |
| Total Naval Personnel | 212 | 205 | 187 | 133 | 108 | Total Naval Personnel | 74 | 70 |
| Total Military Personnel | 87 | 75 | 64 | 55 | 26 | Total Military Personnel | 38 | 32 |
| Grand Total of Ship's Company | 299 | 280 | 250 | 188 | 134 | Grand Total of Ship's Company | 112 | 102 |

[1]*Artilleros de Preferencia.* [2]*Artilleros de Mar.* [3]*Grumetes*, usually with no previous experience afloat. [4]*Pajes*, boys, usually with some seagoing experience.
(Table based on Rolf Mühlmann, *Die Reorganisation der Spanischen* ...)

the eighteenth century in terms of the number and quality of ships in commission – even if not all the fine new *navíos* had the trained crews they needed. However, the fleet's manpower did expand from 24,312 in the naval departments of El Ferrol, Cartagena and Cádiz in 1754 to 31,637 and 1765 and 52,381 in 1786.

Between 1775 and the end of *navío* construction in 1797, the Spanish Navy's total expenditures as a portion of the Spanish Treasury's general budgeting remained high. This was because the largest administrative cost in managing the Indies continued to be the maintenance of a large navy to defend Spanish America. Following the brief and humiliating English occupation of Havana in 1762–63, Spanish naval expenditures had continued to grow despite the efforts by various cost-cutting finance ministers in Madrid to curtail their size. After 1763, the Havana shipyard underwent its greatest expansion to become the largest single producer of ships for the navy from *navíos* to *bergantíns*. By 1790, 74 of the 227 *navíos* bought or built for the navy during the entire eighteenth century had been built in Havana. During the mid-1770s, further naval outlays were made in the Indies to build the new naval base and shipyard at San Blas on Mexico's west coast, both as the new centre for Pacific North-west explorations and for local construction of smaller naval vessels designed for exploration.

Paradoxically, the percentage of naval to overall government spending was at its highest between 1793 and 1795 when Spain was briefly at war with France, its traditional ally. In 1794, the navy's share of total outlays rose to a record 39 per cent. Professor Jacques Barbier writes that between 1776 and 1784, 'the average share of total spending dedicated to the navy hovered around 28 per cent.' This amount increased, he says, to nearly 33 per cent of total spending during the War of American Independence in which Spain played a successful role as a European ally of the American revolutionaries.[15]

The Conde de Lerena, who between 1785 and 1792 was Carlos III's last finance minister and the first of his son Carlos IV, set out to reduce substantially the growing deficit on naval spending. In 1788, Navy Minister Antonio Valdés (1744–1816), the determined aristocrat-sailor, was unable to prevent Lerena's 11 per cent reduction in the naval estimates for that year. Accordingly, he made one of the most astounding suggestions for a large European navy to pay its way. Valdés proposed the Spanish state be exempted totally from financing the fleet and that instead, its funds should come from the colonial tobacco monopoly. Though the idea was approved both by Carlos IV and Lerena, it was opposed by the bureaucrats in the Ministry of War and Finances for the Indies even though Valdés also held the latter portfolio. Their counter-proposals for certain trade-offs between tobacco production and naval expenses and that the Spanish Treasury bear all the extra costs in wartime, were rejected by Lerena.

During the mid- and late-eighteenth century the inter-related ministries of the Navy and the Indies were often held by a single minister who earlier had served as a senior naval officer in the Indies. Their naval duties had included prior administrative authority over the operations of the *Flota* and *Galeones* commercial fleets. Such ministerial linkages made sense for other reasons. Not only did funds for the navy largely come from the considerable revenues of the Indies, but the three largest Spanish mainland arsenals and shipyards at Cádiz, El Ferrol and Cartagena had their own treasuries with funds allocated to them by a treasurer general. However if the Indies' revenues were down, which increasingly was true after the monopolistic *Flota* and *Galeones* experienced foreign competition following the free trade decree of Carlos III in 1778, finance ministers held more control over the expenses of the fleet and its internal treasuries.

Even though the fleet was often unprepared to fight in the chronic European dynastic wars of the century, neither the ex-navy ministers appointed by the king nor their bureaucrats had the power to prevent Spain's participation in them. This development was further exacerbated by the lifelong anglophobia of Carlos III himself which resulted in wars against Britain that could have been prevented. Between 1779 and 1783, Spain militarily supported the revolt of the American colonists against England because Carlos III saw it as a 'just war'. In addition, the huge resources of manpower and ships wasted in the unsuccessful protracted Spanish amphibious assault to recapture Gibraltar between 1779 and 1782, were badly needed for the large and costly fleet expansion that continued throughout his reign. At the same time, a consistently large navy was seen by many bureaucrats in Madrid as an administrative cost that drained off too much of the earnings of the Indies, first from its monopolies of gold and silver and later from sugar and tobacco. The Spanish, too, had their supporters of a view not unknown in Britain that the country could not afford to support a large navy over the years as part of 'the price of empire'. Indeed one can speculate that both the reduced earnings from the

Indies and their final loss to the Spanish Crown between 1810 and 1821 (except for sugar-rich Cuba and Puerto Rico) ended Spanish sea power more effectively than did such devastating naval defeats as Cape St Vincent and Trafalgar.

The negative internal effects of the bureaucractic 'wars' on Spanish naval efficiency can only be surmised – for example during the years 1783 to 1786 when some of the best 74- and 112-gun *navíos* of the eighteenth century fleet were under construction and major fleet changes were under way. Such *navíos* included the 74-gun *Bahama* and *San Ildefonso* (1784 and 1785) and the 112-gun *Santa Ana* and *Mejicano* (1784 and 1786). On 11 September 1783 a business-like letter on building 74-gun ships was sent to Valdés from the naval architect José Romero y Landa. In it, he advises that Plans No 1 and 2 for *navíos* of 74 guns (the *Ildefonsos*) are forwarded to Valdés with recommended structural changes '... in which the total weight of the hull (meaning a finished *navío*) does not exceed 1700 tons.' Valdés constantly requested that senior navy officers and officials such as Romero y Landa keep him informed and be prepared to receive advice on technical developments.[16]

One must wonder to what extent such devoted naval administrators as Vice Admiral José de Mazarredo chafed against the efforts by the bureaucrats to reduce the navy's finances. Such efforts persisted despite the actions of sympathetic navy ministers – such as Valdés, the flag officer turned navy minister – to preserve a large fleet. Mazarredo reported to and received the support of Valdés as one of his former navy commanders when between 1785 and 1787 he instituted the major training and seamanship reforms badly needed throughout the fleet.

The Spanish naval officer of the eighteenth century was as much stirred by patriotism as was his English counterpart. Loyalty to king and country was identical in both fleets. Where the English naval officers of the time served His Britannic Majesty in the Royal Navy, his Spanish counterparts served The Most Catholic of Kings in the *Armada Española*. In 1793, after revolutionary France had committed regicide by executing the Bourbon King Louis XVI and his family and declared war against most of monarchist Europe, Spain and England were briefly allies. Perhaps their monarchs of that year did not amount to much. Spain's Carlos IV showed none of his father's technocratic skills. This inept king abdicated in favour of his son Fernando VII and they both surrendered to Napoleon who placed his brother on the Spanish throne in 1808. Britain's George III, already showing signs of permanent physical infirmity, at least displayed a token interest in maritime affairs. Nevertheless, much genuine camaraderie took place among 'royalist' officers of both Spain and England when they served briefly on the same side between 1793 and 1795.

The Naval Museum of the Spanish Navy Ministry in Madrid contains the full account of the visit to England in 1793 of Rear Admiral Federico Gravina. He was to be the Spanish commander-in-chief at Trafalgar. Like the earlier visit to England of Jorge Juan, Gravina's English trip began as a spying mission. Gravina too, charmed those he met.

In both peace and war English and Spanish naval officers shared a code of loyalty as members of a 'royal' or 'king's' navy. Since 1785 when the new Spanish red–gold–red national flag was adopted for the navy in place of the Bourbon coat-of-arms, the navy became (and still is called) *La Armada Española*, that is the Navy of the Spanish nation. Even though Spain has once more become a monarchy, her fleet is still called the Spanish Navy and not the Royal Navy as in England. Since the Spanish Bourbon royal family was restored to the throne in 1976 with the accession Juan Carlos I, the modern Spanish royal family has quietly adopted a policy instituted in 1758 by Britain's George II of entering the heir to the throne in the navy – called a 'novel and healthy idea' by a Victorian writer. Hence the Principe de Asturias (the Spanish counterpart to the Prince of Wales) has completed his sea time in the Spanish Navy's training ship *Juan Sebastián de Elcano*, named for the first European (not Sir Francis Drake, who was the seventh) to circumnavigate the world. HRH Charles Prince of Wales, who is a Commander RN, has already done considerable service in the Royal Navy. In our own time, when Spain and Britain are friendly allies at sea as fellow NATO member countries, the male heirs of both the Spanish and British monarchs are often seen in their countries' naval uniforms. King Juan Carlos I is a captain general in the *Armada Española*. As a 6-metre boat specialist who was a member of Spain's sailing team in the Summer Olympics of 1972, the king is an accomplished sailor.

The mutual friendship and respect enjoyed by the Spanish and British royal families would have been an anathema to Juan Carlos' ancestor, Carlos III. His hatred of England was based on his personal humiliation by the Royal Navy when he was King of Naples, an experience he never forgot. In 1744 during the War of the Austrian Succession, Commodore Martin and a division of Royal Navy warships were despatched to Naples under orders from Admiral Thomas Matthews, the English commander-in-chief in the Mediterranean, to compel Carlos to withdraw his Neapolitan army of 20,000 troops serving in northern Italy against Austria, an English ally. In his memorable study *The Influence of Sea Power Upon History*, the American naval historian Rear Admiral Alfred T Mahan tells what happened next.

> To the attempts [by Carlos] to negotiate, Martin replied only by pulling out his watch and giving the [Neapolitan] government an hour to come to terms. There was nothing for it but submission and the English fleet left Naples harbour after a stay of twenty-four hours.[17]

For Carlos, there was no alternative but surrender. His army was far away in northern Italy and the Kingdom of Naples had no navy to speak of. Such an immediate ultimatum gave him no time to call upon Spanish naval support. This ultimatum changed the course of history between Spain and Britain until the outbreak of the Peninsular War in 1808. As a result, during the remainder of his reign in Naples, and later in Spain, Carlos III considered Britain to be his 'natural enemy'. When he succeeded to the Spanish throne, Carlos III vowed to build a navy powerful enough that some day it could defeat the British at sea.

The record does not indicate if Carlos III received comfort from the court martial of Admiral Matthews two years later for failing to defeat a Franco-Spanish fleet off Cape Sicié in February 1744. The Spanish fleet was under the command of Juan José Navarro, a most accomplished naval officer. Matthews was dismissed from the service; Navarro was ennobled as the Marqués de la Victoria. The Spanish and the French together could have defeated Matthews and his inadequately trained crews conclusively if they had been willing to fight side by side as allies. That they were not was a sign of the future trouble between the two Bourbon navies which was to take its toll of the Combined Squadron both before and during the Battle of Trafalgar.

On 2 October 1759 Carlos and his Queen Marie Amalie departed from Naples on the ten-day voyage to Barcelona on board the *Fénix* (an 80-gun *navío* built a decade earlier at Havana) to begin his new life as King of Spain. At forty-three, this far-from-handsome monarch of medium height and ruddy complexion was joyously received in Spain, his native land. In gratitude for the safe passage, Carlos conferred the curious title of Marqués del Transporte on Guiérrez Hevia Bustamante y Alonso de Casa, the fleet's commander, a naval

A drawing of a Spanish gun crew moving gun into position. From the *Marqués de la Victoria's Notebook*. (*Museo Naval, Madrid*)

officer whose later career took him to a senior post in Cuba. The title still exists, and is held at present by Juan de Valdés y Suardiáz, a resident of Oviedo.[18]

It is not recorded how the anglophobe Carlos III responded to the fate of the *Fénix*. Captured by the Royal Navy in 1780, she served longer in the Royal Navy as the *Gibraltar* than in the *Armada Española*, and was not broken up until 1836, eighty-seven years after she was launched at Havana. The ship was renamed to celebrate the successful British defence of the Rock which Carlos III tried in vain to restore to Spanish rule.

## THE SEAMEN

The Spanish Navy's Achilles' heel always was its lower standard of seamanship compared with that of the British. Numerous pieces of correspondence in the Spanish naval archives report on crew shortfalls and officers' excuses for the inadequate performance of a ship's company. Lieutenant Commander Peter C Whitlock, a commanding officer of *Victory* in the 1970s and now in charge of her current restoration, estimates that where an English gun's crew required only 90 seconds on average to load, fire, sponge out and re-load a 32-pounder – usually the largest cannon in both fleets – a Spanish 32-pounder gun's crew needed as long as five minutes to do the same. Nevertheless, Nelson's famous remark also contained an element of contempt for Spain's accomplishments at sea, an attitude shared by other senior Royal Navy officers. The famous admiral did not live to see the carnage at Trafalgar resulting from the many individual ships' actions, including the murderous fire exchanged at point-blank range between the Spanish and English ships in that battle.

The truth is that the eighteenth century sailors in all the fleets had more in common than they realized, because they shared common miseries. These included atrocious living conditions on board, bad food, inadequate medical care (which worsened during battle), severe punishment and the ever-present brutality of certain commanding officers. Nowhere was the rudimentary nature of eighteenth century surgical procedure more noticeable than in a naval vessel's cockpit during and after conflict. With spirits such as rum the only anaesthetic, a ship's surgeon during battle was engaged almost entirely in hacking off mangled limbs and staunching the resultant haemorrhaging with crude applications of tar to the arm or leg stumps.

The chronic enemy was not the opponent's battle line, but disease on board or in port, often reaching epidemic proportions. The biggest killers, malaria and yellow fever, were diseases whose cures were beyond the limited knowledge of eighteenth century medicine. In the Caribbean basin, where the European powers vied for control and where whole fleets were stationed and fought during that century, thousands of sailors in all the fleets died of disease on shore and afloat. If a yellow fever epidemic was raging in Havana when the 'fleet was in' from Cádiz, with as many as 5000 men on shore at one time, ships' companies could be decimated.

Professor McNeill is explicit about the Royal Navy's frightening experience with disease in the Caribbean:

> The British Royal Navy which in the eighteenth century had world-wide experience, considered the West Indies the unhealthiest region of all. Yellow fever epidemics broke out in Cuba six times between 1731 and 1762. New arrivals to the West Indies faced a roughly 20 per cent chance of dying within a year; a British garrison at Barbados reported an annual death rate of 18 per cent. Astride the major sea routes of the Atlantic world, Havana functioned as a clearing house for contagion, uniting the disease pools of Europe, Africa and the Americas.[19]

The basic reasons given in English naval histories for the failure in 1740 to capture Cartagena usually do not include the brilliant and stubborn defence of Admiral Blas de Lezo and Viceroy Sebastián de Eslava. Rather they have concentrated on both the decimation of the mixed English and colonial forces by tropical diseases and the differences between the commanders. Because Admiral Edward Vernon's and General Wentworth's mixed naval and land force of 30,000 men was probably the largest sent into the Caribbean until the twentieth century, its losses from disease were consequently higher than in earlier expeditions. John Fortescue, an historian of the British Army, claimed that as many as 9000 English and colonial troops died of yellow fever. The English were fully aware of its ravages. Admiral Charles Knowles wrote that the campaign had to be concluded quickly '... or the Climate soon wages a more destructive War than the Enemy.'

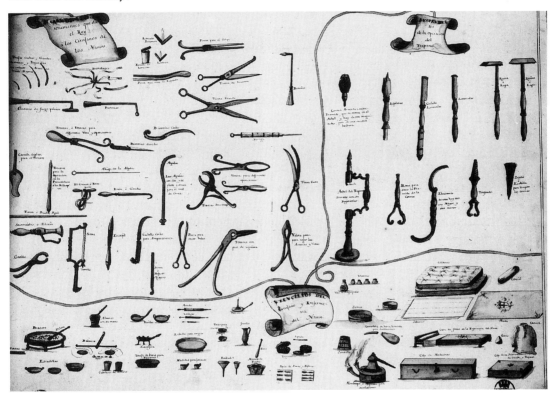

Selection of a Spanish naval surgeon's tools, instruments and basic medicines. From the *Marqués de la Victoria's Notebook*. (*Museo Naval, Madrid*)

Lieutenant Commander Whitlock estimates that of the 133,000 officers and men who served in the Royal Navy from the beginning of the Seven Years' War in 1756 to the end of the American Revolutionary War in 1783, between 30,000 and 50,000 died of diseases, while fewer than 2000 were killed in the sea battles of these two wars. Not even Nelson escaped the killer tropical diseases of the Caribbean. Twice during his early career – at St Nevis where he met his wife, and after his disastrous assault in what is now Nicaragua – the greatest sailor of his day was almost lost to history from disease contracted there.

Unlike Britain, Spain had to cope at home with domestic epidemics of yellow fever and malaria. Cádiz as well as the cities and towns close to it, experienced many tropical disease epidemics throughout the eighteenth century. It is well-known that epidemics sweeping through Andalucía in southern Spain in 1803–1804 (as noted earlier) were a main cause for the depleted and unhealthy crews available to the Spanish naval high command immediately before Trafalgar.

In addition to tropical fevers and scurvy, endemic respiratory diseases resulted from damp, unheated conditions below decks. With the hundreds of bodies needed to handle the rigging and sails and work the guns crowded into wooden ships of between 1500 and at most 5000 deadweight tons, such diseases spread uncontrolled. Added to that, given the amount of smoke inhaled during combat when guns were swung in for reloading, and the fetid conditions beyond belief in bad weather when the gun ports had to be closed for long periods of time, it is not surprising that such unhealthy living conditions took a heavy toll.

Still other medical hazards included hernias and shattered limbs, resulting from manhandling the heavy guns. 'The Royal Navy won the war at sea with the truss,' says Lieutenant Commander Whitlock. No wonder Dr Samuel Johnson and others called the ships of the line floating prisons with a more certain death sentence awaiting many on board than for the inmates in a jail on shore. (Dr Johnson's precise words were 'that no man would be a sailor who had contrivance enough to get himself into gaol.')


## JOSÉ DE MAZARREDO (1745–1812)

The contemporary portrait of Vice Admiral José de Mazarredo offers a familiar face to the British visitor at Madrid's naval museum even though he may never have heard of him. This is because Mazarredo appears in the same official portrait genre as the English paintings of such great sea captains as Hawke, Howe, and Jervis. These honest portraits of admirals hang in perpetuity in the great public art galleries of both England and Spain. Perhaps too portly in middle age for their own good, such Spanish and English admirals of days gone by were painted at the height of their career, and in the fullness of successful professional lives.

Even though he remains largely unknown, Spanish naval historians remind us that Mazarredo was one of the leading naval commanders of his day. In history, Mazarredo was never defeated by the British at sea, unlike the doomed José de Córdoba at Cape St Vincent and the unlucky Admiral Federico Gravina, Spanish commander-in-chief at Trafalgar. Mazarredo never was given command of a Spanish fleet in any of the crucial battles, although he fought in them under other commanders-in-chief.

The *Enciclopedia Universal Ilustrada* wrote of Mazarredo, 'he was one of the most illustrious admirals of the final epoch of the Spanish Navy. A man of much learning, he combined a great spirit of observation with native courage.' Francisco de Paula y Pavia in his four-volume study of Spain's admirals published in Madrid in 1874, says of Mazarredo that 'he was one of the admirals who determined [naval policy] with much credit in the last epoch of our naval operations on a grand scale.' Of Mazarredo's qualities as a leader, Paula y Pavia writes, '… in the fleet the array of his best captains and officers loved and respected him as their father and their teacher.' Are not these the same qualities that we identify with the greatest of the British seamen and admirals?

González-Aller says Mazarredo should have been in command at Trafalgar instead of the more pliant but admittedly courageous Gravina. The reason Mazarredo did not obtain the highest commands – indeed, the reason why he was passed over for them – is that he expressed

Portrait of Vice Admiral José de Mazarredo. (*Museo Naval, Madrid*)

concern publicly over those unsolved crises of training, manning and supply that plagued the Spanish Navy at the end of the eighteenth century and contributed to its many defeats.

Even more serious for Mazarredo than his open attacks against the fleet's chronic disorganization were his frank criticisms of the government's foreign policy. He saw little value for Spain in the renewed Franco-Spanish alliance of 1796. He did this in the full knowledge that it was a result of the pro-French position of Manuel Godoy, the self-styled Príncipe de Paz (Prince of Peace), favourite of the wife of the pliant Charles IV.[20] In addition, the self-indulgent Godoy had elevated himself to the rank of 'generalíssimo' of His Majesty's army and navy. Mazarredo was constantly writing frank letters to both Godoy and the king warning about the decline of the fleet and its crews, now that it was once again fighting a Royal Navy with three times the number of warships as those in the combined fleets of Spain and France. The naval fighting machine of 57 ships of the line and 60 frigates, created during the reign of Carlos III who died in 1788, had been allowed to run down. Before the disaster at Cape St Vincent in 1797, Mazarredo warned Godoy in a foreboding letter that the number of ships in the fleet, as well as the chronic shortage of trained crews, did not add up to a fleet ready to take on the British.

Undoubtedly, Mazarredo was aware of Spain's deteriorating economic position at the end of the century. The spiral of inflation from Europe's constant wars had begun to climb. It continued to mount until the end of the Napoleonic Wars in 1815 and debilitated the economies of all the warring European powers, including Spain's. During 1799, the value of paper money in Spain declined by 40 per cent. Godoy's budgets and self-indulgences were disastrous for the navy. His patronage severely affected the armed forces especially the navy to which he appointed office-seekers on enormous salaries. This trend reached a dismal height after the royal wedding of the Prince of Asturias (heir to the throne) in 1802 when he appointed 57 field marshals, 26 generals including many 'admirals', and 'hundreds of colonels'.

Nor was the Royal Navy as buoyant and ready to fight another major sea war as it had been at earlier times during the century. It is well to bear in mind that 1797 was the year, not only of Cape St Vincent, but of the humiliating mutiny at the Nore. Britain needed another great victory at sea. Michael Lewis, late professor of naval history at the Royal Naval College Greenwich, writes in *The Navy of Britain*,

> '... early in 1797 Britain's position was far from good. Public morale even was at a low ebb. The Spanish were against us as well as the French; we had been forced to evacuate the Mediterranean altogether and were expecting imminent invasion of Ireland if not of England itself. Jervis, commander-in-chief of the evicted Mediterranean fleet, was dangerously weak in ships, having suffered a tragic list of set-backs at the hands of fortune, the weather and short-sighted subordinates. The Spanish fleet, he knew, had orders for Brest and a junction with the French.[21]

Although Spain and England has been allies briefly between 1793 and 1795, the Spanish alliance with France was renewed in 1796 when Spain under Godoy's instructions, joined the French Directory in a new war against England. This newest Franco-Spanish alliance survived the short-lived Peace of Amiens signed in 1802, and was still in force in 1803 when the war against Britain was renewed by Napoleon, now Emperor of the French. This last of the many uneasy alliances during the eighteenth century between France and Spain continued until 1808. At that time Spain was invaded by Napoleon's armies, Godoy was unseated and the unfit Charles IV and Ferdinand VII were forced into exile in France.

Mazarredo, who had held important naval commands both at sea and on shore since joining the corps of marines as a 16-year-old new entry cadet in 1761, had resigned from the navy in 1796, only to be asked by the government to return to service the next year after the disaster at Cape St Vincent. He was assigned to Cádiz to defend it against the anticipated British attack by sea. Because he had organized the fleet and shore facilities to meet such a threat, he was able to repulse just such an attack between 5 and 7 July 1797, two months after Cape St Vincent. In 1798, Mazarredo made what the record calls 'a valiant sally' out of Cádiz to rout an approaching English squadron of eleven vessels and was made captain general of Cádiz.

Since the mid-1780s, Mazarredo had introduced many badly-needed changes in fleet management and the operations of its ships. These paid off in his successful defence of Cádiz against the Royal Navy's raids from the north led by Admiral John Jervis. Mazarredo could see that *Santísima Trinidad* was no longer seaworthy after Cape St Vincent. Almost totally dismasted by smaller English ships, she managed nevertheless to escape under tow. He therefore recommended beaching her as a stationary gun platform as part of the Cádiz harbour defences. His recommendation was ignored. Instead, *Santísima Trinidad* remained in the fleet and was overhauled again, only to fight and be captured at Trafalgar. She then foundered under tow on 23 October 1805 in the great storm that dispersed the surviving ships of both navies in the two days following the battle.

Mazarredo's intimacy with ship performance in the fleet went back to his personal involvement in 1785 with the sea trials and operational efficiency of Romero y Landa's new *navíos* of the *San Ildefonso* 74-gun class. As a new commodore, Mazarredo conducted several 'comparative sea trials' to perfect ship-handling methods and ships' signalling routines in the *San Ildefonsos*. From his notebook of sea trials we read of his navigational runs to determine ships' positions on 9 June 1785. Other similar runs were made during July and August of the same year. On 3 September 1785 Commodore Mazarredo carried out further comparative sea trials with the new *navíos San Ildefonso* and *San Juan Nepomuceno*, as well as with the frigates *Santa Casilda* and *Santa Brigada*. Still other of his documents preserved in Spanish archives include his data analyzing such items as 'overall ships' plans ... ammunition holds and waterline dimensions.'[22]

While in command at Cádiz, he complained about the 'irremediable deficiencies in personnel and materiel' in Spain's major naval base. These same deficiencies, still unresolved eight years later, would plague Gravina and his fleet. For his outspokenness about the unpreparedness that would doom the fleet at Trafalgar, Mazarredo was prevented from ever commanding it.

Mazarredo's open disillusionment with the French began when he was assigned to Paris in 1799 to coordinate naval planning with the Directorate, leaving Gravina in charge of the Spanish squadron at Brest. Later, Gravina too was sent to Paris to serve briefly as the Spanish ambassador. While Napoleon and the admiral shared the common bond of their Italian birth and native tongue, Mazarredo called Napoleon's plans 'imperialistic and despotic'. For this, Charles IV the Spanish monarch under the pro-French influence of Godoy, ordered Mazarredo returned to Cádiz. This was done under the pretext that Mazarredo was needed as captain general there to remedy the chronic problems of manning and fleet supply. Because he persisted in criticizing the inefficiencies that continued to plague the fleet and its main naval base, and the few resources at his disposal to remedy them, Mazarredo was moved to Bilbao in 1802. From that time, he had no further opportunity to make crucial decisions that might have distanced the Spanish Navy from the French in the war that broke out again in 1803 – an alliance that so many Spanish naval officers found unworkable.

Mazarredo's considerable skills as 'one of the most illustrious admirals of the last epoch of the Spanish Navy' must be judged therefore, on his record at sea as well as on his considerable organizational talents.

Despite his open criticisms of the naval systems at the end of his career, Mazarredo had a well-rounded record of sea time, ship command, commander-in-chief of the corps of marines, and responsible posts as aide to senior Spanish commanders at sea. During one of the interminable Spanish wars with Algeria and the North African pirates, against great odds he devised a plan for the safe re-embarkation of the 20,000 Spanish troops that attacked Algiers. He served in the later phase of the unsuccessful siege against Gibraltar, lasting from 1779 to 1782. In 1780, Mazarredo was chief of staff to Luís Córdoba y Córdoba during his attack and capture of the English convoy of 55 merchant ships.

The nature of Mazarredo's fate was not unique to Spain. Like admirals in other navies before him and for many who were to come after, Mazarredo was denied the highest commands when his country needed him most because he openly criticized what he believed to be the wrong public policies for the navy and for the country. Paula y Pavia writes of Mazarredo that 'at the end, [he was] one of our best sailors who knew how to tell the government the entire truth, with neither dissimulation nor reticence.' On 10 May 1801 Mazarredo wrote to the king about coping with an untrained crew when he was captain of the *Conde de Regla* in 1790, eleven years previously. In it, he reported that he had no more than 60 sailors with experience on the high seas in a crew of about 500, the rest being fishermen and crewmen of coastal vessels 'without training or any understanding whatsoever of a ship's rigging or routine on board such as securing a topgallant sail from the yardarm or taking in a reef...' This was quite explicit but undoubtedly too specialized for the landlubberly Charles IV.[23]

However, during the eighteenth and nineteenth centuries as in our own, navies and governments will not countenance or give great command responsibility to senior officers who speak out against the service. The navy in history and in our own time remains the silent service. At the end of the eighteenth century, the Spanish problem with senior naval commanders was that too few of them possessed both the organizational and fighting skills of Vice Admiral José de Mazarredo.

## JUAN FRANCISCO DE LA BODEGA Y QUADRA (1743–1794)

The young Spanish naval captains in their small, locally-built naval vessels, exploring the west coast of North America in the 1770s and 1780s, were the embodiment at sea of the period of intellectual enlightenment in Spain. It is true, there were strong political motives behind the bold voyages of exploration by these youthful officers, based on what is now the west coast of Mexico. By pushing their ships as far north as they could go, they hoped to forestall an attempt by the Russians to move south from their colony in what is now Alaska, and to prevent the British from moving into the Pacific North-west on a permanent basis. The stakes then, were both geopolitical and economic. Where the present British Columbia coast was concerned, their goal was to corner the lucrative sea otter trade.

The British had already indicated that they would no longer tolerate the Pacific remaining a huge 'Spanish lake'. This had prompted Anson's circumnavigation of the world in the early 1740s and his stunning capture of a Manila galleon loaded with gold bullion. In 1762, the British temporarily occupied Manila, capital of the rich Spanish Philippines. Spain in the late eighteenth century no longer had the military resources to keep a region as vast as the Pacific free of European interlopers. The ocean distances from the viceroyalty of New Spain (modern Mexico and much of the modern south-west United States) to Manila was so great that the Manila galleon on its return voyage to Acapulco on Mexico's west coast, and sailing against the prevailing trade winds, could take as long as five months.

Yet, the vigour of the late eighteenth century Spanish renewal was more than enough to justify and then sustain the founding of a new naval base at San Blas in Mexico entirely for the purpose of extending Spanish land and sea claims north from California. A few short years before the Spanish naval explorers began to sail north, Captain James Cook laid claim to the Sandwich Islands (now the Hawaiian Islands) as British territory even though the Spanish later were to claim the same islands as their own. These young Spanish captains sailed, mapped and explored free of the great encumbrances of policy-making and fleet maintenance that plagued the best naval commanders such as Mazarredo. In an age when history disparages Spanish maritime skills because they are associated with lost sea battles, the voyages of such explorers as Juan Francisco de la Bodega y Quadra, Esteban Martínez, Juan Josef Pérez Hernández and Bruno de Hezeta were in the best tradition of Spanish maritime explorers of the sixteenth century.

Their discoveries did not lead to Spanish colonization of the Pacific North-west, but they did take place at the same time as Spain's last burst of new settlements in what is now the

Captain Juan Francisco de la Bodega y Quadra posed
against the backdrop of Nootka on the west coast of
Vancouver Island, with a *goleta* (schooner) and an Indian
war canoe in background. (*Patrick Harbon*)

south-west United States. Many of the Spanish language names of both the *presidios* – Spanish
missions and settlements – and the coastal landfalls named by the exploring captains of their tiny
sloops, remain to this day. The modern metropolis of Los Angeles was founded in 1777 as El
Puerto de Nuestra Señora de Los Angeles. It is an appellation from a deeply Catholic Spanish
past that cannot be lost on that city's growing transplanted population of Hispanics who have
emigrated there from Mexico and Central America. The real opening of the North American
interior was to follow from the overland explorations that began after the voyages of the young
Spanish naval captains had receded into history.

The voyages of Bodega y Quadra and his associates would not have taken place without
the vigour and drive of José de Gálvez, Marqués de Sonora who arrived at Vera Cruz in July
1764 to become the 'Visitor General' of the Viceroyalty of New Spain. Gálvez initiated many
new economic programmes for that vast area, including the building of the small naval base at
San Blas to commence voyages of exploration and investigation of the Russian settlements far to
the north. José de Gálvez was only one of three members of the most remarkable family to serve
on behalf of Spain during her last period of imperial rejuvenation from 1770 to the end of the
century. José de Gálvez left New Spain in 1775 to become Minister of the Indies, with power
in Madrid 'second only to that of King Carlos III himself'. He implemented the king's edict of
1778 that at last opened up the Spanish colonies to free trade. His elder brother Matías had been
captain general of Guatemala adjacent to the Viceroyalty of New Spain. He became its Viceroy
after José was appointed Minister of the Indies.

Matías' son Bernardo de Gálvez outdid his father in his accomplishments for Spain in the
New World. Many of these were concluded before he reached thirty-five years of age, looking
to Uncle José in Madrid for counsel and support. After a brief tour of duty as a lieutenant

colonel at the Avila military academy near Madrid, Bernardo Gálvez was promoted colonel, despatched to Spanish Louisiana and given command of the Louisiana Regiment of Infantry. A year later, aged thirty, he was sworn in as Spanish governor of the vast Louisiana territory. The accomplishments of Bernardo de Gálvez did not end here, but continued as he supported the American colonies fighting for independence against Britain in the American Revolutionary War.

Prior to the Spanish declaration of war against Britain in 1779, Bernardo de Gálvez was responsible for sending funds and supplies to the American rebels from Louisiana and Spanish Cuba. The contemporary Cuban exiled economist Eduardo Tejera writing in a special US bi-centennial supplement of *The New York Times* of 30 May 1976 reported that the £1,200,000 (600,000 Spanish reales) desperately needed by George Washington to finance the Yorktown campaign, came from the ladies of Cuba. 'They freely gave their diamonds, jewellery and gold, singly and through a number of ladies' lodges which proliferated in Cuba and throughout America.'

In 1780, British Florida extended as far west as the east bank of the Mississippi River, with Spanish Louisiana beginning on its other bank. Rather than wait for the English to attack New Orleans, his capital city, Gálvez took the offensive with his racially mixed army of Spanish regular troops, some of the Acadians expelled in 1755 from Nova Scotia, Choctaw Indians and former slaves who had escaped from the English sugar and tobacco plantations in Georgia. By 1781 Gálvez had captured Baton Rouge, the fortified port of Mobile, even though he lost his ships in a storm in the process. He captured the British military base of Pensacola and then all of west Florida. In the humiliating Peace of Paris of 1783 that followed, Britain not only acknowledged the loss of her thirteen American colonies and the existence of the United States of America, but also ceded the rest of Florida to Spain. Florida remained Spanish until it was purchased by the United States in 1819.

Bernardo de Gálvez did not rest on his laurels. After his father's death, he succeeded him as Viceroy of New Spain. Modern Texans who have trouble giving fellow Texans of Mexican and Spanish–American stock their due in the State's history, nevertheless commemorate the brilliant Bernardo de Gálvez in the name of the Texan coastal city of Galveston. Carlos III elevated Bernardo to Conde de Gálvez. Six years after the death of his monarch whose mania was the hunt, Count Bernardo de Gálvez died from over-exertion while hunting.

Bodega, as one of several young naval officers who implemented Spain's policy of curtailing the Russians and the British in the North Pacific, was what we would call today a Spanish–American. He was born in May 1743 in Lima, capital of the Viceroyalty of Peru, a city that was the most aristocratic seat of Spanish power in the New World. Since Peru was Spanish territory at the time, Bodega was born a Spanish subject. He was the son of Tomás de la Bodega y de las Llamas, a senior Spanish government official based at Cuzco in the Peruvian interior. His Peruvian-born mother, Francisca de Mollinedo y Losada, was a member of a prominent colonial family that emigrated from Bilbao, making Bodega yet another of the many Basques who predominated among the ranks of Spain's most famous naval officers. Bodega gave himself the full name Bodega y Quadra adding the last part of his name in honour of his paternal grandmother, Isabel de la Quadra.

Given the Basque origin of his family, it is understandable that the young Juan Francisco left for Spain to enter the newly-opened Escuela de Guardia Marinas at Cádiz. After graduation, he was promoted sub-lieutenant in 1767 and full lieutenant in 1774. He was then assigned to the newly-built naval station *apostadero* at San Blas de Nayarit, which was to be the administrative centre for Spain's west coast operations. The voyages from San Blas that would bring him fame and early promotion began almost at once. At San Blas and during his voyages, Bodega met other young naval officers who like himself, later rose to high rank. This was not the case for Juan Josef Pérez Hernández, already present at San Blas and older than the others. Bodega was only thirty-one when he first sailed north; Pérez, born in Majorca in 1725, was then forty-two. Pérez did not survive the 1770s but died at sea in 1775 on board his sloop *Santiago*, either from scurvy or a fever caught in the unhealthy climate of San Blas, which had been built on a low mosquito-infested coastline.

Rather, Bodega was closer to the other five lieutenants who arrived in San Blas at the same time, all of whom had been classmates in the Escuela de Guardia Marinas at Cádiz. They reached San Blas on 25 October 1774 with a batch of new scientific instruments needed for the far-travelling sloops and corvettes. The 1775 voyage north was under the command of Bruno de Hezeta, one of Quadra's classmates in Cádiz. Hezeta was one of two distinguished Spanish naval officers of the same name. Both of them reached the rank of vice admiral early in the nineteenth century at the end of their naval careers.

In the three-ship fleet under Hezeta's command that left San Blas on 16 March 1775, Bodega was originally second-in-command of the schooner *Sonora*, although after their departure he had to take her over when the captain, Juan de Ayala, 'was stricken by a fit of madness'. As it turned out, Bodega was the only captain to complete the voyage. In early August Hezeta, in ill health, was persuaded by the ship's doctor to turn back. He may have been another victim of the San Blas fever. On his first voyage, Bodega revealed the qualities of persistence, resoluteness and concern for his crew that gained him greater fame than many of his contemporaries. It is important to bear in mind that Bodega sailed thousands of miles to Alaska and back in the *Sonora*, a tiny schooner whose unseaworthiness is recorded in his journal, with 28 members of his crew sick on board. Bodega wrote of the *Sonora*, '. . . there is no hiding her small size, bad steering, frailty, slowness and the fact that I am forced to make more sail than should be necessary.' Clearly, this kind of long range operation into distant, dangerous seas needed newer and stronger ships. However, in *Sonora* he sailed to latitude 58 degrees 30 minutes north. This was well within the region of Russian Alaska and Bodega named the landfall Bucareli Sound. Bodega's map of what he called 'the port of Bucareli' is preserved in the former viceregal palace which is home to the Spanish Ministry of Foreign Affairs in central Madrid. Bodega named the port in honour of Antonio María Bucareli y Ursua, who arrived the same year to become the new viceroy of New Spain based in Mexico City.

Bucareli arrived in Mexico City opposed to the explorations, and even to the existence of San Blas. This was due in part to his dislike of the energetic José de Gálvez. A good deal of high-level correspondence going to Madrid included worrisome letters to Carlos III from the Spanish ambassador in St Petersburg as far back as 1773 concerning the planned moves southwards of the Russians along the Pacific coast of North America. This meant that Bucareli had no alternative but to support the explorations, and to order new ships for them.

While the new corvette *Princesa* was under construction at San Blas, Bucareli ordered Bodega to proceed to Callao, the port of Lima to pick up the new corvette *Favorita*. All the vessels used by these explorers were built in Mexico or Peru. During his 1779 voyage north with Ignacio de Arteaga, Bodega in command of *Favorita* might have crossed sea lanes with the famous English navigator James Cook had not the latter been killed in the Sandwich Islands. Madrid ordered the Arteaga expedition to intercept Cook if he proceded west again to explore or make land claims along what is now the British Columbia coast. In 1776, for his efforts as a valorous and aggressive officer, Bodega was decorated by Carlos III with a military knighthood of the Order of Santiago. In 1780 he was promoted captain. In 1782 he served as commandant at San Blas before his transfer the following year to naval service at Havana. From 1784 until his promotion in 1789 to commandant at San Blas, he served in various fleet duties at Cádiz.

During Bodega's long absence, Estebán José Fernández y Martínez de la Sierra, a fellow officer and pilot from the 1774 Pérez expedition, played a role which almost brought about war between Britain and Spain in 1790. Martínez, a contentious short-tempered man where Bodega was calm and conciliatory, incorrectly warned Manuel Antonio Florez, the Viceroy of New Spain, that the Russians were going to build a base at Nootka. Located on Vancouver Island's western shore, it was situated approximately at the half-way point on the long ocean haul between Alaska and California and was the focal point for the rich sea otter trade. Florez ordered Martínez to proceed to Nootka to build a small but permanent base large enough to support Spain's sovereignty claims. In July 1789 after constructing a battery and a small fort, Martínez foolishly seized two English merchant ships that arrived at Nootka during the month and sent both of them with their crews south to San Blas. This action was probably a result of an argument between Martínez and James Colnett, master of the *Argonaut*, one of the captured English ships, who had a fuse as short as that of Martínez.

John Meares, an English trader with a financial interest in both captured ships, had visited Nootka in 1788. His account of the episode was published in London, creating a new Anglo-Spanish crisis. When Prime Minister William Pitt could not persuade the new Spanish King Carlos IV who succeeded Carlos III in 1788 to make concessions in the Pacific North-west, both sides prepared for war.

British historians give the impression that 'a weakened Spain' backed down when it signed the Nootka Convention in 1790 to prevent a conflict between the two maritime states. From the Spanish Navy's point of view, the year 1790 represented the peak of its modernization and growth during that century. The fine new 74-gun ships and the big 112- and 120-gun three-deckers, designed and built by Gautier and Romero y Landa, were now in service. Despite constant shortages of trained crews that deeply worried Mazarredo, the navy of Spain in the year of the Nootka crisis was a force not to be under-estimated by the British. Nor did they do so.

In early 1790 Admiral Peyton, the British commander-in-chief in the Mediterranean 'placed Spanish strength at 64 ships of the line with 7 building...'. Lord Auckland, a former ambassador in Madrid, reported on the Spanish Navy's revitalized maintenance facilities at Cádiz (undoubtedly a result of Mazarredo's efforts). 'I doubt whether any Power can boast of being on a better footing on this score. The arsenals are well-stocked, every vessel had its own supplies set aside to facilitate fast loading and almost all the ships had been copper-bottomed.'[24]

Bodega, who returned to San Blas for the second time as commandant, was the ideal man to put in charge of Nootka. He arrived there in 1792 to negotiate the terms of the Nootka Convention. Bodega's calm diplomacy was brought into play in his negotiations on the spot with Captain George Vancouver, and the two distinguished naval captains and Pacific explorers became good friends. For years, the large island around which they both navigated, was called Vancouver and Quadra's Island. Indeed, the chief reason for the many Spanish place names that have continued to this day along the Pacific west coast, is because Captain Vancouver included them in his charts. These Spanish names appeared in turn on the charts later produced by the British Admiralty.

Writing in *The Dictionary of Canadian Biography*, Warren Cook, a scholar of Spanish west

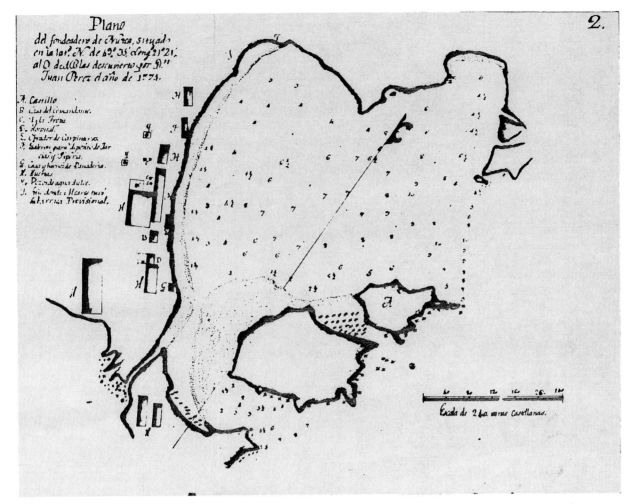

Contemporary plan from 1793 of the Spanish base and fur-
trading station at Nootka, the only permanent Spanish base
north of California on the Pacific west coast. (*Present
private owner unknown*)

coast explorers, says of Bodega's character,

> ... the genial commandant from Lima with the even-tempered governance of the base earned the
> respect and admiration of the British and American fur traders and of the Nootkas ... the tolerance
> and interest Bodega displayed for the Nootkas' customs gained their lasting effect and strengthened
> Spain's hold over the area ...[25]

At the same time, Bodega managed to withhold from Vancouver all but a small portion of
Friendly Cove on Nootka Sound. Bodega spent only one summer as Nootka's governor. The
two succeeding Anglo-Spanish Conventions 'neutralized' the area from colonization by either
power. Serious British settlement in British Columbia did not begin for another half century.

Bodega, a superb mariner and navigator and popular with the crews of his various
commands, was often sick at sea and on shore from the fevers he contracted at San Blas. Bodega

spent the winter of 1792–93 at the delightful Spanish mission of Monterrey in what was then Spanish California, where he hosted a visit from Captain George Vancouver. But he was ill and returned to, of all places, San Blas. Following a period of recuperation in Guadalajara in Mexico, Bodega died on 26 March 1794 in Mexico City, possibly a victim of recurring malaria.

Bodega y Quadra and his fellow naval explorers were more than seamen and would-be Spanish colonizers. In their ships they too, like Cook and Vancouver, carried pilots, cartographers and marine artists. A fine portrait of Bodega exists in which he stands in the full uniform of a navy captain, with the shoreline of Nootka in the background. A Spanish Navy corvette and a Nootka Indian war canoe have been painted behind him from black and white sketches originally drawn by Spanish artists who were with Bodega at Nootka.

Today, young Spaniards at school – as well as Juan Carlos I their modern Bourbon king, himself a keen sailor who unveiled a bust to Bodega's memory at Victoria, British Columbia on 17 March 1984 – remember the young North-west Pacific coast sailors of Spain's last great maritime era as among the best of their race.


## DON BLAS DE LEZO (1688–1741)

When Nelson made his famous but unjustified remark in 1793 that the Dons knew how to make ships and not men, he had forgotten about the doughty Basque admiral Blas de Lezo, who served and fought half a century before Nelson. Like Nelson with one arm and one eye, Blas de Lezo with one eye, one arm and one leg, fought his best battles as a physically handicapped commander. And, as Nelson was to do in his time, Blas de Lezo won most of them.

As the naval commander at Cartagena de Indias in 1741 under Don Sebastián Eslava, Viceroy of New Granada (the present Colombia), Blas de Lezo was largely responsible for the worst defeat suffered by the British during the eighteenth century at the hands of the Spanish. The losers in the attack on Cartagena were certain they would be the victors. The huge military and naval force of 30,000 troops and sailors in 120 ships sent to the Caribbean in the winter of 1740, was probably the largest ever mounted by Britain in the Caribbean. Except for Havana, Cartagena was the strongest fortified port and naval base in Spanish America, as well as an important terminus for the trans-Atlantic commercial fleets. British histories too easily blame the ravages of yellow fever, and not the efforts of the Spanish commander at Cartagena for the failure of Admiral Edward Vernon's and General Wentworth's mixed force of imperial and colonial troops to take the city. Certainly yellow fever was punishing, and killed perhaps 9000 sailors and troops in the British forces. At the same time, the smaller combined forces of about 6000 sailors and troops available to Blas de Lezo and Eslava also suffered greatly from yellow fever, malaria and dysentery.

Failure to take Cartagena constituted Britain's major defeat by Spain in the eighteenth century, at the half-way point between Spain's loss of Gibraltar in 1704 and defeat at Trafalgar a century later. Therefore it is unlikely that only disease and not the innovative, stubborn resistance by the Spanish commander accounted for the British defeat. Indeed, Blas de Lezo displayed all his life those qualities of initiative in battle, stubborn resolve and sound leadership that the Royal Navy's admirals in history rarely attach to their Spanish naval contemporaries. If Blas de Lezo is remembered at all in British records, it is because of his appearance on the victory medals which Vernon ordered struck prior to the battle for his anticipated conquest of Cartagena. On these medals the gallant, and as it turned out, the victorious leader at Cartagena,

Portrait of Vice Admiral Blas de Lezo. (*Museo Naval, Madrid*)

is kneeling before Vernon and surrendering his sword – some feat with only one leg.

German Arciniegas, the twentieth century Colombian intellectual and historian in his study *Caribbean, Sea of the World*, pinpoints why Blas de Lezo defeated the English at Cartagena:

> In 1704 at the battle of Gibraltar Vernon and Don Blas fought on opposite sides. But while Vernon was one of the victors and received a reward of 200 guineas, Don Blas was not only among the defeated but lost his left leg. In Toulon he lost his left eye, in Barcelona, his right arm. In each battle, he left a piece of himself in exchange for a little glory. He was a brave man. In Barcelona, to bring a convoy to the help of the beleaguered city, he set fire to several of his ships and came in under the protection of a double curtain of flame. The English knew all this, and Vernon knew he was dangerous on the offensive. Immediately after the capture of Portobelo, Vernon wrote Don Blas a letter that was a perfect challenge. Don Blas answered him from Cartagena: 'If I had been in Portobelo you would not have assaulted the fortresses of my master the King with impunity, because I could have supplied the valour the defenders of Portobelo lacked, and checked their cowardice...'[26]

Blas de Lezo, another of the many famous Basque sailors of Spain, was born in 1688 in the port town and old shipbuilding centre of Pasajes in Guipúzcoa province. A surviving church record tells us de Lezo was baptized on 6 February 1689 in the parish church of Pasajes de San Pedro. His father Pedro Francisco de Lezo was a sea captain before him and a scion of a seagoing family from the minor Guipúzcoan nobility. Although very little is known about his boyhood, Blas de Lezo undoubtedly was influenced in his choice of a sea career by the many sounds and smells of his native Pasajes, an export centre for Spanish woollens, and port where the local fishing vessels returned from the North Atlantic with their catches of whale meat and codfish. From Pasajes too, aggressive Guipúzcoan traders and businessmen had gone to the Spanish New World to found the *Guipúzcoana Compañía de Caracas*. It quickly became one of the great trading companies created by Spain in her Caribbean possessions during the eighteenth century.

Conde de Llobregat, the early twentieth century Basque historian writing in Irún in 1927, comments on the many influences from the sea that stimulated the young energetic Blas to seek a naval career:

> This background and the fantastic tales that he must have heard from the lips of the ships' captains, most certainly friends of his father and grandfather, like them gentlemen of the sea, influenced not a little the direction of the character of Don Blas who soon began to show his [sea] leanings.[27]

After early education in a French college Blas de Lezo joined the navy as a midshipman in 1702 at the age of fifteen and was assigned to a joint force of the French and Spanish fleets united in the dynastic War of the Spanish Succession. Before that war ended in 1713, Blas de Lezo emerged as one of the toughest young officers in the fleet, brave to the point of almost losing his life on two occasions during bold attacks, and singled out as a result, for early promotion.

In the twenty-year period 1702–1722, Blas de Lezo was to engage in many kinds of naval operations. These included combined operations with the army, fleet service in the New World, both fleet and single-ship actions, promotion to the senior rank of captain and in 1716, command of the *Lanfranco*, his first *navío*. All these activities made him one of the most skilled senior officers in a new Spanish Navy that had begun its eighteenth century rebirth. His experiences under fire were in defence of a Spanish mainland weakened after the defeats during the disastrous reign of Carlos II whose death without heirs brought on the War of the Spanish Succession. The various European enemies arrayed against Spain had captured Gibraltar in 1704 and forced the capitulation of Barcelona in the north in 1706 where the Archduke of Austria had set up court.

Blas de Lezo's active service began as a midshipman in the flagship of the Conde de Tolosa, the Spanish fleet commander who was fighting a Dutch squadron off Málaga. The young de Lezo lost his left leg in that battle, but he recuperated quickly and continued to serve. For his bravery the Conde de Tolosa wrote to the king outlining the action of the young de Lezo and promoted him to sub-lieutenant.

Between 1706 and 1710, when he left the Spanish coast for other duties, de Lezo continued in the navy's support roles to relieve Spain of its invaders. In 1707 he lost an eye during the defence of the fort of Sainte Catharine at the French naval port of Toulon and was promoted lieutenant the next year. In 1710, he was given command of a frigate. De Lezo's capture on the high seas of the English *Stanhope*, a heavily armed privateer or East Indiaman, also captured the imagination of two eighteenth century Spanish marine painters. Cortellini depicted de Lezo's frigate 'crossing the T' and raking *Stanhope*'s stern. Gordillo's offering shows *Stanhope* partially dismasted under tow by de Lezo's frigate. The latter painting features a scene that most Englishmen could not imagine taking place. This is a captured English ship taken in tow by the victorious Spanish frigate with the cream-coloured flag bearing the coat-of-arms of the Spanish Bourbons flying over the Red Ensign of the captured *Stanhope*.

Don Blas de Lezo returned to combined operations and played a part in the recapture of Barcelona. This brought an end to the long Catalan resistance against Felipe V, whose accession to the Spanish throne in 1701 had caused the outbreak of the War of the Spanish Succession. De Lezo suffered his last loss of a limb when his right arm was mangled by grapeshot during the final land and sea assault against Barcelona in September 1714. Captain Cesáreo Fernández Duro (1830–1908), the nineteenth century historian of the Spanish Navy, was inclined to mock de Lezo's physical appearance at this time when he commanded a warship escorting the daughter of the Duke of Parma to Spain for her wedding to Felipe V: 'His shape might have been more appropriate to preside over scenes of terror than to adorn the retinue of a queen.' However, the condition of Blas de Lezo's maimed body did not affect his naval career as he moved to new assignments in Hispanic America, first in convoy protection for the merchant fleets going to the New World, then in naval operations against pirates along the west coast of South America. The 60-gun *Lanfranco*, his first ship of the line command, was one of several warships bought by Spain between 1714 and 1716 before the new *navíos* of Gaztañeta had been completed and commissioned.

By now a captain, de Lezo spent the next fourteen years in continuous sea service along the west coast of South America. The piracy and contraband operations endemic there, especially along the Peruvian coast, were terminated thanks to de Lezo's busy squadron activities. During the new war between Britain and Spain in 1727, de Lezo captured six English and Dutch armed merchantmen that were operating in the Pacific Ocean with cargoes on board worth three million pesos. He then assigned two of his conquests to his own fleet. The historian Llobregat tells us that during de Lezo's lengthy South American sojourn, '... his privileged temperament resisted the climate, shortages of food and lack of comforts [at sea] for such a large period.' Blas de Lezo was married on 2 May 1725 to a Peruvian lady, Josefa Pacheco of Arica. Officiating at the ceremony which took place at the hacienda of Tomás de Salazar near Lima was the Archbishop of Lima, Fray Diego Murcillo. According to existing baptismal records, the de Lezos' first son was baptized on 1 June 1726 in Lima and named for his father.

The archives at Simancas in Spain contain de Lezo's correspondence with José Patiño, the navy minister in Madrid, requesting that he be replaced in his New World command and be returned to Spain for new duties. The de Lezos arrived at Cádiz on 18 August 1730 where the distinguished Spanish captain asked for, and was granted 'a rest in his country for the first time since he began his services.' During his well-deserved leave de Lezo travelled to Seville and met the king, who promoted him to the rank of commodore with seniority in that rank back to February 1726. Blas de Lezo returned to Cádiz and to a new war when he took command of the Mediterranean squadron. History does not tell us how the leaders of the Republic of Genoa felt about the ultimatum delivered to them by de Lezo in 1731. The reason for the Spanish appearance and threat of immediate reprisal was straightforward enough. The Republic of Genoa owed Spain two million pesos, a sum safely stored in Genoa's Banco di San Giorgio and which had not been paid back.

In December 1731 Blas de Lezo arrived at Genoa with a squadron of six *navíos* (a considerable force for the job at hand) and demanded both the surrender of the funds and 'an extraordinary salute' from the city authorities to the Spanish Bourbon flag. When the Genoese Senate indicated it would be delayed in making a decision, de Lezo pointed to his timepiece and threatened that if after several hours no such salute had been made and the money had not been delivered, he 'would raze the city, reducing it to ashes.' Faced by such a determined Spanish naval commander with substantial firepower behind him, the Genoese complied, turned over the money and voted in favour of a salute for the Spanish flag. Then, as one of de Lezo's biographers records, '... immediately on receiving the money he sailed away.' Where de Lezo's Spanish ultimatum is lost to history, the later but similar English one imposed by Commodore Martin of the Royal Navy on Carlos III is well known. As observed earlier, it changed the course of naval history between Spain and Britain by making them enemies for the remainder of the eighteenth century.

As with most senior Spanish naval officers of that era who reached senior shore positions or fleet commands, de Lezo inevitably spent a part of his career in the amphibious operations conducted by Spain against the North African islamic emirates based in Algiers, Tangiers and Oran. Too much precious Spanish manpower and equipment had been expended on these North African raids. The Spanish records prefer to describe them as punitive expeditions against 'the Barbary corsairs', but in Spain's case, they were frequently mounted not only to put down Mediterranean piracy, but to maintain a permanent sphere of influence in neighbouring North Africa.

It is possible that de Lezo's contribution to the defence of Cartagena against such a large amphibious English force owed much to what he learned as a senior fleet commander in the major Spanish campaign against Bey Hassan of Oran between June and November 1732. The Spanish in the Western Mediterranean in 1732, like the British in the Caribbean eight years later, were determined to reduce a large fortified enemy city with a superior amphibious force. Though the large Spanish fleet of 50 ships, 500 transport of various sizes and a huge army of 30,000 men captured Oran, Bey Hassan escaped to return later during the autumn of 1732 when he laid siege to his former capital, then under the control of a Spanish garrison of 8000 commanded by the Marqués de Santa Cruz. Not only did de Lezo help to relieve the garrison, but with his usual courage he pursued the Algerian flagship, a *navío* of 60 guns, hidden in a quiet bay and blew it up. However de Lezo's actions were not without losses, including damage to the guns of his own fleet when the Algerian flagship exploded and the death in action of Santa Cruz during the relief of Oran.

From this extensive yet inconclusive campaign, de Lezo must have realized that amphibious operations can be hazardous and that victory does not always go to the superior invading force. He must have learned too from the later actions of Bey Hassan that the defender of the fortress under attack can himself take the offensive. At Cartagena any naval commander other than de Lezo might have been overwhelmed at the sight of so many English sails appearing on the horizon on 15 March 1741. But the experienced Basque from Pasajes, whose sea time of thirty-nine illustrious years had included service in such an invading fleet, was undaunted by the English strength. Unlike Bey Hassan at Oran, de Lezo at Cartagena never did surrender his city. It was de Lezo's defence of the outer harbour of Cartagena de Indias near the end of the siege that delayed the English forces who began to succumb in alarming numbers to yellow fever and malaria. Unlike the Spanish commanders at Portobelo, which had few defences, de Lezo had no intention of surrendering, though Admiral Vernon had anticipated he would do so.

The details of de Lezo's successful defence of Cartagena are published elsewhere in other histories and do not need repetition at length. He arrived in the city on 11 March 1737 in charge of the naval escort for the regular shipping convoy to that city, three years before its famous defence began. In 1734, Blas de Lezo had been promoted vice admiral for his courageous sea and land assaults at Oran and Algiers. On 23 February 1740 he became governor of Cartagena on the death of Pedro Fidalgo, the previous incumbent. The British

[*112*]

The defence of Cartagena de Indias by the squadron of Blas
de Lezo, 1741. From an oil by L F Gordillo. (*Museo
Naval, Madrid*)

action against Cartagena lasted more than a year, beginning with naval bombardments by the
British fleet in February and March 1740 and ending with Vernon's final failure and
withdrawal on 20 May 1741.[28]

The end of the story offers yet another dramatic irony from the days when Spaniards and
Englishmen were enemies at sea. While the badly defeated Admiral Vernon vindicated himself
and was later entombed with other British heroes in Westminster Abbey, the tough, victorious
Basque has no known grave. His wasted body worn out at last from physical exertions and
tropical disease, finally gave out on 7 September 1741 in the city he saved. He might have been
buried in Cartagena's Convent of San Lorenzo but we will never know as it was later
destroyed. Nor apparently was de Lezo laid to rest in the Vera Cruz Convent containing the
remains of other military officers who died on service in the Viceroyalty of New Granada. It is
recorded that sixty-five years later in March 1806 as he lay dying from wounds following
Trafalgar, Admiral Federico Gravina whispered that 'he now wanted to be with Nelson'. One
wonders if Blas de Lezo one of Spain's greatest fighting sailors, would have wanted to share
eternity with *el pequeño almirante inglés*, the 'little English admiral' who, half a century after de
Lezo's death, would say for posterity that the Spanish knew how to make ships but not men.

PLATE IX
The *navío Catalán* from an oil by Rafael Monleón, 1724, Naval Museum, Madrid. She was one of Gaztañeta's 60-gun ships built in the old Catalonian shipyard at San Felix de Guixols and was stricken as early as 1731. (*Revista General de la Marina, Madrid*)

PLATE X
Portrait of Vice Admiral Blas de Lezo. (*Museo Naval, Madrid*)

PLATE XI
Don Antonio Valdés Fernández Bazán, one of Spain's most competent Ministers of the Navy, who served in the late 1780s and early 1790s during the period of the greatest naval expansion. (*Museo Naval, Madrid*)

PLATE XII
Lieutenant Commander José Martínez, Fernando Martínez de la Sierra, one of the several young commanders based at San Blas who explored the coasts of the Pacific North-west with Quadra in the 1770s.

PLATE XIII
Captain Juan Francisco de la Bodega y Quadra posed against the backdrop of Nootka on the west coast of Vancouver Island, with a *goleta* (schooner) and an Indian war canoe in background. (*Patrick Harbon*)

PLATE XIV
Commodore Cosmé Damián Churruca, as a young officer. (*Oil painting, Museo Naval, Madrid*)

PLATE XV
Painting of Capitán de navío Alejandro Malaspina. (*Museo Naval, Madrid*)

PLATE XVI
Commodore Dionisio Alcalá Galiano, captain of *Bahama* at Trafalgar. (*An oil by an anonymous painter in the Museo Naval, Madrid*)

PLATE XVII
José Espinosa Tello was one of Malaspina's young ship captains during 1789–1794 world circumnavigation. He is shown here at the end of his career, as a Vice Admiral of the Spanish Navy. He died young, in Madrid, aged fifty-two. (*Museo Naval, Madrid*)

PLATE XVIII
The defence of Cartagena de Indias by the squadron of Blas de Lezo, 1741. From an oil by L F Gordillo. (*Museo Naval, Madrid*)

PLATE XIX
Blas de Lezo takes the British *Stanhope* on the high seas, 1710. From oil by Angel Cortellini (*Patrick Harbron*)

PLATE XX
Blas de Lezo's ship has *Stanhope* in tow after its capture in combat. Note Spanish Bourbon family and navy flag of the victor above English Red Ensign. From an oil by L F Gordillo. (*Patrick Harbron*)

PLATE XXI
To British eyes, an unfamiliar post-Trafalgar view of *Victory*. In this reproduction of a Clarkson Stanfield painting on the 1980 Gibraltar 15p stamp commemorating the 175th anniversary of Nelson's death, she is shown under tow to Gibraltar – battered and almost completely dismasted after Trafalgar and the two-day storm that followed it. (*GPO*)

PLATE XXII
The shattered French and Spanish survivors of the Combined Squadron limp back to the protection of Cádiz harbour, portrayed almost as a medieval city. (*Watercolour by José Tomás Córdoba in the collection of Manuel Gómez Moreno*)

X

XI

XII

XIII

XIV

XV

XVI

XVII

XVIII

XIX

XX

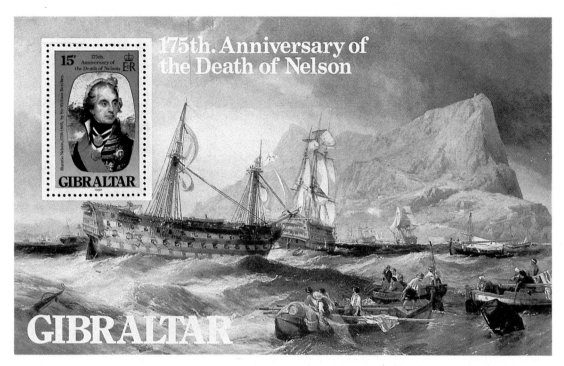

XXI

XXII

# CHAPTER FIVE

## *Trafalgar and the Spanish Captains*

ALTHOUGH TRAFALGAR is one of the most thoroughly analyzed sea battles of history, the Spanish admirals and ship commanders who fought in it come down to us, if at all, as remote figures, inadequate leaders and bad sailors. In the many classic Trafalgar histories, the Spanish captains too often appear as obscure adjuncts to the wider tale of the last great decisive sea battle of the historic age of sail. Such Spanish names as Gravina, Alava, Escaño and Cisneros (the Spanish fleet's four Trafalgar admirals) and Churruca, Alcalá Galiano, MacDonnell and Gastón (four of the fifteen Trafalgar ships' captains) are included in the numerous nineteenth and twentieth century Trafalgar studies, but all too often in such books their personalities and deeds are footnotes to other themes on the battle. The more probing British and American authors of the period make positive but self-conscious references to Spain's ship captains as unusually brave and determined enemies at sea, as though this came as a surprise. They were, after all, among the best of Spain's naval leaders at the end of the century of Spanish naval renewal.

The French, too, have struggled for their proper identification as well as a fair place for the roles of their officers and ships, in the many English-language books published about Trafalgar in the more than 180 years since that battle. The exception, perhaps, is the tragic figure of Vice Admiral Pierre Charles Jean-Baptiste Sylvestre Villeneuve, the overall commander of both the French and Spanish fleets. Villeneuve, a skilled sailor and commander as well as a survivor of the French Royal Navy's experienced officer corps that was largely destroyed by the French Revolution, lost the great and strategic battle following the most gallant defence by his flagship, the 80-gun *Bucentaure*. He died mysteriously – perhaps by suicide – in the Hotel de Patrie in Rennes. He arrived there days after his release as a British prisoner-of-war and return to France in April 1806. He awaited an uncertain fate from Dénis Decrès, the French Minister of Marine and, like Villeneuve, a former officer of the old French Royal Navy.

Villeneuve, too, had employed his own version of the Nelsonian order for battle that in a coming struggle 'the best place to take a Frenchman is alongside.' Villeneuve's own Order of the Day for the Combined Squadron as Nelson's fleet approached in two lines in the light air of the Atlantic on the forenoon of 21 October 1805, was in tone and content Nelsonian:

> *Tout capitaine qui ne serait pas dans le feu ne serait pas a son poste ... et un signal pour l'y rappeler serait pour lui une tâche déshonorante.* [Any captain who is not in the line of fire is not at his post ... and a signal as a reminder would be for him a dishonorable act.]

The Battle of Trafalgar was bloodily won. Single Spanish and French ships' crews and their captains fought furiously against their British counterparts to lose a battle that some of their best ships' commanders stated before the event would probably be lost. The bravery of the mortally wounded and terribly mangled Commodore Cosmé Damián Churruca in command of *San Juan Nepomuceno*; and of Dionisio Alcalá Galiano commanding the *Bahama*, was also Nelsonian. Great gallantry through the insufferable pain before death was not reserved for the cockpit of the *Victory*, where Nelson died horribly wounded. Spaniards and Frenchmen, not only in command but awaiting their orders as guns' crews, were indistinguishable from the British when it came to bravery in the kind of ship-against-ship warfare that, in its intimacy, made fighting at sea more terrifying and more personal than sea warfare in our own era.

Napoleon clearly leaves us with the strong impression that the bravery and gallantry displayed by his fleet and men at Trafalgar were not enough for the land-oriented warrior-emperor. With the battle flags of the vanquished Austrians from their total defeat by him at Ulm and Austerlitz already laid up in Paris, Napoleon, in his Imperial Address to the Corps Législatif on 2 March 1806, brushed off Trafalgar: '*Les tempêtes nous ont fait perdre quelques vaisseaux après un combat imprudemment engagé.*' ... [We have lost several vessels to storms, after a battle imprudently engaged.] Yet in January 1806, Napoleon had ordered the following words painted prominently in all the surviving warships of his imperial fleet which was seriously weakened at Trafalgar: '*La France compte que chacun fera son devoir!*' [France expects that every man will do his duty.] This admonition he told Decrès was '... the best of lessons.'[1]

Nor have the vanquished of Trafalgar – Spanish and French alike – felt the need over time to use a substitute name for the battle, bearing in mind that it came from the ailing English monarch George III. On being informed in early November 1805 when the news first reached England of the Trafalgar victory and the death of Nelson, George III's private secretary announced 'The King is of the opinion that the battle should be styled that of Trafalgar.' And so, indeed, it has been. The French, the centuries-old enemy of England on land and at sea, are readily identified as the enemy at Trafalgar while often the question is asked 'I didn't know the Spanish also fought at Trafalgar. What part did they play?'

The course of both political and military events from 1796 to the year of Trafalgar was prelude to an ultimate showdown sea battle between England, France and Spain. Spain originally was a member of the European monarchist alliance formed in 1793 to contain the aggressive, anti-royalist French revolutionary regime. Called the First Coalition, it was composed of Great Britain, Austria, Spain, Prussia, several smaller German monarchies close to the now hostile French frontiers, the Kingdom of Sardinia and Naples, and Russia. The Spanish Bourbon monarchy had sound reason for originally joining an anti-French coalition of monarchies because the French revolutionaries had beheaded both the French Bourbon King Louis XVI and his wife Marie Antoinette. However, throughout most of the eighteenth century the two Bourbon monarchies – Spanish and French – had been linked in war and peace, a linkage that included, as we have seen, much interchange of naval technology. Paradoxically, the Franco-Spanish Bourbon alliance which continued during most of the century now drawing to a close, had been Britain's strongest opponent at sea.

From the commencement in 1793 of what are loosely called the Napoleonic Wars until Napoleon's final defeat at Waterloo on 18 June 1815, Britain was at war with France for more years than with Spain. Except for the year of uneasy peace between France and England following the Peace of Amiens (signed on 27 May 1802) to the British re-declaration of war against Napoleon on 16 May 1803, Britain and France were at war for twenty-one years. Spain, during the same long period (1793–1815), was Britain's enemy for only eleven years and an ally of England for eight. Anglo-Spanish 'alliances' during the long Napoleonic war era

A superb Spanish painting of Trafalgar by R Monleón, one
of the best of the Spanish marine painters. (*Museo Naval,
Madrid*)

included Spain's brief two-year membership in the First Coalition from 1793 to 1795 and the
six bloody years 1808–1814, when the French – Spain's historic ally – invaded and occupied
Spain during the Peninsular War. History, which is full of dramatic ironies, offers us one from
this war. If the Combined Squadron of Spain and France had not been destroyed at Trafalgar,
its presence after 1808 along the Spanish coast and in control of Spain's major naval bases would
have delayed or even prevented the Duke of Wellington's troop debarkations in Portugal and
Spain. After 1805, it was Britain's supremacy on the seas that also made possible Wellington's
unimpeded landings in Spain to begin his six-year campaign to liberate the country.

In 1795, because of strong fears of aggressive British imperial intentions in the
Mediterranean and the Caribbean, Spain withdrew from the First Coalition. On 19 August
1796 Spain and France signed the Treaty of San Ildefonso (in the palace that was a favourite
summer retreat of the Spanish Bourbons), and on 11 October in the same year, Spain declared
war against Britain. In terms of the re-allocation of the now-considerable Spanish sea power, the
San Ildefonso Treaty was particularly ominous for a hard-pressed Royal Navy. Not only did it
re-establish the powerful Hispano-French squadron at the Brest naval base that again would
require constant blockading by the Royal Navy, but under article 3 of the treaty, Spain could
assign fifteen of its ships of the line to the French fleet:

> Within three months of any such request for assistance the power requiring assistance shall be in receipt of fifteen ships of the line, three of these either three-deckers or ships of 80 cannon, and the remaining twelve of from 70 to 72 cannon, as well as six frigates of corresponding size and firepower, four corvettes or ships of small draught, every one of these equipped with a sufficiency of stores for three months, and rigging enough for one year, all provided by the other party.[2]

Spain was easily capable of such a division of her fleet, since the *Armada Española* was at its apogee of power. By 1794 the dynamic Spanish naval shipbuilding programmes begun in the 1780s, which had produced some of the best warships in Europe, gave Spain the largest fleet in her history.

The Spanish fear that England was planning to annex more of the sugar-rich Caribbean islands at the expense of Spain's West Indian island possessions outweighed other Spanish fears of French expansionism in Europe. Throughout such rich Spanish Caribbean islands as Cuba, Puerto Rico and Trinidad, the sugar industry was expanding at the end of the century to become, in the nineteenth century, Spain's second largest source of income from her colonies after imports of gold and silver.

These Spanish fears were justified in 1797 by the British capture and annexation of Trinidad after hostilities were renewed. Britain did not again attempt to take Havana as it had done successfully in 1762, but such Spanish fears of continued British expansionism were clearly defined in explicit clauses of the Spanish declaration of war against Britain of 11 October 1796:

> ... That ambitious and greedy nation has once more proclaimed to the world that she recognizes no law but that of aggrandizement of her own trade, achieved by her global despotism on the high seas; our patience is spent, our forbearance is exhausted; we must now turn our gaze to the dignity of our throne ... we must declare war on the King of England and on the English nation ...[3]

Spain's re-entry into the war with its large navy – this time on the French side – stretched the Royal Navy's resources to the limit. The British Mediterranean fleet under Admiral John Jervis abandoned its two naval bases at Elba and Corsica. On 1 December 1796 Jervis transferred his command to Gibraltar, and his fleet activites to the Atlantic coasts of Portugal and Spain. However, the stunning English victory at Cape St Vincent on 14 February 1797 against a much larger Spanish fleet not only did much to redress the balance of sea power but helped to place the still substantial *Armada Española* in a secondary position vis-à-vis the French Navy, a role it was forced to play eight years later at Trafalgar.

Although many critical battles took place on land and at sea between 1797 and the Peace of Amiens in 1802, they did not directly involve the Spanish fleet. Two more devastating naval victories by Nelson, the destruction of the French fleet at Aboukir Bay in Egypt on 1 August 1798 and the Danish fleet at Copenhagen on 2 April 1801, did not include the Spanish. The Second Coalition of European powers at war with France (where Napoleon now was the predominant political figure as well as the leading military one) included Austria, Portugal, Naples and Russia. Napoleon's continued hard blows and brilliant victories against the Austrians between 1797 and 1800 brought down the Second Coalition. Napoleon then formed an alliance with Denmark, Sweden and Prussia to close the Baltic to British ships.

The Russian withdrawal was critical for the Royal Navy, which was relying heavily on Baltic pine imports (most of them from Scandinavia and Russia) for the manufacture of masts

## THE SPANISH SHIPS AND CAPTAINS IN THE BATTLE

| Navíos (ships of the line) | Yard | Year | Guns | Crew | Killed | Wounded | Commanding Officers | Fate of Ships |
|---|---|---|---|---|---|---|---|---|
| Principe de Asturias | Havana | 1794 | 118 | 1113 | 52 | 116 | Commodore Rafael de Hore | Returned to Cádiz. |
| Santa Ana | El Ferrol | 1784 | 120 | 1118 | 59 | 169 | Capitán de navío José Gardoquí | Returned to Cádiz. |
| Santísima Trinidad | Havana | 1769 | 136 | 1048 | 205 | 108 | Commodore Francisco Uriarte | Captured by British then lost in the post-Trafalgar storm. |
| Rayo | Havana | 1749 | 100 | 830 | 1 | 11 | Commodore Enrique MacDonnell | Lost in post-Trafalgar storm. |
| Neptuno | El Ferrol | 1795 | 80 | 800 | 12 | 47 | Commodore Cayetano Valdés y Flores Bazán | Damaged in battle and lost in post-Trafalgar storm. |
| Argonauta | El Ferrol | 1798 | 92 | 778 | 100 | 200 | Capitán de navío Antonio Pareja | Lost in post-Trafalgar storm. |
| San Ildefonso | Cartagena | 1785 | 74 | 746 | 24 | 126 | Commodore José de Vargas | Taken as prize, served later in the Royal Navy. |
| Bahama | Havana | 1784 | 74 | 690 | 100 | 150 | Commodore Dionisio Alcalá Galiano | Captured, later served in the Royal Navy. |
| San Juan Nepomuceno | Guarnizo | 1766 | 74 | 693 | 100 | 150 | Commodore Cosmé Damián Churruca | Captured to later serve in the Royal Navy as *San Juan*. |
| San Agustín | Guarnizo | 1768 | 80 | 711 | 150 | 200 | Commodore Felipe Cajigal | Captured by the British and burned. |
| Monarca | El Ferrol | 1794 | 74 | 667 | 100 | 150 | Capitán de navío Teódoro de Argumosa | Lost in post-Trafalgar storm. |
| Montañés | El Ferrol | 1794 | 80 | 715 | 20 | 29 | Capitán de navío Francisco Alcedo | Returned to Cádiz. |
| San Francisco de Asís | Guarnizo | 1767 | 74 | 677 | 5 | 12 | Capitán de navío Luís Antonio de Flores | Damaged in battle then lost in post-Trafalgar storm. |
| San Justo | Cartagena | 1779 | 76 | 694 | 0 | 7 | Capitán de navío Francisco Javíer Gastón | Returned to Cádiz. |
| San Leandro | El Ferrol | 1787 | 74 | 606 | 8 | 22 | Capitán de navío José Quevedo | Returned to Cádiz. |
| | | | | Total: 11,817 | Total: 1025 | Total: 1383 | | |

for Royal Navy warships. Certainly this serious threat to the fleet was one of the reasons it was sent to Copenhagen to punish the Danes by destroying their fleet and re-opening the Baltic. Napoleon had moved quickly to political power in France, as well as to command its constantly victorious land forces. In 1802, as one of the five consuls of the French Consulate, Napoleon appointed himself Consul for Life, an action that preceded the supreme political act of his life when he crowned himself Emperor of the French on 16 May 1804.

By 1802, after a decade of continuous conflict, all the warring powers were exhausted and hoped to benefit from the Peace of Amiens that ended hostilities for one year between Britain and France. Despite Nelson's spectacular naval victories, Britain remained in a precarious position. At sea, the Spanish and French fleets were still intact, despite the devastating defeats at Cape St Vincent and Aboukir Bay. The big French-Spanish squadron based at Brest represented a fleet in being that often raided shipping in the English Channel, and at any time could support the French in their attempts to invade Ireland. In fact, the big Spanish fleet defeated at Cape St Vincent was proceeding to Brest to link up with the French sea and land forces for a planned invasion of England. Though the defeat at Cape St Vincent sent shock waves through the Spanish fleet, unlike Trafalgar it did not remove Spain as a sea power. Of the 29 Spanish *navíos* that fought and lost against 15 English ones at Cape St Vincent, only 4 were actually captured and taken as prizes. By 1802, England's cash subsidies to her unreliable European allies amounted to nineteen million pounds, a huge amount in a day when the annual budget for the Royal Navy represented about a third of that amount.

Meantime, in France during the year of peace 1802–1803, Napoleon continued to build up his land forces and refurbish the fleet. A substantial number of its officers, such as those at the command level (including Admiral Villeneuve, the future Trafalgar commander-in-chief) were officers of the former French Royal Navy who had considerable sea and battle experience. Somehow they had survived the many bloodbaths of the Terror and subsequent violent political changes in France, during which many senior service officers along with the aristocrats they served, had gone to the guillotine. Therefore, a renewal of war between Britain, France and Spain meant that the Royal Navy would face two powerful enemy fleets in which skilled naval officers with long experience would continue to command both the fleets and ships of the line.

'Fighting with the utmost gallantry,' was the generous and accurate observation on the quality of the French and Spanish resistance at Trafalgar as described by the late Sir Arthur Bryant in his *Years of Victory, 1802–1812*, written in 1945 near the end of a later world war. For the four Spanish admirals and fifteen Spanish ships' captains at Trafalgar – professional seamen all and none of them court-appointed favourites – as well as for the French commanders, their individual displays of gallantry were not to win them a victory. The preceding years of indifference to training ships' companies as hard and as long as did the British, the fact that too few of the fifteen *navíos* had been at sea during the two years prior to Trafalgar; the constant drain of disease during 1803–1804 in southern Spain on available manpower and the unhappy French alliance; all of these presaged a defeat for both Spanish and French sea power in a naval battle of such consequence against Nelson.

In their published comments and private correspondence, the Spanish admirals and captains alike attributed disaster to the renewed alliance with France, and more pointedly, to an unbelievable condition for them as sailors with much accumulated sea time in earlier fleets. They had gone to sea as a Combined Squadron of two navies from two different cultures, without once engaging in joint fleet exercises in preparation for combat. On the verge of such a major naval battle, Villeneuve's precipitous order to tack the thirty-three French and Spanish warships from south to north, was done for the first time by his fleet. His ships had never done it before in practice. His manoeuvre, awkwardly made in light winds, helped to turn Trafalgar largely into a melée of individual ships' actions rather than that of a fleet of two navies in correct line-ahead battle order. Further, the Spanish were beholden to a distant upstart French emperor who had no sensitivity about the proper use of sea power and large fleets of ships. Before they set sail from Cádiz on 20 October 1805, also in disarray because of light winds, the Spanish naval commanders knew they were impotent to change events.

The great Nelson as always had a *Plan*, the one he laid out to his admirals and ships' captains only days before the battle. 'We can, my dear Coll, have no jealousies,' he wrote to Collingwood before the battle, 'we have only one great object in view, that of annihilating our enemies and getting a glorious victory for our country.'

The 'ifs' of history that always surround the vanquished have been analyzed many times in the numerous studies of the course of the battle and of the fleet manoeuvrings giving advantage to the British as they approached in two lines the ragged crescent of the French and Spanish ships. If the Spanish had had a different commander-in-chief – say, the cantankerous and ever-critical Mazarredo instead of the pliant and diplomatic Gravina – would the outcome have been different? Or, in effect would there have been no battle at all, if Mazarredo in command had deemed his navy not yet ready to fight the English? We know from the record beginning in the later 1790s of Mazarredo's open anger over the fleet deficiencies in training, sloppy shipyard management and not enough equipment and supplies for the fleet, as well as the need for a higher percentage of *hombres del mar* (seamen) to landlubberly marines that made up the ships' companies of the Spanish Navy.

Gravina certainly made no effort to re-man his ships largely with naval personnel, in part because since 1800 there had been such a shortage of seamen. Also, Gravina was chained to the traditional Spanish naval manning position which so disturbed Mazarredo that the ship of the line must be a shooting platform for troops as well as a fighting naval vessel. On 20 October 1805, the day before Trafalgar, Gravina himself listed the fatal imbalance of troops to sailors in the *Principe de Asturias*:

| | | |
|---|---|---|
| *Tropas de Infantería*   [infantry] | | 382 |
| *Artillería del Mar*   [marine artillery] | | 172 |
| *Marineros y oficiales*   [officers and men] | | 609[4] |

This meant that almost half the 1163 officers and men on board the Spanish flagship at Trafalgar were not seamen.

The other candidate for Spanish commander-in-chief, as suggested by González-Aller, was Domingo P Grandallana, the Minister of the Navy. In 1805 he was forty-eight, the same age as Gravina and sixteenth in seniority on the *Cuerpo General*, or Navy List of twenty-nine vice admirals. Grandallana had a sound reputation in the fleet but, unlike Gravina, was antagonistic to the French. In fact, we know that he had no chance at command based on a letter from Napoleon to Decrès dated 16 June 1805 from Verona: 'I do not wish that Mr Grandallana command my [!] squadron.'

Would Trafalgar have been less of a victory for Nelson if the Spanish and not the French had been in overall command with a Spanish fleet refurbished and renewed as Mazarredo earlier envisaged? Certainly some kind of major fleet action would have taken place, given the alternative of a long blockade of Cádiz by the British. In their own ways, both sides wanted a victory: in late September 1805 Nelson was itching to demolish the two navies that had led him on a pre-Trafalgar diversionary wild-goose chase across the Atlantic to the Caribbean and back; Napoleon wanted the Combined Squadron, not in Cádiz, but at Brest far to the north, to escort his invading armies across the Channel. He needed, but never got, the minimum of twelve hours of clear access – with the Royal Navy either outnumbered or somewhere else – to give the 150,000 troops in his 'Army of England' the clear sea passage they needed to cross the Channel and invade England.

Given Gravina's role as a diplomat in helping to re-establish the Franco-Spanish alliance in 1803, and his part in meeting Napoleon's request that Spain honour her commitments under the San Ildefonso Treaty of 1796 to make ships available to France, any other choice than Gravina for a Spanish fleet commander-in-chief seemed unlikely. On 4 January 1805 Gravina was in Paris promising Decrès that Spain would immediately arm and prepare for war 8 *navíos* and 4 frigates at El Ferrol, 12 *navíos* at Cádiz, with 6 more at Cartagena. 'These ships will be ready

before 20 March and no later than 30 March, all with stores for six months and water for four,' says the Spanish naval document. A month later, on 1 February, Gravina returned to Madrid. At the palace of Aranjuez the next day he outlined and expanded his functions as the Spanish Navy's commander-in-chief and recommended the appointments of the various ships' commanders. According to the record, all of them were approved, *resultaron aprobadas*, by both the King and Godoy.[5]

The following commodores and *capitanes de navío* (captains) were appointed during February and March 1805 to what would become their Trafalgar commands. The commodores were: Rafael de Hore (*Principe de Asturias*), Gravina's future flagship; Francisco Javíer de Uriarte y Borja (*Santísima Trinidad*); Enrique MacDonnell recalled from retirement (*Rayo*); Cosmé Damián Churruca (*San Juan Nepomuceno*); Felipe Jado Cajigal (*San Agustin*). The other captains were José Gardoquí (*Santa Ana*), Luís de Flores (*San Francisco de Asis*), and Francisco Javíer Gaston (*San Justo*). Between June and August 1805 Captains José Quevedo y Cheza, Francisco Alcedo y Bustamente, José de Vargas and Antonio Pareja were appointed commanders of *San Leandro*, *Montañés*, *San Ildefonso* and *Argonauta* respectively. Commodore Dionisio Alcalá Galiano, who had been given command of the *navío Glorioso* in February 1805, was re-appointed to *Bahama*, his Trafalgar command, in June 1805. This left only Commodore Cayetano Valdés, who retained command of the *Neptuno* that he had received in August of the previous year and Captain Teódoro de Argumosa, appointed captain of the *Monarca* in November 1804, to complete the list of Spain's fifteen Trafalgar ship captains.

Gravina's three admirals who joined him during the year 1805 were Vice Admiral Ignacio María de Alava y Navarrete and Rear Admirals Antonio de Escaño and Báltasar Hidalgo de Cisneros. Cisneros was attached to the El Ferrol squadron by his own choice, with his flag in

◁◁ Vice Admiral Federico Gravina, Spanish commander-in-chief at Trafalgar. (*Painting in the Museo Naval, Madrid*)

◁ José Espinosa Tello as one of Malaspina's young ship captains during 1789–1794 world circumnavigation. (*Museo Naval, Madrid*)

Rear Admiral Antonio Escaño, Spanish third-in-command ▷ at Trafalgar. (*Painting in the Museo Naval, Madrid*)

*Neptuno*, on 27 May 1805; but on 12 August he sailed to Cádiz under orders to join the Combined Squadron and reached that naval base on 20 August. On 15 February 1805 Alava was named his second-in-command by Gravina but remained behind in command of the naval units in Cádiz when Gravina left that base on 10 April to join the French Admiral Villeneuve in his pre-Trafalgar diversionary fleet dash to the French West Indies. Escaño, who was placed under Gravina's orders following the Spanish declaration of war against England on 12 December 1804, flew his flag in *Argonauta*, and sailed with Villeneuve to Martinique and back. He also was involved in the skirmish of 22 July 1805 off Cape Finisterre, when Admiral Sir Robert Calder attacked but failed to destroy Villeneuve's Franco-Spanish squadron on its return from the West Indies.

It goes without saying that all these officers were well known to each other as well as to the court. In late-eighteenth century Spain, the military elite was small in contrast with the large bureaucracies of modern European states and their armed forces. In the present day, one cannot imagine the sovereign and the prime minister personally approving the appointments of ships' captains in the Royal Navy, although it is true that all rear admirals' promotions in the United States Navy must be approved by Congress from a captains' list of hundreds of names.

The Spanish naval archives contain the correspondence between Gravina and Godoy relating to the appointment of the Trafalgar ships's captains. Gravina in his letter of 15 February 1805 to the Spanish prime minister is putting up Gaston and MacDonnell to command *San Justo* and *Rayo* respectively. On MacDonnell, who served in two eighteenth century navies, the Swedish and Spanish, Gravina writes, '... his skills, his accredited valour encourage me to request that Your Excellency may restore him to his rank and seniority given the circumstances of the day, to the Navy List.' Godoy's reply in part on 26 February 1805 to

Gravina written from the royal palace at Aranjuez accepts Gravina's choice of MacDonnell: 'I approve ... [Gravina's list and additional request to re-arm *San Justo* and *Rayo*] and I have commanded that Don Enrique MacDonnell may be returned to active service in the fleet in his rank and seniority in order to take over the *Rayo*.'[6]

Cisneros, one of the rear admirals, was indeed well known around the fleet, if for no other reason than his sudden action during Cape St Vincent in recapturing the *Santísima Trinidad* after her surrender to the English. Some British naval histories see this act as quite unworthy because

the big *navío* had already struck her colours, but surely the Royal Navy too must condone – even encourage – the action of an officer determined to retake a ship captured in battle from the enemy. At Cape St Vincent Cisneros was captain of the *San Pablo* in the squadron of Rear Admiral Juan de Lángara. He, in turn, was under the command of the unfortunate Vice Admiral José de Córdoba, the Spanish commander-in-chief who lost that battle. Later, Cisneros gave up command of the *San Pablo* for the *Santa Ana* (a future Trafalgar warship) in a squadron commanded by Vice Admiral Domingo Grandallana (later to become the navy minister), who in turn served under José de Mazarredo, then a fleet commander. In the year of Trafalgar Mazarredo sulked in semi-retirement in Bilbao, passed over like Grandallana for the main job of commander-in-chief of the Spanish Navy.

The Anglo-Saxon histories of the battle that denigrate the Spanish Navy as ill-prepared for the renewed war at sea, usually have not questioned the individual bravery of Spain's Trafalgar captains, and certainly could not do so, given their high casualty rate. Three were killed during the battle: Churruca, Alcalá Galiano and Alcedo; and Gravina died of his wounds five months later. Nine others were wounded, some severely so, but recovered and lived to do other things. These included Vice Admiral Alava and Rear Admirals Escaño and Cisneros (who, after his recovery, had to write the report of proceedings of the battle for Godoy in place of Gravina).

◁ Malaspina's *corbeta* (corvette) *Atrevida* among the icebergs off southern Chile on 28 January 1794. (*Museo Naval, Madrid*)

△ View of the port and part of the city of Acapulco taken from the hospital: Spanish colonial ports by artists of the Malaspina expedition. (*Museo Naval, Madrid*)

▽ Night view of Malaspina's *corbeta* (corvette) *Atrevida* among the icebergs, 1794. (*Museo Naval, Madrid*)

△ Nootka: Indian lodges along the shoreline with more
Indians in their canoes surrounding the two *goletas*
(schooners) *Sútil* and *Mejicano* of the Malaspina expedition.

View of Acapulco and its anchorage as seen from its beach: ▷
Spanish colonial ports by artists of the Malaspina
expedition. (*Museo Naval, Madrid*)

▽ View of the inner part of the small Bay of Friends at the
entrance to Nootka: Spanish colonial ports by artists of the
Malaspina expedition. (*Museo Naval, Madrid*)

Ships' captains who were wounded but survived included Valdés, de Vargas, Francisco Javier de Uriarte, Cajigal, Argumosa, Gardoquí and Pareja. This list does not include the senior officer casualties, dead and wounded, onboard the Spanish frigates that also took part in the battle.

As in all the other Western European maritime states, so in Spain, not all the naval heroes have received the same publicity or priority of place in history. Usually, the national heroes are winners in battle or those who made great discoveries during periods of exploration. Equal place goes to prominent naval figures who have died or were killed at the height of their powers. Among British mariners, Captain James Cook's untimely death in the Sandwich Islands (Hawaii) on 14 February 1779 during his third voyage of discovery, has elevated him in the view of English maritime writers to secular sainthood among long-distance sailors and

navigators. In the foreword to his book *Captain James Cook*, in which Captain Alan Villiers the late Australian author-sailor tells the story of how he repeated Cook's voyages in a modern sailing ship, he describes Cook as 'the most consistent and the greatest sailing ship seaman there ever was.' But was he? Greater than Juan Sebastián Elcano who, in the first decade of the sixteenth century, circumnavigated the world in ships half the size of Cook's? Greater than Sir Francis Drake, who repeated Elcaño's feat toward the end of the same century? Greater than Alejandro Malaspina, Cook's largely unknown Spanish contemporary? Malaspina spent five years circumnavigating the world, gathering together the same kinds of artistic, botanical, anthropological and navigational material as did Cook in his three shorter voyages.

Two of Malaspina's ships' captains, Dionisio Alcalá Galiano and Cayetano Valdés, have fared better in history and in public esteem than the forgotten world circumnavigator. This may be because their other achievements were eclipsed by their valour in the Battle of Trafalgar. Alcalá Galiano is the better remembered of the two. Not only was he killed in command of *Bahama* during the battle but within half a century his son had written a full biography of his gallant father. Dr Donald C Cutter, the American historian of the Malaspina voyages, writes about choices of heroes:

No matter what is done, and even if we are convinced otherwise, Malaspina will never surpass or even approach Cook in the popular mind – certainly not in the English-speaking world. Cook has had the advantage of two centuries of favourable publicity. Place-name geography favours Cook. Malaspina has a glacier and a ferry boat (on Canada's Pacific coast) named for him, but nobody knows who he was. The case for Alcalá Galiano is better – he 'knew when to die' but unfortunately, in a losing cause, which is never as good as going out as a winner, though dead, like Nelson.[7]

Manila: view of the city and its bay, a sizable place even in the late eighteenth century: Spanish colonial ports by artists of the Malaspina expedition. (*Museo Naval, Madrid*)

Actually, Malaspina is better remembered on Canada's west coast than Dr Cutter recalls. His name also is enshrined in other public places in Canada – in a hotel and a community college in Nanaimo, a modern lumber-producing town on Vancouver Island close to where Malaspina passed by long ago.

The last word on Cook comes from the debunking book *The Captain Cook Myth* by Australian Jillian Robertson. She reminds us that Cook was killed on the Hawaiian beach because he lost his temper while trying to take Chief Terre'oboo hostage until his men had returned a cutter they had stolen from his ship the *Resolution*. In reprisal Captain Charles Clerke of the *Discovery*, who took command of Cook's two ships after his murder, went ashore on 17 February with an armed party and in his own words '... set fire to their houses, and shot every person in our way ...' Robertson adds that 200 to 300 natives were killed in his rarely-reported English massacre. She concludes that the cause of his death '... was really Cook's uncontrollable temper.'

Ship's captains Alcalá Galiano and Cosmé Damián Churruca appear in history as greater heroes than their commanding admirals. All of them had pre-Trafalgar careers that included much naval combat, shipwrecks, voyages of exploration in Hispanic America and the Far East, many sea commands from tiny *jabeques* and *urcas* to *navíos* and, in most cases, responsible senior naval administrative posts on shore. Commodore Enrique MacDonnell was one of many Spanish officials of Irish origin in the service of the Spanish Navy. Despite a brilliant career, he ended his life forgotten, sick and in poverty. MacDonnell had held the largest number of pre-Trafalgar ship commands of all nineteen Spanish Trafalgar commanders. These included the *San Felipe, Astuto, Gallardo* and *San Carlos*. Later, he commanded the *San Nicolás*, transferred to the *Angel*, then to the *San Ramón* and returned to the *Angel* for a second time. Including his

Valparaíso: view of the city and port as seen from the Point of the Castle of San Antonio: Spanish colonial ports by artists of the Malaspina expedition. (*Museo Naval, Madrid*)

Trafalgar command *Rayo*, MacDonnell commanded eight *navíos* in all.

Spain's four Trafalgar admirals had parallel careers. They were Vice Admiral Federico Carlos Gravina, Rear Admirals Ignacio María de Alava y Navarrete, Antonio de Escaño and Báltasar Hidalgo de Cisneros. Taking the rear admirals first, Alava was born in 1750 into an upper class local family in Vitoria; the last two were born in Cartagena in the early 1750s. All four admirals had served widely in earlier battles and in defence of Spain's many overseas possessions. They all experienced the inevitable close calls with death when their ships were caught in hurricanes and storms. During a period of service in the Spanish Philippines in 1796–97, when he was in charge of defending the Cavite naval base near Manila, Alava saved the *navío Montañés* from foundering in a hurricane on the nights of 14 and 25 April 1797 by fashioning and installing a new rudder during the storm. The *Montañés* (an improved *San Ildefonso*, and one of the best warships designed and built by Spain in the eighteenth century) later was one of the four Spanish ships of the line to survive Trafalgar. During the brief Spanish alliance with England between 1793 and 1795 at the outbreak of war between revolutionary France and the European monarchies, both Gravina and Alava – at that time a rear admiral and a commodore – fought alongside the British Admiral Samuel Hood in 1793 in the capture of the city centre of Toulon, and the subsequent Hispano-British allied withdrawal from that key French naval base. As outlined earlier, Cisneros was a more effective senior officer in the Battle of Cape St Vincent than was Vice Admiral Luís de Córdoba, the fleet commander-in-chief. Cisneros held several senior administrative posts on shore prior to Trafalgar, both in Madrid and then as commanding general of the Cartagena dockyard. In early 1805 Cisneros requested a sea appointment and on 27 May of that year he raised his rear admiral's flag in *Neptuno*.

Unlike Nelson, who was born in a rural manse and who often had to rely on influential patrons in the navy for his early appointments, Vice Admiral Federico Carlos Gravina came from a noble Sicilian family, well-known to the branch of the Spanish royal family that ruled The Kingdom of the Two Sicilies. His father, Juan Gravina y Moncada, Duke of San Miguel, was a grandee of Spain as was his maternal grandfather. In the year of Gravina's birth on 12 September 1756 Carlos King of Naples had three years left to rule before transferring to Spain in 1759 following the death of his brother. He then began twenty-nine years of enlightened rule as Carlos III of Spain.

Gravina's noble pedigree probably did his career no harm. He was appointed commodore at the age of thirty-three in 1789, vice admiral in 1794, and Spanish ambassador to France in 1802. He was the senior negotiator between the Spanish court and Napoleon in 1804–1805 on the disposition of the Spanish fleet in the new war against Britain. Although Nelson did play politics, and mightily so, on behalf of his own career and promotions, Gravina 'to the manor born' already was part of Spain's ruling elite. As we know from the record, a cultural anomaly smoothed Gravina's course in his direct negotiations with Napoleon. Napoleon and Gravina as leaders in Latin societies not their own, were drawn to each other by their common regional Italian origins, and the fact that they both continued to speak accented Italian as their native tongue – Napoleon the patois of his native Corsica, and Gravina the strong Sicilian accent of his birthplace.

None of this means that Gravina's naval career had been built on sinecure appointments in the fleet. Gravina, in fact, was among the most experienced of all the Spanish admirals of his day in the range of sea and shore appointments and combat experience that must come to the senior officers of any large navy. At Santo Domingo, Martinique, Cartagena de Indias, as well as in the South and North Atlantic and the Mediterranean, Gravina experienced the widest service in war and peace for his fleet and monarch.[8]

Gravina's baptism of fire as a junior naval officer took place during the prolonged Spanish blockade of Gibraltar between 1779 and 1782. As a young officer he did his mandatory sea time in the small ships of his day – *jabeques, goletas,* then frigates. In April 1789 in one of the fastest-recorded voyages of a warship in the age of sail, Gravina in command of the frigate *Paz* sailed from Cádiz to Cartagena de Indias to inform its governor of the accession of Charles IV to the throne. As a senior naval officer, he organized the so-called 'Spanish Armament' during the Anglo-Spanish crisis in 1790 over Nootka on Vancouver Island. As the largest gathering of Spanish warships since the Spanish Armada, the 'Spanish Armament' played a large part in the British decision to negotiate with Spain rather than fight her over the rights to far-off and fur-rich Nootka.

At the end of the century, Gravina took command of the Franco-Spanish 'Ocean Squadron' based at Brest, with Spanish *navíos* committed to it under the San Ildefonso Treaty of 1796. His ability to get along with the French despite increasing resistance by Spanish naval officers to the alliance with France, played a part in his later appointment as ambassador from the court of Carlos IV to France, 1803–1804. Despite his outstanding service on behalf of

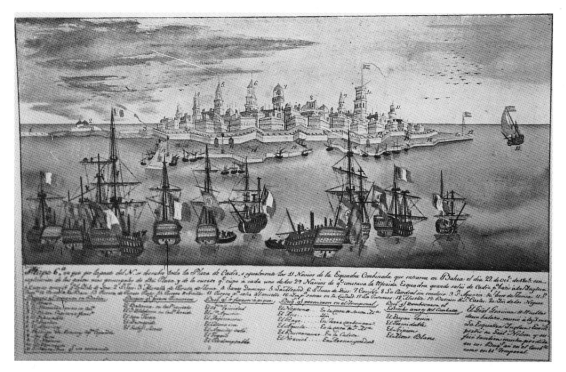

The shattered French and Spanish survivors of the Combined Squadron limp back to the protection of Cádiz harbour, portrayed almost as a medieval city. (*Watercolour* *by José Tomás Córdoba in the collection of Manuel Gómez Moreno*)

Spain, Gravina gets short shrift in Spanish history, perhaps because at the end he lost at Trafalgar, the biggest and most critical task of his career.

For a nation that has so meticulously preserved its naval records from the era of the voyages of Columbus, it is surprising that one of the most important events in Spanish naval history will remain forever shrouded in mystery because the official Spanish record of it has disappeared. That event was the apparently acrimonious pre-Trafalgar conference of senior Spanish and French naval officers held on board *Bucentaure*, the French flagship, on 9 October 1805. One version has it that both Dionisio Alcalá Galiano and Cosmé Damián Churruca were not only present, but both spoke out angrily in opposition to the French insistence of a combined fleet action against Nelson. Alcalá Galiano's biography written by his son in 1850, using secondhand and hearsay references at best, claims that the emotional Alcalá Galiano drew his sword against an insistent senior French officer, only to be restrained by fellow Spanish officers. Yet another version suggested by Dr Julián Zulueta, the modern Spanish medical historian, is that neither Churruca nor Alcalá Galiano (though both commodores) were present at the crucial conference because they were not senior enough in rank. Unlike modern European navies (including the Spanish) in which commodores often hold naval staff positions, in the early nineteenth century commodores were usually individual ship captains.

Unfortunately, we will never know what really took place on this occasion since the Spanish minutes disappeared shortly thereafter. According to Capitán de navío Juan Berenguer y Moreno de Guerra, secretary general of the Institute of History and Naval Culture of the Spanish Navy, Manuel Godoy, the pro-French prime minister for Charles IV, to whom the minutes were sent, handed them over to the French. They in turn destroyed the Spanish-language version because they wished no record preserved of Spanish opposition to a naval action against Nelson during the autumn of 1805.

Another version is that the self-same contentious Spanish account was surrendered by Godoy to the French after they entered Madrid in 1808 and for the same reason. Godoy, a Spanish politician who rose dramatically from officer of the palace guard to generalissimo of Spain as the favourite of both Queen María Luisa and Carlos IV, fled to France after the abdication of the king and his own downfall.

A third but less likely version is that the Trafalgar minutes and other related state documents were destroyed in 1808 when Godoy's palace was sacked by the mob after he fled. Whatever the reason, the Spanish record is lost to history. Nor can the ample papers of the Alcalá Galiano and Churruca families be searched for an answer because both officers were killed during the battle.

Even more important is the question of Gravina's expressed attitude during a far from placid meeting of two naval allies about to fight the last great naval engagement of sailing ships. We know from other surviving Gravina correspondence that in the end he succumbed to the often-destructive principle that honour must prevail, and ordered Spain's unprepared navy to fight alongside Villeneuve's French fleet. Whatever Gravina might have written in his report of the events of 9 October 1805, his grievously shattered arm prevented him from reporting in person to Godoy on the Spanish Navy's defeat. Nor could the wounded Alava, his second-in-command, who had been captured by the British. Rather, that grim duty fell to Rear Admiral Antonio de Escaño, the third-in-command, whose letters of 22 and 23 October 1805 to Manuel Godoy, 'Generalissimo of his Majesty's Land and Sea Forces', have survived and are preserved in full in both the Spanish and British archives.

All of the above correspondence including Escaño's early and inaccurate estimates of ships' and crews' losses on both sides, were published on 5 November 1805 in the *Gaceta de Madrid*. At the opening of his first long submission of 22 October 1805, Escaño explained to Godoy why he, and not Gravina as Spanish commander-in-chief, was submitting the post-battle report: 'His left arm having been shattered by grapeshot at the close of the late action totally incapacitates him from giving your excellency an account of the sanguinary engagement of the 21st instant...'[9]

In eighteenth century naval history the British glorified Nelson, Collingwood, Jervis, Howe and Barham as great warriors and planners. So, too, the Spanish have glorified Blas de Lezo, Ensenada, Mazarredo, Malaspina, Churruca and Alcalá Galiano; but, unlike the British, not their commander-in-chief at Trafalgar. The Nelson cult of personality has never waned. Indeed, his 170-foot statue in London's Trafalgar Square, his tomb in the crypt of St Paul's Cathedral, his flagship *Victory* and the related displays of Nelsoniania in Portsmouth's naval dockyard, all are his permanent and visible memorials, viewed and venerated by millions over the generations. In contrast, Admiral Federico Gravina is all but forgotten to most Spaniards.

Tucked away in a remote dusty corner of Spain's Naval Museum, one can see Gravina's admiral's cocked hat, his Grand Cross of the Order of Carlos III with its faded blue and white ribbon received in 1802 from a grateful Carlos IV and his 'Trafalgar Day' sword. They are jumbled together in an awkwardly shaped pentagonal glass case. The Naval Museum is situated on the main floor of the baroque edifice housing the Spanish Navy Ministry in central Madrid, and listening to the chatter of Madrid's school children as they approach the glass case during guided tours with their teachers and Naval Museum officials, they seem not to know who Gravina was.

A view of Nootka with the ship on the left (either one of Malaspina's corvettes *Atrevida* or *Descubierta*) possibly undergoing repairs or overhaul, with all but the lower masts sent down. This is a photograph of a painting by Fernando Bambila, one of the several artists attached to the Malaspina Expedition. (*Museo Naval, Madrid*)

The Spanish have selected Dionisio Alcalá Galiano, Cosmé Damián Churruca and Cayetano Valdés y Florés Bazán to be the best remembered of the fifteen Spanish Trafalgar captains. Where Alcalá Galiano had an intellectual even elusive quality, Churruca was a tough-minded naval officer, the kind of professional devotee to his craft that every great navy produces. Valdés had a style and ability to adapt that stood him well in the years after Trafalgar and the French invasion of Spain in May 1808 when he served both revolutionary junta fighting the French and, after 1815, the restored Bourbon monarchy.

Valdés and Alcalá Galiano were colleagues as commanding officers of the *Atrevida* and *Descubierta*, the two naval research vessels specially built for Captain Alejandro Malaspina's expedition around the world. During the Malaspina expedition, Alcalá Galiano briefly held an independent command, when he was detached at Callao to sail north and do further inshore exploratory work around the Strait of Juan de Fuca in the locally-built *goletas Sútil* and *Mexicana*. He wrote his own book on the activities of these two tiny sailing vessels under his command. Always more of a navigator and mathematician than a warrior per se, Alcalá Galiano's further studies on navigation, astronomy and charting were published during his lifetime by the newly-formed Naval Hydrographic Depository in Cádiz. These further works were finished while he was in command of the frigate *Sabina* during an official visit to negotiate with the ever-contentious Barbary chieftains in Algiers. In Spanish maritime history Alcalá Galiano is accurately described as *et sabio marino*, 'the learnèd sailor'.

The ten lesser known Spanish Trafalgar captains were all distinguished in their own way. Flores and Gaston were what we today would call Latin Americans. They were born in the cities of Buenos Aires and Cartagena de Indias. Gaston's father Miguel was a senior officer in the navy. In the early 1790s the son served in the *navío San Isidro* under his father's command when he was captain general of the Cádiz naval department. The younger Gaston must have known the more famous Churruca since they did naval hydrographic studies together in the Cádiz astronomical observatory. Like Churruca, but after the battle which his

△ Photograph of a painting by the painter José Cardero, also with the Malaspina Expedition with his excellent presentation of Indian war canoes at Nootka. The frigate on the right in this print could be the *Concepción* that arrived at Nootka from San Blás on 13 August 1791. In background, are the two schooners *Sútil* and *Mejicano*.

A rough but nevertheless accurate sketch of the ships. It ▷ could have been done by José del Pozo, who was the artist for a time with the Malaspina Expedition. It shows *Descubierta* and *Atrevida* in the calm waters off Mount Elias in the present State of Washington in the US Pacific Northwest. (*Museo Naval, Madrid*)

fellow ship commander did not survive, Gaston was publicly critical of his crew's inadequate training, saying that they were to blame for the *San Justo* 'falling to leeward' during the battle.

Several of these captains had served as junior officers and captains of frigates in earlier Spanish naval conflicts. At Cape St Vincent, Argumosa commanded the *navío San Isidro*, and Pareja the frigate *Perla*. Gardoquí, who must have been held in high regard as a seaman since he commanded three of the big three-deckers between 1796 and 1805 (*Mexicano, Reina Luisa* and *Santa Ana*), also took part in the capture of the 64-gun *Ardent* taken in the English Channel in 1779 by the Franco-Spanish fleet.

Cajigal, a Basque born near Santander, came from a family which already had distinguished itself in military command roles in Cuba and during the successful Spanish combined operations against the British in the American Revolutionary War that resulted in the Spanish conquest of Pensacola and West Florida in 1781. Cajigal had more continuous seatime than some of his Trafalgar contemporaries having served extensively in frigates as a junior and middle rank officer. Also, like many of his contemporaries, he had been wounded in naval actions long before Trafalgar. Prior to that battle he served at El Ferrol under the command of Vice Admiral Grandallana.

Like Gravina, Francisco Javier de Uriarte y Borja (born on 5 October 1753 near Cádiz where he would spend so many of his forty-nine years of naval service) came from a noble family, the house of the Dukes of Gandia. He lived until the age of eighty-nine, dying on 29 November 1842 in the same house where he was born. Uriarte was the longest lived of all the Spanish Trafalgar captains. In 1838, thirty-three years after the battle, Uriarte a patrician and a man of style, wrote his own account of the last fighting days of the *Santísima Trinidad*. It is one

of the most poignant accounts of the dismal state of his ship, and the grim condition of the wounded and the dying under his command. Like so many of the Spanish commanding officers, he was badly wounded himself. Later, as a prisoner of the English at Gibraltar, Uriarte wrote to his wife Francisca on 27 October 1805 in a laconic style not often used by the Spanish: 'My dear Frasquita, I have continued with life and honour. Your husband, Javier.'

For three of its four admirals, and ten of its fifteen *navío* commanders, the battle of Trafalgar did not end their careers. Instead, it opened the way to new ones. Some of the Trafalgar captains are more famous for what they accomplished after that event than for their brave actions during it. Their mixed fleet experiences, not only in command at sea but as shipyard and naval base administrators, paved the way for their unexpected post-Trafalgar roles.

The event that traumatized Spain was the Napoleonic invasion in 1808. It was an event that tested the loyalty of all Spaniards in authority, from the King himself to the leaders of the military and the intelligentsia who had served absolutist Spain at the end of the age of enlightenment. Napoleon sent the Bourbons Carlos IV and Fernando VII into exile and placed his brother Joseph on the thorne, a regime that lasted for six years. Joseph I, a liberal and a modernist, proved to be a better ruler than the departed, ineffectual Carlos IV. Although Joseph was able to win the support of many Spanish intellectuals, politicians and some military leaders – called in Spanish history *los francesados* (literally, those who turned to the French) – none of them was a Trafalgar captain.

For Spain's royalist naval officers loyalty to Spain meant offering their services and taking

Vice Admiral Ignacio María de Alava, Spanish second-in-command at Trafalgar. (From engraved plate in *Combate de Trafalgar* by Manuel Marliani, Madrid, 1850)

the oath to the new patriotic juntas being formed throughout 'unoccupied Spain' to oppose the French invaders. In 1812 the principal junta based at Cádiz (which never fell to the French), promulgated Spain's first liberal constitution, to which Ferdinand, son of Carlos IV, pledged his support. The records contain the bold letter written to Joseph I from Madrid in 1808 by Francisco Javier de Uriarte y Borja:

> Neither my honour nor my conscience permits me to change my oath of allegiance to my legitimate sovereign, given the instructions by your excellency (to do so) and I am ready to lose my employment and my life before acceding to what your excellency requests in your office that I must contest.
>
> Madrid, 22 July 1808. Uriarte.[10]

The letter dispatched, he fled south to Seville to join the resistance junta in the city from which Spain's explorers and navigators had sailed from the end of the Middle Ages across the Atlantic to claim and settle Spanish America.

Of the five other Trafalgar captains so far not covered, José de Vargas, commanding officer of the *San Ildefonso*, was murdered in 1808 by a disgruntled sailor. Rafael de Hore, captain of the *Principe de Asturias*, Gravina's flagship, died the same year. The remaining three, Cosmé Damián Churruca, commanding officer of the *San Juan Nepomuceno*, Dionisio Alcalá Galiano of the *Bahama*, and the little-known Francisco Alcedo y Bustamente of the *Montañés*, were all killed on board their commands during the battle. If he had lived, there is no doubt that Churruca too would have joined the forces resisting the French invaders, given his lifelong disdain for the French as Spain's allies at sea.

If it seems strange that the surviving commanding officers were promoted to commodore's rank and both Escaño and Cisneros to vice admirals, rather than court-martialled and dismissed

Commodore Cayetano Valdés y Flores Bazán, captain of the *Neptuno*. In this painting he appears later in life in the uniform of Captain General de la Armada (Admiral of the Fleet) and temporarily Regent of the Monarchy wearing the stars of two orders. (*Museo Naval, Madrid*)

the service because they lost the battle of Trafalgar, one must recall the attitude that Spain has adopted about that defeat. Unlike the French the Spanish never have viewed their defeat at Trafalgar as a national disaster, but rather as a naval engagement fought and lost, as Uriarte put it, 'with honour'. Accordingly, on 9 November 1805 all the surviving Trafalgar captains who had commanded *navíos* were promoted to the rank of commodore by Carlos IV. These promotions placed them in line for important posts with the revolutionary junta and after 1814, with the restored monarchy under Fernando VII.[11]

José Quevedo y Cheza took part in the seizure of the surviving French ships of the line that had fled into Cádiz after Trafalgar and were still there three years later. Quevedo also commanded the Spanish Navy units that carried the French naval crews as prisoners of war into captivity in the Canary Islands. After the war, he was promoted to vice admiral and was made captain general of Cádiz, following a term in the Viceroyalty of New Spain where he was named military governor of Vera Cruz in 1812 by the revolutionary junta based in Cádiz.

José Gardoquí was the only Trafalgar veteran to command a surviving Trafalgar warship in the years after the battle – namely his own, the 112-gun *Santa Ana* to which he was re-assigned in 1809. *Santa Ana* was one of only four Spanish Navy ships of the line to survive both the battle and the ensuing storm that drove on shore several of the ships still in French and Spanish hands. Later, the Cádiz junta gave Gardoquí naval and military command positions in Cuba and the Philippines where he died in 1814 at the age of fifty-nine.

For others, the two decades after Trafalgar meant promotions to senior state positions, including that of navy minister. A few concluded their careers full of honours as admirals of the fleet not only as a result of their post-Trafalgar service, but because they had been successful administrators for the civilian-run junta. Alava and MacDonnell, for example, later were made members of the Supreme Council of Admiralty when that body was reconstituted in 1817.

Gaston, a native of Cartagena de Indias, never returned there. That once-great Spanish naval bastion had become the new naval base of the new Republic of Colombia, one of the many successor Hispanic American republics formed during and after the Wars of Independence (1812–1825) that resulted in the break-up of most of Spain's American empire. Perhaps because Spain was not his native land, Gaston as a loyal Spanish naval officer was appointed military commander of Havana, the capital of a Spanish Cuba. It was not lost to Spain during those wars. Cuba's sugar exports replaced the gold and silver shipments which would no longer flow to Spain from Mexico and Peru. Gaston returned to Cádiz in 1828 upon his promotion to vice admiral. However, ill health prompted him to request retirement in Havana, where he died in 1839 an old man at seventy-three.

The impressive Don Cayetano Valdés, called *el intrépido Valdés* in Spain, had surrendered *Neptuno* to the British only when her rigging was shot away and her sails were in tatters. After his return from a brief period as a British prisoner of war, Valdés rejected Spain's French ally when Napoleon invaded Spain in 1808 and was appointed to the rank of general in the opposing Spanish army. He was made governor of Cádiz and later admiral of the fleet in the post-1815 navy. Still later he was appointed president of the Spanish Cortes, then a Regent of Spain during the infancy of Queen Isabella. He died on 2 February 1834, aged seventy-seven.

In 1808 the dramatic irony could not have been lost on the French that Cádiz, from which the Combined Squadron under French command sailed to its doom in 1805, now became the main centre of Spanish resistance to Napoleon. Within three years of the unhappy and unwanted alliance with France that aroused so much opposition in the fleet, Spain's Trafalgar commanders were fighting the one-time allies who had invaded their homeland. Cádiz was the headquarters of the most important of the many revolutionary juntas that fought the invading French. Between 1808 and 1814, the year of the French expulsion from Spain, Cádiz also had become the seat of a Spanish government 'in exile'.

It is interesting to place the dilemma of these military and naval officers in a hypothetical British context. Imagine that a former European ally of Britain suddenly turned enemy and conqueror, say Prussia, had successfully invaded England from the north to capture London, but had been stopped in the south. This grim development would have left Portsmouth free as a functioning naval base and major seat of resistance, with much of the Royal Navy still intact. Under these conditions Portsmouth in 1808 would have been identified as the capital of 'unoccupied England'. The Royal Navy's admirals and ships' captains who had fought at Trafalgar three years earlier, along with the rest of their fellow officers who had survived the 'Prussian invasion', would have joined the English equivalents to the forces of the free Spanish juntas.

Accounts of brave men cannot end without a mention of the dramatic ironies which always enlighten and charm the historical record – in this case for an aide de camp and a liaison officer to Gravina, one French and the other Spanish, for whom the fortunes of war redirected their careers in strange ways. The Spaniard was Miguel de Alava, cousin of Vice Admiral Alava and a naval commander on board the *Principe de Asturias*. An aide de camp to Gravina, he was to serve later on the staff of the Duke of Wellington at Waterloo. The Frenchman was Major Antoine Drouot of Napoleon's corps of artillery at Trafalgar and a liaison officer to Gravina. Drouot escaped with Gravina from Trafalgar, returned to France and joined Napoleon's Grand Army where he commanded artillery units with great bravery and skill at such land battles as Jéna, Friedland and Wagram. At Hohenlinden, he changed the French fortunes of the day with his magnificent handling of the artillery. Of Drouot it was said, 'he washed his face and shaved in the open air, affixing his looking glass to a gun carriage every day.' On 18 June 1815 he was the general who commanded the doomed French Imperial Guard at Waterloo.[12]

Alava's career was just as spectacular. After 1808, he joined the Spanish patriot army, was promoted colonel and in this capacity served as an aide de camp to Wellington throughout the Peninsular War in Spain. In 1814, he was appointed Spanish Minister Plenipotentiary to Holland. In that function, he was present in Wellington's headquarters at Waterloo. On Wellington's personal recommendation, Alava was decorated an honourary Knight Commander of the Bath (KCB) by the Prince Regent, later King George IV. In the late 1820s, His Excellency Don Miguel de Alava was Spanish Ambassador to the Court of St James. At its royal receptions, he often wore the British Peninsular Gold Medal with Bars for the British victories at Badajoz, Ciudad Rodrigo, Salamanca, Victoria and Toulouse, with which he had been honoured by the Prince Regent in 1814.

## COSMÉ DAMIÁN CHURRUCA

Commodore Cosmé Damián Churruca, one of Spain's great sailors in the age of sail and a doomed captain at Trafalgar, combined Spanish pride and strong religiosity with superb seamanship and naval professionalism. A devout, fatalistic Roman Catholic and a modern naval officer at the same time, he was determined to have the best ship and crew in a Spanish Navy that always moved too slowly to thoroughly train its sailors. His final admonition to his crew before Trafalgar – eternal glory for those who will die in battle, but summary execution for any who shirked the fight – was harsher than Nelson's direction that every man is expected to do his duty.

In November 1803, almost two years before the disastrous and fatal mid-afternoon of 21 October 1805 off Cape Trafalgar, Churruca had requested the command of the *San Juan Nepomuceno* because he wanted to turn it into as efficient a ship as he had done with earlier commands. Fleet commanders in all European navies allowed their ship captains little leeway for disobedience on board the uncomfortable, unhealthy wooden warships in which, for months on end, officers and men were cooped up in small and unsanitary spaces. Both Churruca and Nelson displayed the mixed characteristics of hardness and humanitarianism. Nelson's last words of concern and tenderness for Lady Hamilton came from the same man who, earlier in his career at sea, hanged disobedient miscreants aboard one of his commands.

Churruca's last letter, written on 11 October 1805 in his cabin in the *San Juan Nepomuceno* to his brother, is filled with seamanlike assessments of the enemy and the situation of the fleet for the battle to come; but also with his innermost worries about his poor finances and family needs at home. Like Nelson, he had unpaid debts. Churruca had often been paid irregularly or not at all during the four years of his naval career leading up to Trafalgar. Indeed, he went into that battle with his officer's frock coat tattered and worn in places.

Churruca was worried about his bride of only five months, Doña María Dolores de Luís Apodaca, daughter of Vicente Apodaca, another commodore. Churruca went to sea and to his death at Trafalgar with the assurance that 'a rich friend' (unnamed) in El Ferrol, Spain's Galician naval base, would help her if such financial aid was required. As indeed it was. Nevertheless, the day before his funeral, Churruca's widow had to write a humiliating plea to Carlos IV from El Ferrol that her husband be paid the same back salary and pension awarded to other senior officers killed at Trafalgar.[13] Her pension was granted as well as back pay that

Commodore Cosmé Damián Churruca at the time of Trafalgar. (*From an engraved plate in* Combate de Trafalgar *by Manuel Marliani, Madrid 1850*)

some say was due to Churruca from as far back as 1800. As with Nelson, Churruca was plucked away in the prime of life – the great English admiral at forty-nine, Churruca newly-wed at forty-five.

Nelson came to Trafalgar with a record of numerous brilliant sea victories before achieving the rank of vice admiral. As a commodore Churruca was never more than chief-of-staff to an admiral in charge, but undoubtedly he equalled Nelson's best ships' captains in professionalism and style. He came to his last command after a brilliant career in the awkward and unhandy two- and three-decker wooden warships of his day. The most famous of these was *Conquistador*, the third ship to carry that name in the Spanish Navy before 1800, in which both his seamanship and skill in training a crew were the outcome of a lifetime of working and fighting at sea. Under his command *Conquistador* survived a heavy gale off Oran, Algeria on 16 May 1799. According to the record in the naval archives in Madrid, '... three or four other [ships] entered the port of Cartagena dismasted ... [but he] was able to return his ship to the fleet within 40 days ... perfectly repaired.'

Churruca's prowess as a ship-handler impressed France, Spain's ally, even though the French Navy found it hard, if not impossible, to learn lessons of seamanship from the Spanish. When Churruca was attached to the Franco-Spanish squadron at Brest, he was often on duty in Paris as a consultant to the French Navy and technical institutes on naval science, especially after Spanish ships of the line were assigned to the French Navy. 'The reputation of the *Conquistador* was so great,' says Manuel Marliani in his classic study of the Spanish captains of Trafalgar written half a century after the battle, that 'he was considered as a model by the French sailors.'

Churruca opposed the offer of fifteen of Spain's ships of the line to France under the San

The young Dionisio Alcalá Galiano as a lieutenant and ship commander during his years of service with the Malaspina expedition, 1789-1794. (*Anonymous ink etching, Museo Naval, Madrid*)

Ildefonso Treaty of 1796, especially since those sent included his beloved *Conquistador*. In time, he came to dislike both the French and the upstart Corsican who by 1800 had become First Consul of France. 'But his sadness knew no limits,' writes Marliani 'when he had to separate himself from his beloved ship in which he had, in a certain manner, created changes after a course of three years of constant effort.' Churruca returned to Cádiz as a passenger in the ship of the line *Concepción*, arriving there on 25 May 1802. He asked for, and received, permission to return to his birthplace, the small Basque village of Motrico. There, he busied himself with family and financial matters. His home there remains in his family to this day.

Churruca also requested authorization from the king 'that he might detain himself' in Madrid for four or five days, also 'to resolve personal affairs' in the summer of 1803. By November of that year, he had returned to sea in command of the *San Juan Nepomuceno*. He requested her in place of the *Principe de Asturias*, the ship to which he was originally assigned as captain. Prior to his leave in May 1802 and his return to active service 18 months later, Churruca was consistently at sea or busy with the fleet as he had been since 1799. In that year, he was promoted to full captain and was made chief-of-staff to Vice Admiral José de Mazarredo's squadron.

Nevertheless, home leave in Motrico was no rest for Churruca returned from the sea. The local citizens poured honours on him including a short stint as mayor in a town that knew earlier Spanish naval heroes. The leading maritime families of the Basque province of Guipúzcoa had been involved with shipbuilding, fishing and sea commerce for centuries. Motrico was also the birthplace in 1656 of Admiral Antonio Gaztañeta, the first great architect of the new eighteenth century Spanish Navy. Not far from it lie the equally tiny villages of Guetaría and Zaraúz. From the former, 250 years before Churruca's birth, came Juan Sebastián

Commodore Cosmé Damián Churruca, as a young officer.
(*Oil painting, Museo Naval, Madrid*)

Elcano, the first man to circumnavigate the earth, in 1522. His historic, tiny and fragile ship *Victoria* was launched from Zaraúz. Shipbuilding in the region extended back to the fifteenth century, when the plentiful oak forests of that time restricted agriculture and the growing of olive trees.

If oil for the lamps of late mediaeval Spain could not be acquired at home, then the small ships constructed by the energetic seamen of Motrico, Guetaría and Zaraúz would bring back the whale oil from as far away as the Grand Banks of Newfoundland, voyages that strained to the limits the ships, navigational skills and stamina of Basque sailors at the dawn of the age of exploration. The list of famous Guipúzcoans who added to the splendour and performance of Spain at sea begins with Elcano and continued through Churruca. From Pasajes, another village of Guipúzcoa, came Admiral Blas de Lezo, the defender of Cartagena in 1741 against the British. So too, from Zumárraga, yet another village of the region came Miguel López de Legazpi, senior civil servant of the Spanish crown in Mexico City, chosen by Philip II to complete the conquest of the Spanish Philippines in 1564. Legazpi remained as governor of the Philippines and died in Manila, never to see his homeland again.

In his biography of Elcano, the English writer Mairin Mitchell sees these tiny Basque villages as a lyrical kind of haven for their great seamen, who drove the ships and men to the far corners of the globe to make new discoveries and conquests and to open new markets for Spain. 'They look down from the heights of heroes onto the pleasantly protected urban life . . . whose unruffled waters would have seemed Elysium to them at any moment in the tempests of their lives at sea.' For Churruca at the beginning of his career, there would not be such a dreamy growing-up. Then as now, becoming a naval officer meant joining the naval academy at Cádiz, there to start the long gruelling path of shore and sea training which could led to a coveted command at sea.

All of Churruca's letters home from 1778 until his final correspondence shortly before Trafalgar, indicate that 'dreamy' was far from his response to life at sea. Rather, his 168 surviving letters to his family, twenty-seven years of personal correspondence from cadet to commodore, reveal him to be tough-minded, filled with self-examination and a deep sense of duty and honour. He was seventeen when he wrote to his father in 1778:

> You will know that the French *Gazette* carries [information] that six English ships of the line, some frigates, continue cruising throughout the Bay of Biscay, observing the Spanish armament. There is no doubt that an armament like the one in Cádiz (to which they are adding *navíos*) has no equal in Spain. They explain why war [will be] bloody with the English ... it is the time, my father, that we all wish to be men or be finished like the wretched [who won't fight]. It would please me very much if more of the peasants would volunteer for the King's service. It is the most honourable career. No one has to tell me that he has a better career than I, nor how they may better service the King ...
>
> Your most humble son, Cosmé.[14]

Cosmé Damián Churruca y Elorza was born on 21 September 1761 into a Motrico family already distinguished by the role of its forebears in the military and civilian life of the province as far back as the fifteenth century. At fifteen, after a short period of study in the Conciliar Seminary at Burgos, he joined the newly expanding *Armada Española* as a cadet, graduated as a midshipman in 1778 and joined his first ship, the *navío San Vicente*, as a sub-lieutenant. Having completed his basic sea time, Churruca then fought in the long and unsuccessful Spanish blockade of Gibraltar, 1779–1782. During that event, he showed not only his skill in gunnery, but personally rescued the crews of some of the floating batteries which the Spanish launched unsuccessfully against the British defences of Gibraltar. On returning to Cádiz in 1783 Churruca embarked on a period of advanced studies in mathematics and navigation. In time, this would bring him almost as much fame in the fleet as his skills in seamanship.

Another early letter, written to his father from Lansana on 12 February 1782 near the end of Spain's naval involvement in the American Revolutionary War, not only speculates on the movement of Admiral Rodney's fleet, but relates what happened to Churruca in port from 'the strongest wind since a year ago, from which we surely might have been crippled ... I am sure that yesterday being on duty when another frigate was breaking its moorings gave me a bad enough day.' The 'bad enough day' resulted from a larger frigate almost colliding with his own but doing much damage to her nevertheless.

This letter, like so many others of his, reveals to us technical information about ships' histories that apparently is not recorded in the official documents. One is surprised to read here that as early as 1782, *Santísima Trinidad* was completely refitted and coppered a short thirteen years after her launching in Havana. Churruca writes:

> The squadron includes four *navíos* ... taking in enough water that they needed docking. *Santa Isabel* went to Cartagena to be careened, the *navío Trinidad* is entirely refitted and coppered and soon we would find her at [our] disposal and able to sail with us, though she still lacks artillery and rigging.[15]

At the naval school at El Ferrol in Galicia, Churruca continued to study astronomy, mathematics, geography and mechanics until 1788, when he was assigned to the first of several naval scientific expeditions to Spanish America that consumed his career until the mid-1790s. Under the command of Captain (later Vice Admiral) Antonio de Córdoba, this New World expedition completed a re-examination of the dangerous waters of the Straits of Magellan. Churruca's diary of this voyage was published in Madrid in 1795 as an appendix to a book about the first voyage of Fernando Magellan. It was this publication which brought Churruca to the attention of the Spanish public as well as to a wider community of his fellow officers.

A second scientific expedition sailed from Cádiz on 17 June 1792. It consisted of two brigantines, *Descubridor* and *Vigilante*, bound for the Spanish-owned island of Trinidad in the eastern Caribbean. A small observatory was built on the island to mark meridians for navigational purposes and to help in the making of new maps of the Spanish Antilles, especially the island of Puerto Rico.

These important activities were interrupted by the outbreak of war between the new French revolutionary regime and the royalist states of Western Europe, including Spain. The Spanish naval units already in the Caribbean prepared to defend their territories against possible French attack. For the Spanish Navy, there was much irony in a brief alliance with Britain and a declaration of war against France. Although that country had been an ally of Spain in all the major naval battles of the eighteenth century, for a brief time at the beginning of the French Revolutionary War (in 1793–95) it was the enemy of Spain.

After 1796, royalist Spain soon found itself once again an ally of France with Napoleon as first consul. As observed earlier, Churruca served in senior capacities in Paris and with the Ocean Squadron at Brest, alongside a French naval ally for whom he had little respect. As with many of his contemporaries, Churruca nurtured a lifelong dislike and suspicion of the French, not only as allies but as competent ship-handlers. In his case, these attitudes towards the French appear throughout all the years of his correspondence home. The following is one of the very few letters he wrote at sea, this time on board the frigate *Santa Barbara*, referring to the failure of a joint Spanish-French blockade to prevent three English ships from reaching Gibraltar:

> The certainty is that if the French had done what they were ordered, we would have taken to Cádiz three other enemy frigates that entered [the Straits of Gibraltar] the following day with powder and artillery troops. In Gibraltar, we found out later that one of them was a warship of 38 guns, the other a packet ship of 28 guns, and the third a merchant ship. You can see what a nice little action we have lost. I can assure you that in all my life [at that time, he was only twenty-one] I have not had a worse time than that of the night of the 19th. With the sole consideration that we lost such a neat fight and a certain victory ... the fault of others, I was so disgusted that my bad mood has lasted until now. The same [was true] with the other officers, and the commander [ship's captain] was extremely vexed that night.[16]

Churruca agrees that the failure of the French to coordinate with his squadron could have been even worse. 'I give thanks to God for having been released from the shame of seeing myself a prisoner [after] having lost my frigate.'

Given his lifelong antipathy to the French it is small wonder that Churruca was so unhappy about fighting with them as allies at Trafalgar. In 1782 he did not like the prospect of the peace that was about to come although it did not take place formally until the following year with the Treaty of Paris in 1783.

> I have never heard so much talk of peace as in these days ... if this news turns out to be certain, it is good for the nation; but for those who make their career with sword in hand, it [the talk] is not good.

In 1794, worn out from his labours, Churruca – not always physically strong and beset with a melancholia that would increase in later life – was invalided home.

A complete version of Churruca's scientific and navigational studies of the early 1790s was finally published in 1802 and reproduced again in the *Almanaque Náutico*. Among Churruca's less-publicized activity on behalf of navigation was his improvement of the maritime chronometer, a super-accurate timepiece essential for calculating longitude. Today, the name of Churruca is preserved in the Straits of Magellán region at the entrance to a canal with the more prosaic name of Smyth.

The *navío San Juan Nepomuceno* which Churruca asked to command, was already thirty-seven years old when he first came aboard in 1803, a warship not excessively ancient by the longevity standards of ships of the line of that time. For example, *Santísima Trinidad* was thirty-four years old in that year. Churruca's movements at this time are outlined in detail, with some frank comments, in a letter to his brother from El Ferrol on 13 February 1804. He reveals much of the pre-Trafalgar composition of Spain's navy as well as its substantial unpreparedness for new hostilities:

> Dear brother,
> In the last mail arrived an order from the Generalíssimo Godoy (the Prince of Peace) relieving me of the command of the *Principe* with that of the *San Nepomuceno* confirmed, accordingly as I had requested it – and authorizing me without reference to the regulations – to arrange the interior fittings and to arm her to my entire satisfaction. The rear admiral of this squadron is the squadron's chief, Cisneros, who must come from Cartagena. Gravina has left Madrid to command the Cádiz squadron that must be twelve *navíos*, and his rear admiral is Escaño, who is here and has orders to go [to Cádiz] by land. The Cartagena squadron should be made up of six *navíos* under the command of Vice Admiral Juan de la Nava, and the one here of eight. I doubt that one can find crews for a strength of twenty-six ships that make up the three squadrons, despite the fact that we have sent some 1200 seamen to Cádiz from Galicia. . . . In Cádiz, the trades in that place are being given one million *pesos fuertes* for [ships'] supplies. But here [in El Ferrol] there is neither flour, nor meats, nor wine, nor olive oil, nor firewood, nor charcoal for the forges. Iron is very scarce, and in such a way that there is a lack of the most essential articles; it is impossible that one can confirm the departure of the squadron until next winter.[17]

Subsequent events proved otherwise, and the El Ferrol squadron had to join the fleet at Cádiz earlier than expected. Nevertheless, Churruca, who was on the spot and given authority to restore and provision the *San Juan Nepomuceno* as he saw fit, was saying that the El Ferrol-based *navíos* would not be ready for sea until a year after this letter had been written. From his vantage point in El Ferrol in the north-west corner of Spain, Churruca was optimistic about the ability of Cádiz merchants (on Spain's south coast) to victual the fleet before Trafalgar. Also unknown to him at the time of this letter was the fact that, in the following year, the French fleet would join the enlarged Spanish one at Cádiz. As a result, the already hard-pressed resources for the many Spanish *navíos* could not handle the even larger fleet replenishment needs for food and ammunition of no fewer than thirty-three *navíos*, French and Spanish.

Churruca took over the *San Juan Nepomuceno*, which one mid-nineteenth century Spanish source says was 'newly docked'. Churruca the ever-conscientious naval captain was determined to train her crew to become a fighting unit as he had done earlier with the ship's company of the *Conquistador*. The fact that he was not able to completely prepare his crew for action, is more than hinted at in the harsh alternatives he offered his men at Trafalgar and from his own gloomy pre-battle assessment that the Spanish would be defeated by the better-disciplined British.

It is likely that Churruca was prevented from shaping up his crew, not only because of the

*San Juan Nepomuceno*, Churruca's Trafalgar command with his commodore's broad pennant at main mast peak. Painter Alejo de Berlinguero, a naval lieutenant and professor in the Cartagena Naval Pilots' School who also painted *Santísima Trinidad*, *Real Carlos* and *San Telmo* in this same unique stylized manner, always painted his *navíos* in correct sailing positions. *San Juan Nepomuceno* is sailing before the wind and appears to be approaching land. Only her fore, main and mizzen topsails are set. Crew members scrambling along her bowsprit, appear ready to take in the jib and flying jib. (*Museo Naval, Madrid*)

sudden formation of the Combined Squadron of the French and Spanish fleets at Cádiz, but also because of the lack of manpower for crews, a result of malaria epidemics that had raged through the maritime regions of southern Spain since 1802. Churruca's harsh admonishment of his men before Trafalgar had much to do both with his previous record as a firm disciplinarian and because of the part he played as a member of the fleet commission that investigated the Cape St Vincent defeat – as has been said, a battle the Spanish should have won. Churruca wrote a hasty dispatch to his cousin on 28 March 1797 with the news of his appointment to the commission.

> I write you in haste. At the moment I am charging out of bed to go and live in the León Island for in this mail we have a royal order naming me attorney general [in Spain at that time, the term meant ex-officio representing the king] with the rear admiral [not named] of the Armada and Commodore Juan José García to form a judicial board relative to the last naval battle [Cape St Vincent] with the three having equal responsibility.[18]

Churruca was understandably proud to serve and to be at his country's call to investigate a defeat at sea that was going to besmirch his navy's name and that of Spain. In the rest of the letter this concern emerges loud and clear:

> The commission honours me greatly. But it is very delicate and [will have] much difficulty. We will have much adventure with it. But the honour of the corps, that of the nation, the expectation of all of Europe, all excite, or should excite, justice and action in us. Let us then do our duty and let the chips fall where they may.[19]

The revelation of his great pride in his service and his nation as well as his lifelong sense of honour makes these perhaps the most moving words in all the letters Churruca wrote to his family over nearly thirty years.

British and Spanish historians differ in their accounts of Churruca's last day, as well as of the fighting record of his ship at Trafalgar. One British historian claims that Churruca's ship was put out of action and dismasted in fifteen minutes, with Churruca dead on his quarterdeck. It is true that his ship took an early pummelling immediately after the action began since she was in the lead of the French-Spanish squadron. Not only was Churruca mortally wounded on his deck but along with him, one other officer and 100 of the crew were killed; a further 7 officers and 150 crew also had been wounded. The British clearly wanted to deliver a *coup de grâce* to this ship but did not do so in fifteen minutes. At two o'clock in the afternoon, half way through the battle and after Churruca had been killed, his ship was still being pounded by seven English ships. According to a Spanish source, Churruca died when he returned to his quarterdeck after 'adjusting a gun' on the forecastle. His right leg was mangled by shot, a wound that haemorrhaged so badly, he knew he would not live.

He had made personal pre-battle arrangements with his brother-in-law, Lieutenant José Ruiz Apodaca, who was on board, for his replacement as captain. On 19 October, two days before Trafalgar, Churruca advised him, '... write to your parents that you are about to enter a battle that will be bloody. Say farewell to them, that my fate will be your own...'[20] After Churruca was killed, Apodaca approached Lieutenant Joaquín Ibáñez de Corbera to assume command to be told in turn by him that First Lieutenant Joaquín Núñez Falcón was the most senior officer left alive and that he should take command. Núñez then gathered together three other officers in addition to himself, including Ibáñez de Corbera, who made a joint decision to surrender the ship.

It was now impossible for the *San Juan Nepomuceno* to extricate herself from the battle. The close-in salvos from the many British ships firing into the Spanish vessel had seriously crippled her. Most of the rigging had disappeared; only the sails on the fore mast remained in order and the rudder was unworkable. The *San Juan Nepomuceno* surrendered to the *Dreadnought* and was towed to Gibraltar where she remained until 1808 as a floating museum in memory of Churruca, who was held in high esteem by the Royal Navy. Churruca's cabin was maintained intact as he had lived in it and kept closed to all but official guests, his name inscribed on the outside cabin door in large gold letters. His former ship entered the Royal Navy as the *San Juan* until she was paid off in 1818, three years after the end of the long Napoleonic Wars. This British recognition of Churruca as a Spanish naval hero was yet another example of the magnanimity that the English and Spanish extended to each other after battle.

Churruca's funeral was held a month after his death, on 21 November 1805 in the chapel of San Fernando de Esteiro in El Ferrol and in 1812 he was posthumously promoted to vice admiral in the Spanish Navy. Where Nelson's family descended into relative obscurity soon after his death (and in 1945 finally lost the pension granted to it by Parliament in 1805 as one of the cost-cutting measures of Prime Minister Clement Attlee's postwar Labour government), the Churruca family down the years has remained prominent in Spanish public and professional life, including the navy.

Because Commodore Churruca died childless, members of the Churruca family who have been active in both the nineteenth and twentieth centuries, are the descendants of his brother Julián. In 1909, King Alfonso XIII conferred the title of Conde de Motrico (Count of Motrico) on Evaristo de Churruca y Brunet the grandson of Julián, a brilliant public works engineer, for his modernization of port facilities in Spain and the Spanish Caribbean and his re-design of the harbour of Bilbao, one of Spain's busiest ports. Julián's son José Churruca, a distinguished mid-nineteenth century Basque jurist, author and congressman, had eight children, one of whom, Alejandro, spent fifty-eight years in the *Armada Española* between 1846 and 1904. He served as captain general of the major naval base at Cádiz and was promoted vice admiral in 1898, the year of the Spanish–American War.

Titled 'The Last Hours of the *Santísima Trinidad*' this painting by R R Spencer shows the ship in the storm following the battle, a storm in which the ship foundered. (*Museo Naval, Madrid*)

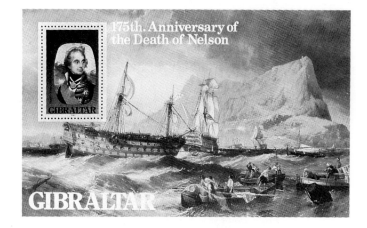

Clarkson Stanfield's painting of the damaged *Victory* being towed into Gibraltar after Trafalgar. (See also Plate XXI.)

The title Count of Motrico presently is held by the family of the wife of José María de Areilza y Martínez Rodas, born in the Basque province of Vizcaya. Appointed the youngest mayor of Bilbao at twenty-seven in 1937, Areilza later became one of Spain's most distinguished retired diplomats. In 1975, he was the first foreign minister of the restored Bourbon monarchy of Juan Carlos I. In 1987 as a distinguished essayist and author, he was elected a Member of the elite Royal Spanish Academy. Señora Areilza, who is the granddaughter of Evaristo de Churruca, inherited the title after her brother was killed during the Spanish Civil War. (In Spain, the female as senior in line, inherits the title.) Doña Areilza's son, Enrique Areilza Churruca, a corporation lawyer in Madrid who has served as an officer in the navy reserve, will inherit the title from his mother. Because the Churruca family name and reputation have been synonymous with the town and seaport of Motrico since the time long ago when Juan de Pérez Churruca first resided there in 1415, Alfonso XIII approved the name Motrico for the family title.

In the small world of Guipúzcoan families of renown, the Churruca ties extend further to a family association in the late seventeenth and early eighteenth century with Antonio Gaztañeta, the great Basque admiral and ship designer. The Areilza family archives not only contain Commodore Cosmé Damián Churruca's many letters written to his family during a lifetime in the navy, but some of Gaztañeta's technical notes and drawings from the early years of the eighteenth century when he was designing the 60-gun *San Luís* class of *navíos*. Since Trafalgar, the Spanish Navy has always named a warship *Churruca*, the current being the former United States Second World War destroyer *Eugene S Greene*, one of many former US warships acquired by the Spanish Navy during the early 1970s. A resolution passed by the Spanish Cortés (Parliament) stipulates that a ship of the *Armada Española* will always bear the name *Churruca*. Other former US Navy vessels of today's Spanish Navy are called *Gravina, Blas de Lezo, Lángara, Alcalá Galiano* and *Jorge Juan*. The Marqués de Ensenada's name is carried by a Spanish-built destroyer.

Because of the later titles and honours bestowed on his descendants and himself after death, as well as his record as one of Spain's leading seaman, Cosmé Damián Churruca's place as 'scholar, hero and man' is secure in the firmament of great Spanish and European sailors and warriors of the age of sail.

The last survivors of Trafalgar from the British and Spanish fleets lived very long lives, the final one dying in 1898. *Victory*'s last surviving seaman was James Chapman, who died at

Dundee in 1876 in his ninety-second year. Sir George Westphal, *Victory*'s longest living officer died in 1875 as a full admiral. The last two English survivors of Trafalgar were both officers: Admiral Sir George Sartorius, a midshipman in the *Tonnant*, died in 1885 at the age of ninety-five; Lieutenant Colonel James Fynmore, Royal Marines, was a midshipman at Trafalgar in the *Africa* and died in April 1887. The Spanish Navy's last Trafalgar survivors were seamen: cabin boys and, in one case, a caulker. As late as November 1870, four of them were listed in a Cádiz document as naval veterans with their ages, duties at Trafalgar and trades. One, Manuel Alonso Múñoz of ninety years, belonged to the *Monarca* as a soldier. Francisco Méndez y Sánchez was a cabin boy in *Santísima Trinidad*. Finally, Pedro Antonio Zía Martínez, a Vizcayan like his long-gone captain Damián Churruca and a cabin boy in his ship *San Juan Nepomuceno*, died in Dallas, Texas on 1 February 1898, at what the Spanish record calls 'the respectable age' of 109, an almost ninety-three incredible years after Trafalgar. Señor Zía did not quite make it to 23 April 1898 the day Spain declared war against the United States. If he had, a few weeks more of such a long, long life would have made him the Spanish Navy's only living link between Trafalgar and the Spanish–American War.[21]

The very last direct link we have with Trafalgar is, of course, the great *Victory*, preserved forever at her permanent berth inside the Portsmouth naval dockyard. Each year, she too must become less and less of a 'Trafalgar original'. So much new wood has gone into constant repairs to her external portions, bow and stern areas and deck construction in order to survive the wind and weather that today less than 40 per cent of the *Victory* timbers we see were in the ship at Trafalgar. Nevertheless, we stroke a wooden pillar, bulkhead or gangway as we pass through the ship, almost wishing the act would put us in mystical communion with one of *Victory*'s long-dead crew who could whisper to us first-hand from the ship's dark shadows what it really was like to live or die in that ship on that day of days, 21 October 1805.

For the Spanish, there can be no such ritual. The original plans for *Santísima Trinidad* have vanished forever, as indeed has that mighty ship of the line which sank after breaking her tow as an English prize in the fierce post-Trafalgar storm. It was the same storm that denied the victorious Royal Navy so many of its other French and Spanish ship prizes, lost during that ferocious gale. Had *Santísima Trinidad* been preserved like *Victory* in perpetuity, the spirits of a long-dead Spanish sailor or captain would have whispered different stories to the visitor about their great navy than the dismal ones so familiar in the English-speaking world.

Surely they would say from the mist that Spain, too, had a fleet, staunch ships' captains and ships to be proud of, although victory in the greatest sea battles of the eighteenth century too often eluded them.

# Epilogue:
## The Spanish Presence in the Royal Navy

In one instance only has an eighteenth century Spanish ship of the line survived to the age of photography. She was the *San Josef*, the 112-gun ship captured by Nelson at Cape St Vincent in 1797. She appears in Wilfrid Pym Trotter's *The Royal Navy in Old Photographs*, clearly a very old lady close to the end of her days, as a hulk at Devonport Dockyard. The photo was taken shortly before she was broken up in 1849. Although this is the only photograph we shall probably ever see of an eighteenth century Spanish warship, the book's author is entitled to identify the print as '. . . reputed to be the earliest photograph of one of HM Ships.'

Indeed, most of her sixty-six years of life were spent in the Royal Navy as the *San Josef*. She flew the red-gold-red flag of the *Armada Española* for a mere fourteen years from the time of her launching at El Ferrol in 1783 to her capture at Cape St Vincent. The rest of it, more than half a century, was passed as a serving capital ship in the Royal Navy from the time she completed her post-battle refit at Portsmouth on 6 November 1797 until 3 October 1803 when she was reduced to a hulk. The sturdy, wide tumblehome features, as well as a figurehead (though probably not her original) of this once-great 112-gun ship, are both clearly visible in this early Victorian photograph.

The great *San Josef* lasted long past the lifetime of her famous builder, José Romero y Landa, the engineer-in-chief at El Ferrol who died in 1794. She also outlasted Admiral Horatio Nelson by forty-three years. The *San Josef* was only one of the many captured Spanish ships of the line that saw service in the Royal Navy and which were coveted by British ship captains who, more than once during the century, expressed a preference in writing for the command of a captured Spanish *navío*. According to Christian de Saint Hubert's list 'Spanish Ships of the Line, 1714–1825' (see appendix), twenty-five Spanish ships of the line were captured and refitted to serve in the Royal Navy between the Battle off Cape Passaro in 1718 and Trafalgar. This figure does not include frigates or the many smaller craft captured by the British or lost in storms (as was the case with several Trafalgar prizes) or which, for other reasons did not serve in the Royal Navy.

Among the *navíos* he lists was the 80-gun *Fénix*, captured in the Battle of Santa Maria in 1780 and incorporated into the Royal Navy as the ship of the line *Gibraltar*, later to be reduced to a powder hulk and lazaretto until she was broken up in 1836. The 80-gun *San Rafael*, built at Havana in 1772, was captured in Calder's action off Cape Finisterre, entered the Royal Navy as a ship of the line with the same name, and served as such until she was reduced to a prison ship in 1806; the *San Rafael* was sold in 1810.

There were others among them. For example, the 74-gun *Infante* built at Havana in 1750, was captured there during the brief English occupation of that city in 1762. She too kept her

Spanish name while serving in the Royal Navy, and was sold in 1775. The case of the 74-gun *San Antonio* offered a most curious way of securing for the Royal Navy a new Spanish-built ship. The *San Antonio* was built in Cartagena in 1785 but was captured as a transfer to the French Navy with French name *Saint Antoine*. Nevertheless, her Spanish name was restored as *San Antonio*. Like *San Rafael*, she was reduced to a prison hulk (in 1808) and then sold in 1828.

Much more is known about the history of the 70-gun ship *Glorioso*, captured off Cape St Vincent on 8 October 1747 by the *Russell* under the command of Captain Matthew Buckle, a successful Royal Navy officer who was made a post-captain in 1745 when he was thirty-seven. After her capture, he commented most favourably on the qualities of yet another Havana-built *navío*, saying that her beams and planks 'looked as fresh as when they were built.' He was one of many English ship captains who would praise Spanish naval shipbuilding. Nevertheless, Commodore Pedro Mesía de la Zeada, commanding officer of the *Glorioso*, had the last word. While Captain Buckle had indeed captured Mesía de la Zeada's command, the Spanish treasure she had carried was safe in Spain. The commodore's reportedly pungent comment to Buckle was 'You have got the nut but not the kernel.'

Nor was Captain Buckle the first Royal Navy captain to try to take the *Glorioso*. On 14 July 1747 she evaded capture after an engagement off the Azores with the 60-gun *Warwick* and the 44-gun *Lark*. Captain Cruikshank of the *Lark* was court-martialled and dismissed the service for letting her escape. Later *Glorioso* forced her way past another small British squadron, and was attacked with great temerity by a British privateer, before falling in with the *Russell*. Would that Captain Buckle had experienced the same quick success in disposing of the *Glorioso* as he did in capturing her. A vacillating Admiralty lost the chance to sell the *Glorioso* to an interested King of Portugal for £30,000 pounds, then quibbled later about the cost of obtaining a crew to sail her to England and for essential repairs before the damaged *Glorioso* was ready to sail back to England. According to E G Thomas in his revealing paper 'Captain Buckle and the Capture of the Glorioso' in *The Mariner's Mirror* of February 1982, the navy refused to buy the *Glorioso* and she 'was sold at Lloyd's Coffee House on 13 April 1749 for £12,100 pounds.'[2]

In a few truly odd cases, British warships found their way into the Spanish Navy as a third-party fleet. Hence the *Cumberland*, built in 1695 and captured by the French, was sold first to Genoa and then to Spain in 1717 to serve as the first *Principe de Asturias*. As such, she was in turn captured by the English at Cape Passaro in 1718, and was sold to Austria to survive fifteen years until her breaking up in 1733. *Gloucester*, a 60-gun ship captured by the French during the War of the Spanish Succession, was sold to Genoa in 1711, whose navy in turn sold it to Spain. Until the 1730s she served in the Spanish Navy as the first *Conquistador*.

Various English commanders over the years unabashedly sang the praises of their Spanish-built commands. Captain Augustus Hervey wrote in his diary *The Intimate Account of the Life of a Captain in the Royal Navy Ashore and Afloat, 1746–1759*: 'The 17th [of May, 1746] I was to my great joy sworn in Captain of the *Princesa*. She was at Portsmouth, and a glorious ship she was, but rather too large for my wishes of cruising.' On 27 October 1746 Admiral Lestock on taking over *Princesa* as his flagship, wrote to the Admiralty, 'I have the pleasure to assure your Lordships, there never was a finer ship of war than this I am now on board...'

Captain Hervey's remark about the size of the *Princesa* relates to the reaction of her British captors in April 1740 when three British 70-gun ships, *Kent*, *Lennox* and *Orford* took over six hours to force the surrender of the *Princesa*, even though she had lost one of her topmasts. *Princesa* proved to be as large as an English 90-gun ship of the period, measuring 165 feet on the gun deck and nearly 50 feet in breadth. At a time when the 74-gun ship was emerging as the basic *navío* of all European fleets, few in England had seen such a large 70-gunner. She was an early product of the Guarnizo yard and was completed there in 1730.

The assumption that her design influenced future Royal Navy ship designs is found in both British and Spanish writings. González-Aller sees influences of the *Princesa* design in the *Victory*, which was launched fifteen years after *Princesa*'s capture. Others hint that *Princesa*, of which there are no surviving drawings, influenced the design of the famous and ultimately doomed *Royal George* that foundered in 1782. In 1850, Fincham writes that 'one step in the improvement [of the design of English ships of the line] resulted from the capture in 1740 of the *Princesa* ... The excellence of this ship it was desired to equal, and with this view the *Royal George* was constructed and laid down at Woolwich in 1746, but she was not launched until 1756.'

Brian Lavery, the modern British author and specialist on the British ship of the line accepts the reported influence of the size of the *Princesa* on mid-eighteenth century English shipbuilding, but strongly discountenances the idea that her design was copied. The lines of both *Royal George* and *Victory* were completed in what he calls 'traditional British style'.

A second Spanish *navío* named *Princesa*, this time a conventional 74-gun ship built at Havana in 1750, was also captured by the British to serve as the *Princessa* until 1784, when she was reduced to a hulk and then broken up in 1809. Her longevity thereby perpetuated the English experience of having a Spanish bottom that served years longer in the Royal Navy than in the Spanish fleet. Indeed, so many captured Spanish *navíos* did long service in the Royal Navy that Joaquín Aguirre, a Spanish observer, commented early in the century that 'one is to observe the Navy that England sustains is none other than the old Spanish one.' Of course, he greatly exaggerated.[3]

English dockyard officials involved in the repair of captured Spanish *navíos* are often less praiseworthy of the quality of Spanish naval construction than are the Royal Navy ship captains who commanded Spanish prizes. This must be because dockyard officials saw only Spanish *navíos* after they had been severely pounded by the gunfire of a sea battle. An example is the *San Damaso*, a 74-gun ship built at Cartagena in 1776 and captured at Cape St Vincent in 1797. She was the only Cape St Vincent prize to be sent to Portsmouth for repair. She arrived there on 1 September 1797, was docked on 6 October and 'undocked' on 6 November of the same year. She was not re-coppered like most of the other Cape St Vincent prizes because the dockyard officials decided she could not be fully restored. On 14 October 1797 Messrs E Tippet, R J Nelson and J Ansell wrote to the Navy Board at its request:

> In answer to your letter of the 11th [of October] respecting the defects of his Majesty's ship the *San Damaso* we here agreeable thereto, spotted over the whole and cut out some of the defective ceiling in different parts of the hold and find the timbers of the frame (which are of oak) appear sound, but in general very shaky, the whole of the ceiling appears defective and will require to be shifted; and being chiefly of fir except her frame, from her general appearance she will require a great deal of work done to make her fit for service. We are therefore humbly of opinion it will not be advisable to enter her repairs, but she may be made fit for any harbour service in her present state, without entering into any repair.[4]

A few weeks later, her fitting as a prison ship began. Later, she was sold to a private owner, but not until 1814.

However, the naval career in English hands of the more famous *San Josef*, one of Nelson's favourite ships, was quite different from that of the *San Damaso*. Nelson's first letters in the year 1801 to fellow officers, relatives, Lady Hamilton and Admiral the Earl of St Vincent were written from the *San Josef*, in which he hoisted his flag at Plymouth on 17 January 1801. Most of these letters were written, not from his own cabin which was undergoing repairs, but from Captain Hardy's cabin. On that day he wrote to the admiral, commander-in-chief of the Channel Fleet, to which Nelson would be attached as a new Vice Admiral of the Blue:

> My dear Lord,
> My flag is up on board the *San Josef* and Wednesday next I have fixed her for going to Cawsand Bay, where, as she must be for two days or three, she shall be finished by the joiners, who have not begun my cabin; but I shall live in Hardy's.[5]

Thomas Masterman Hardy, Nelson's famous captain of his flagship *Victory* at Trafalgar, was also captain of the *San Josef*, with a large crew of 900 officers, marines and men. Actually, the *San Josef* flew two new flags on that day: Nelson's as Vice Admiral of the Blue from the ship's fore mast; and the new Union Jack on the jackstay above the bowsprit.

The Act of Union that marked the creation of the United Kingdom of England, Scotland and Ireland came into force on 1 January 1801 and with it, the need for a new flag. In the century just passed, Royal Navy ships fighting against the red-gold-red banner of the Spanish Navy, itself instituted in 1785, had flown the Union Standard. This had been the St George's red cross superimposed on the white saltire cross on the blue ground of Scotland's St Andrew. Now for the first time in this former Spanish *navío*, the new Union Jack fluttered, with the red saltire cross of Ireland's St Patrick, to compose the red and white diagonals on blue.

Nelson must have known that the big *San Josef*, with her deeper draught, would not be suitable for the planned naval operations in the shallow waters off Copenhagen in 1801. An unpopular pre-emptive strike against Danes, not an historic enemy of England, was considered necessary when the Russian Tsar Paul I won the support of Denmark, Prussia and Sweden to embargo British shipping. Since much of the pine for the Royal Navy's masts was being imported from Scandinavia and Russia, Britain had to take naval action in the Baltic to guarantee this vital source of supply. Hence *San Josef* did not sail to Denmark with Nelson as second-in-command of the British fleet, even though she was his choice.

Preparations for an assault against the Danish fleet were under way when Nelson wrote to the Rt Hon Earl Spencer, also on 17 January 1801 from Hardy's cabin in *San Josef*:

> Next to getting a command which I was a candidate for, whenever Lord Keith [Admiral, later Viscount George Elphinstone, then a commander of naval forces blockading French ports] gave up his, of course my pleasure would have been to serve under him, but that circumstances had so altered since my arrival, that it was almost certain I should go to the Baltic ... The Earl [St Vincent] was very handsome to me, and hoped that, by a temporary absence of a few months [in the Baltic] I should not lose my *San Josef*, the finest ship in the world...[6]

Nelson would not return to *San Josef*, nor would *San Josef*, rebuilt at great cost, be returned to a serving ship of the line. On 3 October 1803 she was reduced to a hulk for various shoreside uses, a role she fulfilled for forty-six years, almost half a century, when all who gave her life were themselves long gone.

By 1825, Spain had become a much-reduced colonial power. She no longer needed a big fleet, even if a Battle of Trafalgar had not intervened to destroy it. At the same time, after the loss of most of Spanish America, there was still enough of the empire left to justify calling Spain a major colonial power. The Spanish Caribbean still included Cuba, already one of the richest of early nineteenth century European colonies, and Puerto Rico. In the Pacific, the island archipelagos of the Marianas, Marshalls (called the Ladrones or 'Thieves' Islands' by the Spanish) and Palaus remained Spanish until 1898, as did the sugar-rich Philippine Islands.

During the nineteenth century with the arrival of the age of steam, Spain created two small colonial naval squadrons for her navy based in Cuba and the Philippines; except for the brief naval build-up at Cavite in the Philippines and Santiago de Cuba during the Spanish–American War in 1898, neither of them was large enough ever again to require major warships on station.

# NOTES AND REFERENCES

Abbreviations for the Spanish Archives identified in the references are:

AGI – Archivo General de Indias (General Archives of the Indies), Sevilla.
AGS – Archivo General de Simancas (General Archives of Simancas), near Valladolid.
AHN – Archivo Histórico de la Nación (Historic Archive of the Nation), Madrid.
ARAH – Archivo de la Real Academia de la Historia (Archive of the Royal Academy of History), Madrid.
Museo Naval – Naval Museum in the Spanish Ministry of the Navy, Madrid.
Viso del Marqués – Archivo 'Don Alvaro de Bazán' El Viso de Marqués, close to the village of the same name and administered by the Museo Naval in Madrid.

## CHAPTER ONE

There are no references for Chapter One.

## CHAPTER TWO

[1] From 'How Britannia Came to Rule the Waves', a review of Rodger's *The Wooden World, An Anatomy of The Georgian Navy* by William Golding in *The Manchester Guardian Weekly*, 4 January 1987, p22.

[2] John Robert McNeill, *Atlantic Empires of France and Spain, Louisburg and Havana, 1700–1763*, p61.

[3] Bernardo Tinajero de la Escalera, Legajo 2313, Archivo Histórico de la Nación, AHN, Madrid, 1714.

[4] José P Merino, *La Armada Española en el Siglo XVIII*, pp350–1.

[5] See the author's 'The Spanish Ship of the Line', *The Scientific American*, New York, December 1984, Vol 251, No 6, pp116–124.

[6] List from 'La distribución de los pesos por conceptos en un navío' (The distribution of the weights by categories in a *navío*) in *El Buque en la Armada Española*, p246.

[7] From lists of first editions of eighteenth century *Ordenanzas Reales) (Royal Ordinances)* for the navy as preserved in the Museo Naval, Spanish Navy Ministry, Madrid.

[8] 'Sobre construcción de navíos de 58 cañones' (regarding the construction of navíos of 58 guns), Julián de Arriaga y Rivera al Marqués de la Victoria. Copía autorizada, Madrid, 15 de mayo de 1757, Manuscrito 1214, Colección Guillén y Tato, documento 10 de 16, Museo Naval, Madrid.

[9] G Douglas Inglis, his unpublished essay 'The Spanish Naval Shipyard at Havana in the Eighteenth Century', Texas State Archives, Austin, 1981, p4.

[10] Alfred Thayer Mahan, *The Influences of Sea Power upon History 1660–1783*, p209.

[11] Spanish and English Fleet Lists from Pablo Emilio Pérez-Maillana Bueno, *Política Naval Española en el Atlántico 1700–1715*, p410.

[12] *Ibid*, p210.

[13] 'El Navío de Tres Puentes en La Armada Española', Capitan de Fragata (Commander) José Ignácio González-Aller Hierro, *Revista de Historia Naval*, Año III, No 9, 1985, p52.

[14] *El Buque en la Armada Española*, pp192–93.

[15] D Jorge Juan, 'Instrucción del Marqués de Ensenada a Jorge Juan para la Comisión que ha de empeñar en Inglaterra de reconocimiento de puertos, y regimen de arsenales contacto de dos constructores, un maestro de fábrica de jarcia ... instrumentos marítimos' (For the commission of enquiry he is to undertake in England of ports, shipyard systems, contact two (ship) constructors, a master of rigging ... (and) maritime instruments), San Lorenzo de Real, 27 October 1748. Manuscrito 2162, Miscelánea, Doc 2, Folio 2–6, Museo Naval, Madrid.

This is one of the most important documents in Anglo-Spanish naval and maritime relations of the eighteenth century in that Jorge Juan, one of the best Spanish ship designers of the era was despatched on a major spying mission to England by the shrewd and purposeful Ensenada. Juan was instructed to report on much more than on the condition of the English fleet and naval shipbuilding and to hire specialists in shipbuilding during one of the rare periods when Spain and England were at peace. Ensenada empowers him still further to find out to what extent the English were violating the rigid rules of Spanish mercantilism by secretly importing textiles from Spain and Spanish America for manufacture into end-products in England. In this strategically-put memorandum, Ensenada directs Juan to do all of the following while in England:

You will procure the dimensions and secretly if possible, acquire data on the best known methods of construction of warships of that Monarchy, validating [such] methods.

You will visit the first-line [*de mayor nombre*] shipyards in England and always cloaking [your interest] as mere curiosity ... you will examine all the works [warships] that might be under way as well as those that might be in the dockyards, drydocks ... methods of preserving the woods and of construction, rigging and masts, other sites and (ships') supplies.

You will proceed to acquire ... the composition of the fleet, what is made or is perfected in England with pre-eminence over the same [goods] that are made in other countries of Europe.

You will make efforts to find out what dry goods of Spain and even of [Spanish] America that only the King [of Spain] has in his Dominions, [their] prices to the English and how they may value them for manufacture.

You will determine with possible care what contraband the English are carrying out in our America, in what ways they practice it and what methods of security they employ ...

[16] Merino, *op cit*, pp100–102.

[17] There were, according to the Spanish archives, six previous ships with the name *Santísima Trinidad*. These included a merchant ship dated 1675, a seventeenth century *navío*, a commercial *goleta* of the mid-eighteenth century, a *jabega* fishing vessel (not to be confused with a *jabeque*) from the early eighteenth century and a coastal merchant vessel serving the textile merchants of Colindres in the late seventeenth century. Manuscritos Nos 142, 1294, 2110, 2238, 469 and 1293, Museo Naval, Madrid.

[18] Carta que dejó escrita el Jefe de Escuadra D Jorge Juan al Rey Carlos III cuando murió acompaña el texto de la inscripción hecho sobre su tumba (Letter which Commodore D Jorge Juan had leave to write when he died to King Carlos III accompanying the text of the inscription made on his tomb). Copias 1773, Manuscrito 2164, Miscelánea, Doc 6, Folio 23–26, 1773, Museo Naval, Madrid.

[19] Merino, *op cit*, pp13–14.

[20] From *Cuaderno de Pruebas* of 1785 (Log Book of Runs of 1785). See item for 9 June 1785, navigational runs to deteremine ships' positions. Manuscrito No 2278 (*San Ildefonso, navío*), Madrid.

## CHAPTER THREE

[1] Page 29: Levi Marrero, *Cuba: Economía y Sociedad (Azúcar, Ilustración y Conciencia, 1763–1868)*, p68.

[2] Lord Hugh Thomas, *Cuba, or the Pursuit of Freedom*, pp2–3.

[3] José A García Ordóñez, 'La Familia Montalvo', unpublished typewritten manuscript, Concord, New Hampshire, 1983–84, p5.

[4] John Robert McNeill, *op cit*, p174.

[5] McNeill, *ibid*, p175.

[6] G Douglas Inglis, *op cit*, p6.

[7] 'The Minister's Mariner: The Marqués de Matallana,' Lowel W Newton, *Revista de Historia de América*, Pan American Institute of History and Geography, Mexico City, No 93, January–June 1982, p21.

[8] See selected legajos under classification 'Officiales de Guerra y Marina' in the Sección de la Marina, Archivo General de Simancas, AGS, 1717–1783, Simancas.

[9] Archivo General de Indias, AGI, Sección Contratación Papeles del General Don Rodrigo de Torres, año 1733, legajo 5, 102.

[10] Major Thomas Mante, *The History of the Late War in North America and the Islands of the West Indies*, p411.

[11] Mante, *ibid*, p411.

[12] In his fine and detailed essay 'The Ministers' Mariner: The Marqués de Matallana,' Dr Newton has written one of the few full biographical essays available of a senior Spanish naval commander of the eighteenth century *Armada Española* based on the Spanish archival records.

[13] Inglis, *op cit*, p10.

[14] Ordóñez, *op cit*, p22.

[15] 'In Havana, in 1790 there existed thirteen noble titles and seventeen proceeding to titles, all of them native-born (in Cuba). It was an oligarachy made rich, of the first order with much political-social power and it was surmised, (with) a structural axis inside the old regime which is an exceptional case in Latin America,' writes Moreno Fraganals, the colonial Cuban historian in an essay in *El País*, Madrid, 26 July 1987, p11.

## CHAPTER FOUR

[1] Manuel Marliani, *Combate de Trafalgar Vindicación de la Armada Española*, p472. 'Hay desastres que honran tanto como una victoria' (There are disasters that may be honoured as much as a victory).

[2] From the editorial in *!Arriba!* (now defunct) Madrid, Sunday, 5 July 1942. During and after World War Two, *!Arriba!* was the party paper of Franco's Spanish Fascist Falange Party, the only political party permitted in Spain between 1939 and 1975.

[3] See the Royal Canadian Mint's illustrated advertisement in *Barron's*, New York, 12 September 1983.

[4] In *Nelson* by David Walder, p236, but also appears along with much of Nelson's correspondence in the seven volumes of *Letters and Despatches* edited by Sir Harris Nicolas.

[5] Marliani, *op cit*, pp478–9.

[6] Warren Tute, *The True Glory: The Story of the Royal Navy over a Thousand Years*, p73.

[7] 'Trafalgar: the Spanish View,' Julián de Zulueta, *The Mariner's Mirror*, November 1980, p298.

[8] Zulueta, *ibid*, p303.

[9] Carta del Presidente de la Suprema Junta de Sanidad referente a la cuarentena establecida como consecuencia de una epidemia declarada en Cádiz (Letter from the Chairman

of the Senior Board of Health referring to the quarantine established as a consequence of the epidemic declared in Cádiz). Manuscrito 10590, Cádiz, 30 October 1804, Doc 13, pp89–90.

[10] Tute, *op cit*, p98.

[11] Interview with Brian Lavery, author and eighteenth century naval specialist, in London, 1 November 1986.

[12] 'La Politica del Reformismo de los Primeros Borbones en la Marina de Guerra Española' (The Policy of Reformism in the Spanish Navy by the First Bourbons), Vicente Rodríguez Casado, *Anuário de Estudios Americanos*, Sevilla, Vol XXV, 1968, p9.

[13] From the review of Dr Rodger's *The Wooden World: An Anatomy of the Georgian Navy*, *loc cit*, p22.

[14] 'La Matricula del Mar bajo Carlos III' (The Seaman's Register under Carlos III), Angel O'Dogherty, *Anuario de Estudios Americanos*, Sevilla, Vol IX, 1952, p13.

[15] 'Indies Revenue and Naval Spending: The Cost of Colonialism for the Spanish Bourbons, 1763–1805,' Jacques A Barbier, *Jahrbuch für Geschichte von Staat, Wirtschaft und Gesellschaft Lateinamerikas* (*Yearbook for the History of State, Economy and Society of Latin America*), Vol 21, 1984, Böhlau Verlag, Köln, pp179–181. (Though the source is a German-language journal, Barbier's essay in it was published in English.)

[16] Josef Romero y Landa's letter to Navy Minister Antonio Valdés from Villalva of 11 September 1783. Manuscrito 1945, Construcción naval 1, doc dictamen de 74 cañones, Folio 117–8, 1783.

[17] Alfred Thayer Mahan, *op cit*, p232.

[18] In addition to Marquis of the Royal Transport, Carlos III granted other very curiously named noble titles to worthy senior public officials of the 1760s and 1770s, all of which are preserved today in Spain by their present title holders. They include the Marquis of Royal Defence, The Royal Mercy, The Royal Proclamation, The Royal Succour and The Royal Treasure!

[19] John Robert McNeill, *op cit*, p41.

[20] There are several major studies of Godoy. The best is *Godoy, Master of Spain, 1792–1808* by Jacques Chastenet, CBE, originally in French, translated by J F Huntington, Kennikat Press, Port Washington, NY, 1972.

[21] Michael Lewis, *The Navy of Britain A Historical Portrait*, p551.

[22] These and other references to Mazarredo's effort to improve seamanship methods during the mid- and late-1780s, are found in the Mazarredo papers donated by the present family to the Museo Naval, Spanish Navy Ministry, Madrid, 1973, as well as in *Navíos en Secuestro: La Escuadra Española del Océano en Brest, 1799–1802 (Warships in Hiding: The Spanish Navy Ocean Squadron in Brest, 1799–1802)*, J M Carlan, pp18–19.

[23] See Note [22].

[24] An important analysis in English of the Spanish position in the region appeared in 'The Transient Presence: A Re-Appraisal of Spanish Attitudes Toward the Northwest Coast in the Eighteenth Century,' by Christon I Archer, *BC Studies*, Vancouver, BC, No 18, Summer 1973, pp3–32.

[25] See 'Bodega' by Warren L Cook in *The Canadian Dictionary of Biography*, Vol IV, University of Toronto Press, 1979, pp72–3.

[26] German Arciniegas, *Caribbean Sea of the New World*, p299.

[27] Conde de Llobregat, *Un General Español Cojo, Manco y Tuerto, Don Blas de Lezo: Natural de Pasajes (A Spanish General Lame, One-Handed and One-Eyed: Don Blas de Lezo, Native of Pasajes)*, p2.

[28] Dr J C M Ogelsby, the Canadian Latin-American historian, has analyzed at length the Spanish position during the many mid-century English attacks against cities of the Spanish Caribbean. His studies used for this book include 'England vs Spain in America, 1739–1748, the Spanish Side of the Hill,' *Historical Papers*, The Canadian Historical Association, Toronto, 1979, pp147–157.

## CHAPTER FIVE

[1] Edward Fraser, *The Enemy at Trafalgar: An Account of the Battle from Eye-Witnesses' Narratives and Letters and Despatches from the French and Spanish Fleets*, p375.

[2] 'Treaty of Alliance between His Catholic Majesty and the French Republic signed at San Ildefonso on 18 August, and treating of matters both offensive and defensive.' English translation of this treaty in Document No 74, *Spain under the Bourbons, 1700–1833*, W N Hargreaves-Mawdsley, pp178–9.

[3] Hargreaves-Mawdsley, *ibid*, Document No 75, pp180–1.

[4] From Manuscrito 10905 in Museo Naval, Madrid containing details of Gravina's memorandum on the Spanish Navy's manpower and crew composition in his flagship *Principe de Asturias*.

[5] Details of Gravina's movements in the months before Trafalgar as well the pre-Trafalgar movements and appointments of senior Spanish naval officers in 'Trafalgar: Genesis de Una Selección,' Lieutenant Hermengildo Franco Castañon, *Revista de Historia Naval*, Año III, Num 8, 1985, Madrid, pp55–79. Gravina in Paris in January 1805 is reported on p59.

[6] H Franco Castañón, *loc cit*, p61.

[7] Quoted from two-page letter to the author from Dr Donald Cutter, the distinguished US historian of the Alejandro Malaspina voyages, 28 April 1987.

[8] Carmen, Sor (Sister), *El Almirante Sin Tacha y Sin Miedo: Vida del Capitán General de la Armada Española, Don Federico Gravina*.

[9] Escaño's full report to Godoy also appears as 'Translation of a Dispatch to the Prince of Peace from Don Antonio de Escaño, Rear Admiral of the Combined Fleet' in *Letters of Lord Nelson*, Sir Harris Nicolas, pp283–300.

[10] In Manuel Marliani, *El Combate de Trafalgar: Vindicación de la Armada Española*, pp526–7. Uriarte's bold letter of refusal

to King Joseph Bonaparte begins: 'Ni mi honra ni mi conciencia me permiten renovar acudiendo al mandato de V E juramento que tengo hecho a mi legítimo soberano...'

[11] The full list of these post-Trafalgar promotions appears in Manuscrito 2238, Combate de Trafalgar, Cartagena Departmento, Doc 73, Folio 254–8 in the Museo Naval, Madrid as follows: 'Relación de los oficiales que han sido promovido en su clase inmediata en 9 de noviembre de 1805 por haber tomado parte en el combate de Trafalgar y por otras circunstancias especiales' (Report of the officers who have been promoted in their (new) rank immediately on 9 November 1805 for having taken part in the Battle of Trafalgar and for other special circumstances).

[12] Fraser, *op cit*, pp250–1.

[13] 'Mariá Dolores Ruíz de Apodaca, viuda de Churruca, solicita se le de ... pensión, el sueldo ... de su marido muerto en Trafalgar' (Mariá Dolores Ruíz de Apodaca widow of Churruca requests that she be given the pension and salary of her husband killed at Trafalgar). Manuscrito 2200, Miscelánea, Doc 51, Folio 119, Museo Naval, Madrid.

[14] Churruca de El Ferrol, 24 de junio de 1778.

[15] Churruca de Lansana, 12 de febrero de 1782.

[16] Churruca de la fragata *Santa Bárbara*, 28 de mayo de 1782.

[17] Churruca de El Ferrol, 13 de febrero de 1804.

[18] Churruca de Cádiz, 28 de marzo de 1797.

[19] Churruca de Cádiz, 28 de marzo de 1797.

[20] Churruca de Cádiz, 19 de octubre de 1805 [his last letter].

[21] Details on the last Spanish survivors of Trafalgar from two Spanish sources. The first is Manuscrito 2513, Documento 60, 11 pages, Museo Naval, Madrid signed at Cádiz on 28 November 1870 by Victoriano Sánchez as the 'Report on the individuals who at present exist in this province (Cádiz) and who were present at the Battle of Trafalgar.' The second is the small booklet *Los Ultimos Sobrevivientes de Trafalgar (The Last Survivors of Trafalgar)*, Juan Llabres y Bernal, Imprenta Viuda de F Soler, Palma de Mallorca, 1949, 16 pages.

## CHAPTER SIX

[1] 'Captain Buckle and the Capture of the *Glorioso*,' E G Thomas, *The Mariner's Mirror*, Vol 68, No 1, February 1982, p51.

[2] E G Thomas, *loc cit*, p55.

[3] 'Es de advertir que la Marina subsistente a Inglaterra, no es otra que la antigua española,' Discurso general sobre la Marina, por Joaquín Aguirre, Archivo General de Indias (AGI), Indiferente General (or Miscellaneous General) 3167. (In his day, Aguirre was known to exaggerate the plight of the Spanish Navy.)

[4] *The Progress Books*, Volumes 5 and 6, 1797. Copies held by National Maritime Museum, Greenwich.

[5] From Nelson's letters written while on board *San Josef*, in *Letters of Lord Nelson*, Sir Harris Nicolas, Vol VI, p273.

[6] Nicolas, *ibid*, p274.

# SOURCES

## A) PRIMARY SOURCES

(1) Public Documents, Spain, England and Canada

ARCHIVO 'DON ALVARO DE BAZÁN, EL VISO DE MARQUÉS' (VISO DEL MARQUÉS)
ARCHIVO DEL MUSEO NAVAL (MADRID)

Representative examples follow of extensive research in these two major sources of original eighteenth century Spanish naval documents. Historic Spanish government documents are loosely held together in *legajos*, the leather-bound volumes of papers under such general classifications as 'Administration' or 'Construction'. In addition, a single *legajo* on naval subjects can contain original documents and correspondence extending from the decade after the defeat of the Spanish Armada in 1588 to the late eighteenth century immediately prior to Trafalgar.

*Arsenals and shipyards* – organization, personnel, ordinance at Cádiz, Cartagena, El Ferrol, Guarnizo, Havana.

*Theories and plans of naval construction* – by Garrote, Gaztañeta, Jorge Juan and Romero y Landa.

*Diaries and letters* – Commodore Dionísio Alcalá Galiano, Commodore Cosmé Damián Churruca, Jorge Juan, Capitán de navío Alejandro Malaspina, Vice Admiral José de Mazarredo.

*Trafalgar* – Gravina's pre-Trafalgar correspondence with Godoy held by both archives.

*Ships* – in both archives, considerable drawings, cost estimates and official correspondence on individual *navíos* between 1720 and 1800.

*Exploration* – excerpts from the diaries and official correspondence on the major voyages of discovery and exploration between 1770 and 1800, for example, those of Capitán de navío Juan Francisco de la Bodega y Quadra.

*Selections from the Mazarredo collection* – manuscript material of Vice Admiral José de Mazarredo; his diary of events from on board the *navío Condé de Regla* in 1790; his correspondence with the Minister of the Navy, and the Prince of Peace (Godoy) about affairs of the Mediterranean Squadron under command of Mazarredo, 1795–96; Mazarredo correspondence on various subjects, 1801–1812.

ARCHIVO GENERAL DE SIMANCAS (SIMANCAS)

*Naval construction* – documents, 1787 to 1797.

*Various documents* – on Battle of Cape Sicié, 1744; diary of the Gibraltar blockade; *matriculas del mar*, that is seamens' list for the Indies, Lima, Canaries and Havana.

*Navy Ministry correspondence and dispatches* – 1718 to 1783.

REAL ACADEMIA DE LA HISTORIA (MADRID)

BRITISH LIBRARY, DEPARTMENT OF MANUSCRIPTS (LONDON)

*Admiral Norris papers* – his report on the capture of the Spanish *Princesa* from on board the *Orford*, 8 April 1740.

*Nelson's Memorandum* – from on board *Victory*, off Cádiz, 9 October 1805.

NATIONAL MARITIME MUSEUM (GREENWICH)

*The Progress Books* – Vols 5 and 6. Shipwrights' reports of reconstruction and repairs made to Spanish *navío* prizes taken at both Cape St Vincent, 14 February 1797 and Trafalgar, 21 October 1805.

*Lord Nelson* – dispatches and correspondence from on board his new flagship, and ex-Spanish *navío*, *San Josef*, 1800–1801.

*Trafalgar* – official report of proceedings of the Spanish fleet performance from Rear Admiral Antonio de Escaño to Godoy, November 1805. (This important and lengthy document appears in full in the Spanish and English languages in both the Spanish and British archives.)

UNIVERSITY OF TORONTO, THE ROBARTS LIBRARY (TORONTO)

– Photocopies of selected eighteenth century manuscripts of originals held in the Spanish archival system.

(2) Private Documents Held by Families in Spain and the United States

CHURRUCA

The private correspondence of Commodore Cosmé Damián Churruca. Between 1778 and 1805, Churruca wrote 168 letters, mainly to members of his family during his long naval career. These letters made available to the author are in the possession of the Areilza and Churruca families (Madrid and Motrico).

LA FAMILIA MONTALVO

Unpublished genealogical lists of the Montalvo family of Cuba by José A García Ordóñez y Montalvo. Based on official state and private records of the Hispano-Cuban Montalvo family from 1750 to 1959 (Madrid, Havana and Concord, New Hampshire).

# B) SECONDARY SOURCES

Acerra Martine, Merino Navarro, José P, Meyer, Jean *Les Marines de Guerre Européennes XVII–XVIIIe Siècles*, Presses de l'Université de Paris-Sorbonne, Paris 1985.

Albion, Robert Greenhalgh, *Forests and Sea Power: The Timber Problem of the Royal Navy 1652–1862*, Harvard University Press, Cambridge, Mass 1926.

Alcalá Galiano, Pelayo, *El Combate de Trafalgar*, 2 vols, Imprenta del Depósito Hidrográfico, Madrid 1930.

Alden, John Richard, *The American Revolution 1775–1783*, Harper & Row, New York 1954.

Amiconi, Jacopo, *El Marqués de la Ensenada*, Diputación de la Rioja, Logroño 1981.

Archivo General de Simancas, *Guía del Investigador*, Angel de la Plaza Bores, Valladolid 1962.

Arciniegas, Germán, *Caribbean Sea of the New World*, Alfred A Knopf, New York 1946.

Artiñaño y de Galdacano, Gervásio de, *La Arquitectura Naval Española (en Madera)*, Madrid 1920.

Bamford, Paul Walden, *Forests and French Sea Power 1660–1789*, University of Toronto Press, Toronto 1956.

Bennett, Geoffrey, *Nelson The Commander*, Charles Scribner's Sons, New York 1972.

Bethencourt Massieu, Antonio, *Patiño en la Política Exterior de Felipe V*, Valladolid 1954.

Bobb, Bernard E, *The Vice-Regency of Antonio María Bucareli in New Spain, 1771–1779*, University of Texas Press, Austin 1962.

*El Buque en la Armada Española*, Editorial Silex, Madrid 1981.

Carlan, J M, *Navios en Secuestro: La Escuadra Española del Océano en Brest 1789–1802*, Instituto Histórico de Marina, Madrid 1951.

Carmen, Sor, *El Almirante Sin Tacha y Sin Miedo: Vida del Capitán General de la Armada Española, Don Federico Gravina*, Editorial Esclicer, Cadiz 1957.

Carr, Sir Raymond, *Spain 1808–1939*, Clarendon Press, Oxford 1966.

Carter, Henry Rose, *Yellow Fever: An Epistemological and Historical Study of its Place and Origin*, Wilkins and Wilkins, Baltimore 1931.

Castiella, Fernando M, *Razones de España sobre Gibraltar*, Aguilar, Madrid 1966.

Caughey, John Walton, *Bernardo de Gálvez in Louisiana 1776–1783*, Pelican Publishing Co, Gretna 1972.

Charnock, John, *An History of Naval Architecture*, 3 vols, R Faulder, London 1800–02.

Chaunu, Pierre, *Seville et l'Atlantique 1504–1650*, 8 vols, Paris 1955–57.

Chevalier, E, *Histoire de la Marine Française sous le Consulat et l'Empire*, Hachette, Paris 1886.

Churruca, Cosmé Damián, Capitán de navío, *Instrucción sobre Punterias*, Imprenta Real, Madrid 1805.

Comisión de Estudios Historicos de Obras Públicas y Urbanismo, *Catálogo para la Exposición Puertos y Fortificaciones en América y Filipinas*, Madrid 1985.

Condeminas, Francisco, *La Gesta Hispánica en el Océano Atlántico*, Museo Marítimo de Barcelona 1948.

Conn, Stetson, *Gibraltar in British Diplomacy in the Eighteenth Century*, Yale University Press, New Haven 1942.

Corbett, Julian S, *The Campaign of Trafalgar*, Longmans & Co, London 1910.

Desbrière, Edouard, *La Campagne Maritime de 1805*, Paris 1933.

Díaz-Plaja, Fernando, *La Sociedad Española desde 1500 hasta Nuestros Dias*, Universidad de Puerto Rico, San Juan 1968.

Elliott, J H, *Imperial Spain 1469–1716*, Penguin Books, London 1983.

Fernández Duro, Cesáreo, Capitán de navío, *A la Mar Madera Libro Quinto de las Disquisiciones Nauticas*, Imprenta de Aribau y Cía, Madrid 1880.

Fernández Duro, Cesáreo, Capitán de navío, *Armada Española desde la Unión de los Reinos de Castilla y Aragon*, 15 vols, Museo Naval reprint, Madrid 1973.

Ferrer de Couto, José, *Historia del Combate Naval de Trafalgar*, Imprenta de D Wenceslao Ayguals de Izco, Madrid 1851.

Fraser, Edward, *The Enemy at Trafalgar*, Hodder and Stoughton, London 1906.

García-Baquero, Antonio Gonzalez, *Cádiz y el Atlántico (1717–1778)*, 2 vols, Escuela de Estudios Hispano-Americanos, Sevilla 1976.

Garrote, Francisco Antonio, Capitan de navío, *Recopilación para la Nueva Fábrica de Vexeles Españoles*, Madrid 1691.

Gaztañeta y de Iturribálzaga, Antonio de, Admiral, *Proporciones de las Medidas más Esenciales ... para a Fábrica de Navíos y Fragatas de Guerra, que Puedan Montar desde Ochenta Cañones hace Diez ...* Imprenta Phelipe Alonso, Madrid 1720.

Hamilton, Earl J, *War and Prices in Spain, 1650–1800*, Harvard University Press, Cambridge, Mass 1947.

Hargreaves-Mawdsley, William N, *Eighteenth Century Spain 1700–1788*, The Macmillan Press Ltd, London 1979.

Hargreaves-Mawdsley, William N, *Spain Under the Bourbons, 1700–1833*, University of South Carolina Press, Columbia 1973.

Harland, John, *Seamanship in the Age of Sail*, Conway Maritime Press Limited, London 1984.

Herr, Richard, *The Eighteenth Century Revolution in Spain*, Princeton University Press, Princeton 1958.

Herring, Hubert, *A History of Latin America from the Beginnings to the Present*, Alfred A Knopf, New York 1968.

Hodges, H W and Hughes, E A, *Select Naval Documents*, Cambridge University Press, Cambridge 1936.

Hull, Anthony H, *Charles III and the Revival of Spain*, University Presses of America, Washington, DC 1980.

Johnson, Victoria Stapells, *Corsairs of Santo Domingo: A Socio-Economic Study, 1718–1779*. Unpublished MA thesis for Dept of Political Science, University of Ottawa, Ottawa 1985.

Juan, Jorge, *Examen Marítimo Theórico Práctico, o Tratado de Mechánica Aplicado a la Construcción, Conocimiento y Manejo de los Navios y Demás Embarcaciones*, 2 vols, Imprenta Francisco Manuel de Mena, Madrid 1771–72.

Kany, C E, *Life and Manners in Madrid, 1750–1800*, AMS Press, New York 1970.

Kendrick, John, *The Men with Wooden Feet: The Spanish Exploration of the Pacific North-west*, NC Press Limited, Toronto 1985.

Kennedy, Paul M, *The Rise and Fall of British Naval Mastery*, B T Batsford Limited, London 1983.

Knight, R J B (Editor), *Guide to the Manuscripts in the National Maritime Museum*, Vol 1, Mansell, London 1977.

Lasso de la Vega, Jorge, *La Marina Real de España a Finés del Siglo XVIII y Principios del XIX*, 2 vols, Imprenta Viuda de Calero, Madrid 1856–1863.

Lavery, Brian, *The Ship of the Line, Volume II: Design, Construction and Fittings*, Conway Maritime Press Limited, London 1984.

Ledesma, Miranda, *Gibraltar La Roca de Calpe*, Ediciones del Movimiento, Madrid 1957.

Lemaître, Eduardo, *A Brief History of Cartagena*, Producciones Eduardo Lemaître y Co Ltda, Cartagena 1985.

Levi, Marrero, *Cuba, Economía y Sociedad del Monopolio Hacía La Libertad Comercial 1701–1763*, Editorial Playor, Madrid 1980.

Lewis, Michael, *The Navy of Britain: A Historical Portrait*, George Allen and Unwin Ltd, London 1948.

Lewis, Michael, *A Social History of the Royal Navy, 1793–1815*, George Allen and Unwin Ltd, London 1960.

Llobregat, Conde de, *Un General Español Cojo, Manco y Tuerto: Don Blas de Lezo, Natural de Pasajes*, Viuda de B Valverde, Irún 1927.

Madariaga, Salvador de, *The Fall of the Spanish American Empire*, Hollis & Carter, London 1947.

Mahan, Alfred Thayer, *The Influence of Sea Power Upon History 1660–1783*, Sagamore Press Inc, New York 1957.

Mante, Thomas Major, *The History of the Late War in North America and the Islands of the West Indies*, W Strahan and T Cadell, London 1772.

Marliani, Manuel, *Combate de Trafalgar Vindicación de la Armada Española*, Impreso de Orden Superior, Madrid 1850.

Marrers, Levi, *Cuba: Economía y Sociedad (Azúcar, Illustración y Conciencia, 1763–1868)*, IV Editorial Playor SA, Madrid 1985.

McDermott, John Francis, *The Spanish in the Mississippi Valley 1762–1804*, University of Illinois Press, Urbana 1974.

McGowan, Alan, *The Ship: The Century before Steam, The Development of the Sailing Ship 1700–1820*, HMSO and National Maritime Museum, Greenwich 1980.

McNeill, John Robert, *Atlantic Empires of France and Spain, Louisburg and Havana, 1700–1763*, The University of North Carolina Press, Chapel Hill 1985.

Menéndez Pidal, Ramón, *The Spaniards in Their History*, translated with an introduction by Walter Starkie, The Norton Library, New York 1966.

Merino Navarro, Jose P, *La Armada Española en el Siglo XVIII*, Fundación Universitária Española, Madrid 1981.

Ministerio de Asuntos Exteriores de España, *Negotiations on Gibraltar (A New Spanish Red Book)*, Madrid 1967.

Ministerio de Cultura de España, *Catálogo La Expedición Malaspina 1789–1794 Viaje a America y Oceania de las Corbetas 'Descubierta' y 'Atrevida'*, Centro Cultural de la Villa, Madrid 1984.

Ministerio de Cultura de España and Ministerio de Cultura de Cuba, *Catálogo de La Habana Vieja Mapas y Planos en Los Archivos de España*, Castillo de la Fuerza, Havana, Cuba 1985.

Ministerio de Transportes, Turismo y Comunicaciones and the Pavilion of Spain, 1986 World Exposition, Vancouver, *To the Totem Shore: The Spanish Presence on the Northwest Coast*, Ediciones El Viso, Madrid 1986.

Mitchell, Mairin, *Elcano The First Circumnavigator*, Herder Publications, London 1958.

Morton, H V, *A Stranger in Spain*, Methuen, London 1955.

Mühlmann, Rolf, *Die Reorganisation der Spanischen Kriegsmarine im 18 Jahrhundert*, Böhlau Verlag, Köln 1975.

Museo Naval, *Banderas de la Marina de España*, José Fernández Gaytán, Madrid 1985.

Naish, George B (Editor), *Nelson's Letters to His Wife*, Routledge and Kegan Paul (Navy Records Society), London 1958.

Nicolas, Sir Harris, *Dispatches and Letters of Vice Admiral Lord Viscount Nelson*, 7 vols, Henry Colburn, London 1840.

Novo y Colson, Pedro de, *Viaje Político-Científico Alrededor del Mundo por las Corbetas Descubierta y Atrevida al mando de los Capitanes de Navio D Alejandro Malaspina y Don José de Bustamente y Guerra desde 1789 a 1794*, Imprenta de la Viuda e Hijos de Abienzo, Madrid 1885.

Ogelsby, J C M, *War at Sea in the West Indies 1739–1748*, Doctoral thesis in history, University of Washington, Seattle 1963. Published on microfilm, University Microfilms International, Ann Arbor, Michigan 1963.

Olesa Muñido, Francisco-Felipe, *La Organización Naval de los Estados Mediterráneos y en Especial de España Durante Los Siglos XVI and XVII*, 2 vols, Editorial Naval, Madrid 1968.

Oman, Carola, *Nelson*, The Reprint Society, London 1950.

O'Scanlan, Timóteo, *Diccionário Marítimo Español*, Museo Naval, Madrid 1974.

Oyarzun, Javier, *Expediciones Españolas al Estrecho de Magallanes y Tierra del Fuego*, Ediciones Cultura Hispánica, Madrid 1972.

Parry, J H, *The Spanish Seaborne Empire*, Alfred A Knopf, New York 1966.

Pérez, Galdos Benito, *Trafalgar (Episodios Nacionales)*, Editorial Orbe, Santiago de Chile 1970.

Pérez-Maillana, Pablo Emilio Bueno, *Política Naval Española en el Atlántico 1700–1715*, Escuela de Estudios Hispano-Americanos, Sevilla 1982.

Petrie, Sir Charles, *King Charles III of Spain: An Enlightened Despot*, Constable, London 1971.

Portell-Vilá, Herminio, *Historia de Cuba en sus Relaciones con los Estados Unidos y España*, 4 vols, Havana 1938.

Ratto, Hector Paul, *La Expedición de Malaspina en el Siglo XVIII*, Editores Emecé SA, Buenos Aires 1945.

Richmond, Admiral Herbert W, *The Navy in the War of 1739–1748*, 3 vols, Cambridge University Press, Cambridge 1920.

Rivas, Fabal José Enrique, *Historia de la Infantería de Marina Española*, Editorial Naval, Madrid 1969.

Rodger, N A M, *The Wooden World: An Anatomy of the Georgian Navy*, Collins, London 1986.

Rodríquez, Villa Antonio, *Don Cenón de Somodevilla Marqués de la Ensenada*, Librería de M Murillo, Madrid 1878.

Rodríquez, Villa Antonio, *Patiño y Campillo, Reseña Histórica Biografía de Estos Dos Ministros de Felipe V*, Madrid 1882.

Sariego del Castillo, J L, *De Sevilla a Vera Cruz, Historia de la Marina Española en la América Septentrional y Pacífico*, Sevilla 1975.

Schurz, William Lytle, *The Manila Galleon*, E P Dutton & Company, New York 1939.

Thomas, Lord Hugh, *Cuba, or the Pursuit of Freedom*, Eyre & Spottiswoode, London 1971.

Thurman, Michael E, *The Naval Department of San Blas: New Spain's Bastion for Alta California and Nootka 1767 to 1798*, The Arthur H Clark Company, Glendale, California 1967.

Tute, Warren, *The True Glory: The Story of the Royal Navy over a Thousand Years*, Macdonald, London 1984.

Universidad Politécnica de Madrid, *Jorge Juan y La Marina Española del Siglo XVIII*, II Centenário de las Enseñanzas de Ingeniero Naval, Madrid 1973.

Uztariz, Geronymo de, *Theórica y Práctica de Comercio y de Marina*, A Sanz, Madrid 1742. Reprinted by the Editorial Aguilar, Madrid 1968.

Vernet, Ginés Juan, *Historia de Ciencia Española*, Editorial Instituto de España, Madrid 1975.

Villiers, Alan, *Captain James Cook*, Charles Scribner's Sons, New York 1964.

Villiers, Patrick, *La Marine de Louis XVI: Vaisseaux et Frégates de Choiseul a Sartine*, Paris 1983.

Wagner, Henry R, *Spanish Explorations in the Strait of Juan de Fuca*, Santa Ana Fine Arts Press, 1933.

Walder, David, *Nelson*, The Dial Press/James Wade, New York 1978.

Walker, Geoffrey J, *Spanish Politics and Imperial Trade 1700–1789*, Indiana University Press, Bloomington 1979.

Wilgus, Curtis A, *Latin America, Spain and Portugal: An Annotated Guide to the Books Published in the USA, 1954, 1974 and 1977*.

de Ybarra y Berge, Javier, *De California a Alaska Historia de un Descubrimiento*, Madrid 1945.

# Ships of the line of the Spanish Navy (1714–1825)

**Prepared by C de Saint Hubert**

| Name | Also called | Service | Ld. | Guns | Yard | Fate | Remarks |
|------|-------------|---------|-----|------|------|------|---------|
| 1 SANTA ROSA | – | 1677-1718 | 1677 | 56 | ? | Captured by the British at Cape Passaro, taken to Minorca and laid up (1718). In 1731, Britain offered to return the ships captured at Cape Passaro but they were found to be rotten and BU | One of the few ships left over from the reign of Carlos II |
| 2 RUBI (1) | – | 1700-1727 | ? | 50 | ? | Wrecked off S coast of Cuba (1727) | Acquired 1700 |
| 3 GUADALUPE | – | 1703-1724 | ? | 50/58 | Tallapiedra (near Havana) | Wrecked off Sto Domingo (1724) | Acquired 1703 |
| 4 REAL MAZI | El Real | 1714-1718 | ? | 60 | ? | Captured by the British at Cape Passaro (1718) etc (see No 1) | Acquired 1714 |
| 5 N S de BEGOÑA | – | 1714-1724 | 1703 | 54/70 | Genoa | Stricken 1724 | Acquired Genoa 1714 |
| 6 PEIBO del ler SAN FRANCISCO | | 1714-1716 | ? | 60 | Genoa | Wrecked off Patagonia (1716) | Acquired Genoa 1714 |
| 7 PEMBROKE | | 1714–1718 | 1694 (?) | 60 | Deptford (England) | Wrecked in Rio de la Plata (1718) | Acquired Genoa 1714 |
| 8 LANFRANCO (1) | – | 1714-1716 | ? | 60 | ? | Wrecked off Patagonia (1716) | Acquired from private owners 1716 |
| 9 N S de LAS VINAS | – | 1715-1717 | ? | 60 | ? | Wrecked? | Acquired or built? |
| 10 SAN PEDRO | – | 1716-1718 | 1716 | 60 | Pasajes | Wrecked in Gulf of Taranto (12/1718) | 1st ship built Pasajes |
| 11 HERMIONE | | 1716-1721 | ? | 50 | ? | Stricken 1721 | Acquired 1716 |
| 12 SAN ISIDRO (1) | – | 1716-1718 | 1716 | 50 | Pasajes | Captured by the British at Cape Passaro (1718), etc (see No 1) | |
| 13 SANTA ISABEL (1) | – | 1716-1718 | 1716 | 60 | Pasajes | Ditto | |
| 14 SAN FELIPE (1) | El Real | 1716-1718 | 1716 | 70/80 | S Feliu de Guixols | Captured by the British at Cape Passaro (1718). Blew up while being towed to Minorca | |
| 15 SAN CARLOS (1) | – | 1716-1718 | 1716 | 60 | Santander | Captured by the British at Cape Passaro (1718), etc (see No 1) | |
| 16 HERCULES (1) | – | 1716-1718 | ? | 50 | ? | Stricken 1718 | Acquired 1716 |
| 17 SAN LUIS (1) | – | 1717-1720 | 1717 | 60 | Orio | Wrecked in America (1720) | 1st ship built at Orio |
| 18 SAN FERNANDO (1) | – | 1717-1719 | 1717 | 60 | Orio | Scuttled at Messina to prevent capture by the Austrians (1719) | |

| Name | Also called | Service | Ld. | Guns | Yard | Fate | Remarks |
|---|---|---|---|---|---|---|---|
| 19 PRINCIPE DE ASTURIAS (1) | *Cumberland* (former name) | 1717-1718 | 1695 | 70 | Bursledon (England) | Ex-British *Cumberland* (80). Captured by the French 1707, served in their Navy under the same name. Sold to Genoa 1715. Sold to Spain 1717. Captured by the British at Cape Passaro 1718. Sold to Austria 1720. Based at Naples and renamed *San Carlos*. BU 1733. This ship thus served under 5 flags! | |
| 20 SAN JUAN BAUTISTA (1) | – | 1718-1719 | 1717 (?) | 60 | Palermo | Wrecked off Italian coast (1719) | A Piedmontese warship captured by the Spanish at Palermo (1718) |
| 21 Sta ROSA PALERMO | *Sta Rosalia* | 1718-1719 | 1717 (?) | 60 | Palermo | Scuttled at Mesina (1719) etc (see No 18) | Ditto |
| 22 TRIUNFO | – | 1718-1719 | 1717 (?) | 60/66 | Palermo | Ditto | Ditto |
| 23 CAMBI | – | 1718-1725 | 1718 | 60/66 | S Feliu de Guixols | Accidentally burnt in Gulf of Mexico (1725) | |
| 24 CATALAN | – | 1719-1731 | 1719 | 62 | S Feliu de Guixols | Stricken 1731 | |
| 24 CONDE DE TOLOSA | *San Jose* | 1719-1724 | ? | 56/58 | Toulon | Wrecked off Sto Domingo (1724) | Acquired 1719 |
| 26 CONQUIST-ADOR (1) | – | 1720-1738 | ? | 62/64 | Rotherhithe (England) | Stricken 1738 | British *Gloucester* (60), captured by the French 1709, sold at Genoa 1711, resold to Spain 1720 |
| 27 SAN FRANCISCO | – | 1720-1739 | ? | 62 | Genoa | Wrecked at Veracruz (1739) | Acquired Genoa 1720 |
| 28 ESTRELLA DEL MAR | – | 1720-1730 | ? | 64 | Genoa | Stricken 1730 | Acquired Genoa 1720 |
| 29 LANFRANCO (2) | – | 1720-1739 | ? | 62 | ? | Wrecked at Veracruz (1739) | Acquired at Genoa 1720 |
| 30 SAN FOIT | – | 1721-1722 | ? | 60 | Amsterdam (?) | Stricken 1722 (rotten) | Acquired Amsterdam 1721 |
| 31 GALLO INDIANO | – | 1723-1733 | 1723 (?) | 58 | Santander (?) | Wrecked off N coast of Cuba (1733) | Acquired 1723 |
| 32 POTENCIA | – | 1723-1738 | ? | 58 | ? | Stricken 1738 | Acquired 1723 |
| 33 SAN FERNANDO (2) | – | 1723-1748 | 1723 | 62 | Guarnizo | Hulked 1746 | 1st ship built at Guarnizo |
| 34 SAN ESTEBAN | – | 1723-1745 | 1723 | 50 | Guarnizo | Stricken 1745 | |
| 35 SAN LUIS (2) | – | 1723-1745 | 1723 | 62/66 | Guarnizo | Stricken 1745 | |
| 36 GRAN PRINCESA de los CIELOS | – | 1723-1726 | ? | 80 | | Wrecked off N coast of S America (1726) | Acquired 1723 |
| 37 SAN CARLOS (2) | – | 1724-1741 | 1724 | 66 | Guarnizo | Scuttled at Cartagena de Indias to block harbour entrance (1741) | |
| 38 SAN FRANCISCO JAVIER (1) | – | 1724-1749 | 1724 | 50/52 | Guarnizo | Hulked 1749 | |
| 39 SAN JUAN | – | 1724-1741 | 1724 | 54/60 | Havana | Stricken 1741 | 1st ship built at Havana |
| 40 INFANTE (1) | – | 1724-1733 | ? | 60 | Genoa | Wrecked off N coast Cuba (1733) | Acquired Genoa 1724 |
| 41 SAN FELIPE (2) | – | 1726-1741 | 1726 | 70 | Guarnizo | Scuttled at Cartagena de Indias (1741), etc (see No 37) | |

| Name | Also called | Service | Ld. | Guns | Yard | Fate | Remarks |
|---|---|---|---|---|---|---|---|
| 42 INCENDIO | *San Lorenzo* | 1726-1739 | 1726 | 58 | Havana | Wrecked at Veracruz (1739) | |
| 43 SAN FRANCISCO de ASIS (1) | – | 1726-1735 | ? | 52 | Holland | Hulked 1735 | Dutch privateer captured off N coast of S America by *Potencia* (see No 32) (5/1726) |
| 44 SAN ANTONIO (1) | – | 1727-1750 | 1727 | 60 | Guarnizo | Stricken 1750 | |
| 45 RETIRO | *San Geronimo* | 1727-1737 | 1727 | 54 | Havana | Sold 1737 | |
| 46 CONSTANTE (1) | *San Dionisio* | 1727–1727 | 1727 | 60 | Havana | Wrecked in Gulf of Mexico on her 1st Commission | |
| 47 ROSA | – | 1727-1736 | 1727 | 56 | Pasajes | Wrecked at Veracruz (1736) | |
| 48 PALOMA INDIANA | – | 1727-1745 | 1727 | 52 | ? | Stricken 1745 | Acquired 1727 |
| 49 FUERTE | *N S de Guadalupe* | 1728-1739 | 1728 | 60 | Havana | Sold 1739 | |
| 50 SANTA ANA (1) | – | 1729-1745 | 1729 | 70 | Guarnizo | Stricken 1745 | |
| 51 SANTIAGO | – | 1729-1745 | 1729 | 60 | Guarnizo | Stricken 1745 | |
| 52 REINA (1) | – | 1729-1743 | 1729 | 70 | Guarnizo | Stricken 1743 | |
| 53 SANTA ISABEL (2) | | 1730-1747 | 1730 | 80 | Guarnizo | Stricken 1747 | |
| 54 SAN ISIDORO (1) | – | 1730-1742 | 1730 | 62 | Guarnizo | Burnt off Corsica to prevent capture by the British (1743) | |
| 55 CASTILLA (1) | – | 1730-1736 | 1730 | 62 | Guarnizo | Stricken 1736 | |
| 56 ANDALUCIA | *N S del Carmen* | 1730-1740 | 1730 | 62 | Havana | Wrecked off N coast of Cuba (1740) | |
| 57 SANTA TERESA | | 1730-1743 | 1730 | 60/62 | Guarnizo | Stricken 1743 | |
| 58 HERCULES (2) | – | 1729-1749 | 1729 | 60 | Puntales (Cadiz) | Stricken 1749 | 1st ship built in the Cadiz area |
| 59 VICTORIA | – | 1730-1738 | 1730 | 50 | Guarnizo | Wrecked off Veracruz (1738) | |
| 60 GALICIA (1) | – | 1730-1741 | 1730 | 60/70 | La Graña (near Ferrol) | Scuttled at Cartagena de Indias to block the the harbour entrance (1741). Raised by the British, *Galicia Prize* then burned by them when they raised the siege of Cartagena | 1st ship built in the Ferrol area |
| 61 PRINCESA (1) | – | 1730-1741 | 1730 | 70 | Guarnizo | Captured off Finisterre (19.4.1740) after a long and gallant fight against *Oxford* (70), *Kent* (70) and *Lennox* (70); became *Princessa* (70) (hulk 1760, sold 1784) | |
| 62 PRINCIPE (1) | – | 1730-1746 | 1730 | 70 | Guarnizo | Stricken 1746 | |
| 63 CONQUIST-ADOR (2) | – | 1730-1741 | 1730 | 62 | Havana | Scuttled at Cartagena de Indias (1741), etc. (see No 37) | |
| 64 RUBI (2) | – | 1730-1733 | 1730 | 60 | Pasajes | Wrecked off Florida (1733) | |
| 65 GENOVES | – | 1730-1740 | ? | 54 | Genoa | Wrecked off Yucatan (1740) | Acquired Genoa 1730 |

| Name | Also called | Service | Ld. | Guns | Yard | Fate | Remarks |
|---|---|---|---|---|---|---|---|
| 66 CARMEN | – | 1730-1764 | 1730 | 64 | Havana | BU 1764 | |
| 67 FAMA VOLANTE | – | 1730-1740 | ? | 52 | Genoa | Stricken 1740 | Acquired Genoa 1730 |
| 68 LEON | – | 1731-1749 | 1731 | 70 | La Graña (near Ferrol) | Stricken 1749 | |
| 69 GUIPUZCOA | – | 1731-1741 | 1731 | 60/64 | Pasajes | Wrecked off Sta Catalina Is (Brazil) (1741) | |
| 70 GALGA | – | 1731-1750 | 1731 | 56 | Puntales (Cadiz) | Wrecked off the coast of Virginia (1750) | |
| 71 REAL FELIPE | – | 1732-1750 | 1732 | 112 | Guarnizo | Stricken 1750 | The first Spanish three-decker. |
| 72 CONSTANTE (2) | San Cristobal | 1732-1746 | 1732 | 64/66 | Havana | Sold 1746 | |
| 73 AFRICA (1) | San Jose | 1732-1741 | 1732 | 64 | Havana | Scuttled at Cartagena de Indias (1741), etc. | |
| 74 REAL FAMILIA | – | 1732-1750 | 1732 | 60 | Carraca (Cadiz) | BU 1750 | 1st ship built Carraca |
| 75 EUROPA (1) | N S del Pilar | 1734-1762 | 1734 | 64 | Havana | Scuttled at Havana to block the harbour entrance (1762) | |
| 76 ASIA (1) | N S de Loreto | 1735-1746 | 1735 | 64 | Havana | Stricken 1746 | |
| 77 NUEVA ESPAÑA (1) | – | 1735-1752 | 1735 | 60 | Coatzacoalcos (Mexico) | Sold 1752 | The only s/l built in Mexico |
| 78 AMERICA (1) | N S de Belen | 1736-1762 | 1736 | 64 | Havana | Captured at Havana (1762) by the British. Not taken over. | |
| 79 ESPERANZA | – | 1736-1747 | 1736 | 50 | Havana | Stricken 1747 | |
| 80 DRAGON (1) | Sta Rosa de Lima | 1737-1741 | 1737 | 64 | Havana | Scuttled at Cartagena de Indias (1741) (See No 37) | |
| 81 CASTILLA (2) | Sto Cristo de Burgos | 1737-1747 | 1737 | 60 | Havana | Wrecked on Spanish Mediterranean coast (1747) | |
| 82 INVENCIBLE (1) | San Ignacio | 1739-1741 | 1739 | 70 | Havana | Accidentally burnt at Havana (1741) | |
| 83 GLORIOSO (1) | N S de Belen (2) | 1739-1747 | 1739 | 70 | Havana | Captured (19.10.1747) at the end of the 3rd action of this ship alone against separate British Squadrons: off Flores (25.7.47), off Finisterre (14.8.47) and off Cape St Vincent (8.10.47). Not taken over by the RN | |
| 84 BIZARRO | N S de Guadalupe | 1739-1759 | 1739 | 50 | Havana | Stricken 1759 | |
| 85 PODER | – | 1740-1744 | ? | 66 | ? | Captured by the British at Cape Sicié, recaptured by the Spanish, then burned to prevent recapture by the British (1744) | Acquired 1740 |
| 86 SOBERBIO (1) | – | 1740-1746 | ? | 66 | ? | Sold 1746 | Acquired 1740 |
| 87 BRILLANTE (1) | – | 1740-1746 | ? | 66 | ? | Sold 1746 | Acquired 1740 |
| 88 NEPTUNO (1) | – | 1740-1748 | ? | 66 | ? | Sold 1748 | Acquired 1740 |
| 89 HALCON | – | 1740-1748 | ? | 60 | ? | Sold 1748 | Acquired 1740 |
| 90 ORIENTE (1) | – | 1740-1746 | ? | 64 | ? | Sold 1746 | Acquired 1740 |
| 91 DRAGON (2) | – | 1742-1783 | 1742 | 60 | Havana | Wrecked in West Indies (5/83) | |

| Name | Also called | Service | Ld. | Guns | Yard | Fate | Remarks |
|------|-------------|---------|-----|------|------|------|---------|
| 92 AVE de GRACIA | – | 1742-1744 | ? | 50 | ? | Sold 1744 | Acquired 1742 |
| 93 NUEVA ESPAÑA (2) | – | 1743-1752 | 1743 | 70 | Havana | Sold 1752 | |
| 94 REINA (2) | – | 1743-1762 | 1743 | 70 | Havana | Captured by the British at Havana (1762) British *Reina* (74) (sold 1775) | |
| 95 INVENCIBLE (2) | *San Jose* | 1744-1750 | 1744 | 70 | Havana | Accidentally burned at Ferrol (1750) | |
| 96 CONQUIST-ADOR (3) | *Jesus, Maria y Jose* | 1745-1748 | 1745 | 64 | Havana | Captured by the British Havana (1748). Not taken over by the RN | |
| 97 SAN FELIPE (3) | – | 1745-1761 | 1745 | 70 | Guarnizo | Stricken 1761 | |
| 98 AFRICA (2) | *San Francisco de Asis* | 1746-1748 | 1746 | 70 | Havana | Damaged in action off Havana and burned to prevent capture by the British (1748) | |
| 99 VENCEDOR (1) | *Sto Tomas* | 1746-1750 | 1746 | 70 | Havana | Accidentally burned at Ferrol (1750) | |
| 100 TIGRE | *San Lorenzo* | 1747-1762 | 1747 | 70/74 | Havana | Captured by the British at Havana (1762). British *Tigre* (74) (sold 1784) | |
| 101 RAYO | *San Padro* | 1749-1805 | 1749 | 80 | Havana | Damaged at Trafalgar. Stranded, near Rota, in the storm which followed the battle (1805) | |
| 102 FENIX | *San Alejandro* | 1749-1780 | 1749 | 80 | Havana | Captured by the British in Battle of Cape Sta Maria (1780). British *Gibraltar* (80) (powder hulk 1813, lazaretto 1824, BU 1836) | |
| 103 PRINCESA (2) | *Sta Barbara* | 1750-1780 | 1750 | 74 | Havana | Captured as above. British *Princessa* (hulk 1784, BU 1809) | |
| 104 GALICIA (2) | *Santiago el Mayor* | 1750-1797 | 1750 | 70/74 | Havana | Stricken 1797 | |
| 105 INFANTE (2) | *S Luis Gonzaga* | 1750-1762 | 1750 | 70/74 | Havana | Captured by the British at Havana (1762). British *Infanta* (74) (sold 1775) | |
| 106 SAN FERNANDO (3) | – | 1751-1758 | 1751 | 70 | Ferrol | Wrecked? | 1st s/l built at Ferrol |
| 107 CASTILLA (3) | – | 1751-1771 | 1751 | 64 | Ferrol | Wrecked at Veracruz (1771) | |
| 108 ASIA (2) | – | 1752-1762 | 1752 | 62/64 | Ferrol | Scuttled at Havana to block the harbour entrance (1762) | |
| 109 AFRICA (3) | – | 1752-1809 | 1752 | 74 | Cadiz | BU 1809 | |
| 110 ORIENTE (2) | *San Diego de Alcala* | 1753-1806 | 1753 | 74 | Ferrol | Stricken 1806 | |
| 111 EOLO | *San Juan de Dios* | 1753-1760 | 1753 | 68 | Ferrol | Stricken 1760 | |
| 112 SEPTENT-RION | – | 1751-1783 | 1751 | 60 | Cartagena | Wrecked off Velez Malaga (1783) | 1st ship built at Cartagena |
| 113 TRIDENTE | – | 1754-1771 | 1754 | 74 | Cartagena | Stricken 1771 | |
| 114 NEPTUNO (2) | *San Justo* | 1754-1762 | 1754 | 68 | Ferrol | Scuttled at Havana to block harbour entrance (1762) | |
| 115 MAGNANIMO | *San Pastor* | 1754-1794 | 1754 | 74 | Ferrol | Wrecked off Galicia (Spain) (1794) | |
| 116 AQUILON | *San Damaso* | 1754-1762 | 1754 | 68 | Ferrol | Captured by the British at Havana (1762) British *Aquilon* later *Moro* 74. Broken up 1770 | |
| 117 GALLARDO | *San Juan de Sahagun* | 1754-1797 | 1754 | 74 | Ferrol | Burnt at Trinidad to prevent capture by the British (1797) | |
| 118 BRILLANTE (2) | *San Dionisio* | 1754-1790 | 1754 | 74 | Ferrol | Accidentally burnt at Cartagena 1790 | |

| Name | Also called | Service | Ld. | Guns | Yard | Fate | Remarks |
|---|---|---|---|---|---|---|---|
| 119 PODEROSO | – | 1754-1779 | 1754 | 70/74 | Guarnizo | Wrecked off the Azores 1779 | |
| 120 SERIO | – | 1754-1805 | 1754 | 74 | Guarnizo | Broken up 1805 | |
| 121 SOBERBIO (2) | – | 1754-1764 | 1754 | 68/74 | Guarnizo | Stricken 1764 | |
| 122 FIRME (1) | – | 1754-1805 | 1754 | 74 | Carraca | Captured by the British in action off Finisterre (1805). British *Firme* (74). Prison hulk 1806, stricken 1810. BU 1814 | |
| 123 AQUILES | – | 1754-1790 | 1754 | 74 | Carraca | Stricken 1790 | |
| 124 ARROGANTE | – | 1754-1797 | 1754 | 68 | Guarnizo | Burned at Trinidad to prevent capture by the British 1797 | |
| 125 ATLANTE (later, ATLAS) | – | 1754-1801 1808-1817 | 1754 | 74 | Cartagena | Transferred to France 1801, renamed *Atlas* (1803). Captured by the Spanish at Vigo 1808, name unchanged, BU 1817 | |
| 126 TERRIBLE | – | 1754-1811 | 1754 | 74 | Cartagena | Stricken 1811 | |
| 127 VENCEDOR (2) | San Julian | 1755-1806 1808-1810 | 1755 | 74 | Ferrol | Transferred to France 1806 in exchange for *Argonaute* (see No 221), renamed *Argonaute*. Captured by the Spanish at Cadiz (1808), renamed *Vencedor*. Wrecked off Sardinia 1810 | |
| 128 GLORIOSO (2) | San Francisco Javier | 1755-1818 | 1755 | 74 | Ferrol | BU 1818 | |
| 129 GUERRERO | San Raimundo | 1755-1844 | 1755 | 74 | Ferrol | BU 1844 | Was 89 years old when broken up! |
| 130 HECTOR | San Bernardo | 1755-1770 | 1755 | 68/74 | Ferrol | BU 1790 | |
| 131 SOBERANO (2) | San Gregorio | 1755-1762 | 1755 | 74 | Ferrol | Captured by the British at Havana (1762). British *Soberano* 74. BU 1770 | |
| 132 DICHOSO | – | 1756-1781 | 1756 | 70/74 | Ferrol | Stricken 1781 | |
| 133 DILIGENTE | – | 1756-1780 | 1756 | 68/74 | Ferrol | Captured by the British at Cape Santa Maria (1780). British *Diligence* (68). BU 1784 | |
| 134 TRIUNFANTE | – | 1756-1795 | 1756 | 70/74 | Ferrol | Wrecked off Rosas (Spain) 1795 | |
| 135 MONARCA (1) | – | 1756-1780 | 1756 | 70/74 | Ferrol | Captured by the British at Cape Santa Maria (1780). British *Monarca* (68). Sold 1791 | |
| 136 HERCULES (3) | – | 1756-1780 | 1756 | 68/74 | Guarnizo | BU 1780 | |
| 137 VICTORIOSO | – | 1756-1776 | 1756 | 74 | Guarnizo | BU 1776 | |
| 138 CONSTANTE (3) | – | 1756-1790 | 1756 | 68 | Guarnizo | Stricken 1790 | |
| 139 CONTENTO | – | 1758-1759 | 1756 | 70 | Guarnizo | Stricken 1759 | |
| 140 ESPANA (1) | – | 1757-1807 | 1757 | 68 | Carraca | BU 1807 | |
| 141 PERUANO | – | 1757-1790 | 1757 | 50 | Guayaquil | Sold 1790 | The only ship of the line built on the Pacific coast of Spanish America |
| 142 CONQUIST-ADOR (4) | – | 1758-1762 | 1758 | 74 | Carraca | Captured by the British at Havana (1762). British *Conquistador* 74. Stricken 1782. | |
| 143 CAMPEON | – | 1758-1778 | 1758 | 60 | Ferrol | Hulked 1778 | |
| 144 ASTUTO | San Eustaquio | 1759-1810 | 1759 | 58/60 | Havana | BU 1810 | |
| 145 PRINCIPE (2) | – | 1759-1776 | 1759 | 74 | Guarnizo | Sold 1776 | |
| 146 SAN GENARO (1) | – | 1761-1762 | 1761 | 60 | Havana | Captured by the British at Havana (1762). British *San Genaro* 60. Lost 1763 | |
| 147 SAN ANTONIO (2) | – | 1761-1762 | 1761 | 60 | Havana | Captured by the British at Havana (1762). British *San Antonio* 64. Sold 1775 | |
| 148 VELASCO (1) | – | 1764-1801 | 1764 | 74 | Cartagena | BU 1801 | |
| 149 BUEN CONSEJO | – | 1764-1768 | ? | 60 | Genoa (?) | Sold 1768 | Acquired Genoa 1764 |

| Name | Also called | Service | Ld. | Guns | Yard | Fate | Remarks |
|------|-------------|---------|-----|------|------|------|---------|
| 150 SAN CARLOS (3) | – | 1765-1819 | 1765 | 94 (later 112) | Havana | BU 1819 | Built as 2-decker (94) converted to 3-decker (112) at Cartagena (1801) |
| 151 SAN FERNANDO (4) | – | 1765-1815 | 1765 | 94 | Havana | Sold 1815 | |
| 152 SAN GENARO (2) | – | 1765-1801 | 1765 | 74 | Cartagena | Transferred to France 1801, renamed *Ulysse*, later *Tourville*. Stricken 1822. | |
| 153 SAN JUAN NEPO- MUCENO | – | 1766-1805 | 1766 | 74 | Guarnizo | Captured by the British at Trafalgar (1805). British *San Juan* 74. Receiving ship 1808, sold 1818. | |
| 154 SAN PASCUAL | – | 1766-1797 | 1766 | 74 | Guarnizo | BU 1797 | |
| 155 AMERICA (2) | *Santiago* | 1766-1823 | 1766 | 68 | Havana | BU 1823 | |
| 156 SAN LUIS (3) | – | 1767-1789 | 1767 | 94 | Havana | BU 1789 | |
| 157 SANTA ISABEL (3) | – | 1767-1803 | 1767 | 74 | Havana | BU 1803 | |
| 158 S FRANCISCO de ASIS (2) | – | 1767-1805 | 1767 | 74 | Guarnizo | Damaged at Trafalgar, wrecked in the storm which followed (1805) | |
| 159 SAN JULIAN (1) | – | 1768-1780 | 1768 | 74 | Ferrol | Captured by the British at Cape Santa Maria, recaptured by her crew but wrecked two days later | |
| 160 SAN ISIDRO (2) | – | 1768-1797 | 1768 | 74 | Ferrol | Captured by the British at Cape St Vincent (1797). British *San Isidro* (74) (prison hulk 1798, sold 1814) | |
| 161 SAN FRANCISCO de PAULA (1) | – | 1768-1784 | 1768 | 70/74 | Havana | Accidentally burned at Carraca (1784) | |
| 162 SAN JOSE (1) | – | 1768-1780 | 1768 | 74/76 | Havana | Wrecked off Brest (1780) | |
| 163 SAN LORENZO | – | 1768-1815 | 1768 | 74 | Guarnizo | BU 1815 | |
| 164 SAN VICENTE | – | 1768-1797 | 1768 | 80 | Cartagena | Burned at Trinidad to prevent capture by the British 1797 | |
| 165 SAN AGUSTIN | – | 1768-1776 1777-1805 | 1768 | 74/80 | Guarnizo | Captured by the Portugese off Rio de la Plata (1776), returned by peace treaty (1777). Captured by the British at Trafalgar and burned by them (1805) | |
| 166 SANTO DOMINGO (1) | – | 1769-1780 | 1769 | 74 | Guarnizo | Blew up at Cape Santa Maria (1780) (1 survivor!) | |
| 167 SANTISIMA TRINIDAD | – | 1769-1805 | 1769 | 120 (later 136) | Havana | Captured by the British at Trafalgar, sank in the storm (1805) | Built as 3-decker (120), converted to 4-decker (136) at Cadiz 1796. The world's only 4-decker |
| 168 SAN NICOLAS | – | 1769-1797 | 1769 | 80 | Cartagena | Captured by the British at Cape St Vincent (1797). British *San Nicholas*. Prison hulk 1800, sold 1814. | |
| 169 SAN PEDRO APOSTOL | – | 1770-1801 | 1770 | 74 | Ferrol | Stricken 1801 | |
| 170 SAN PABLO (renamed SOBERANO (3) 1814) | – | 1771-1854 | 1771 | 74 | Ferrol | BU 1854 | Served 83 years! |
| 171 SAN PEDRO ALCANTARA (1) | – | 1771-1786 | 1771 | 68 | Havana | Wrecked off Peniche (Portugal) (1786) | |
| 172 SAN JOAQUIN | – | 1771-1817 | 1771 | 74 | Cartagena | Broken up 1817 | |

| Name | Also called | Service | Ld. | Guns | Yard | Fate | Remarks |
|------|-------------|---------|-----|------|------|------|---------|
| 173 SAN RAFAEL | – | 1772-1805 | 1772 | 80 | Havana | Captured by the British at Cape Finisterre (1805). British *San Rafael* (80). Prison hulk 1808, sold 1810 | |
| 174 SAN JUAN BAUTISTA (2) | – | 1772-1809 | 1772 | 74 | Cartagena | Stricken 1809 | |
| 175 SAN GABRIEL | – | 1772-1808 | 1772 | 74 | Ferrol | Broken up 1808 | |
| 176 SAN MIGUEL | – | 1773-1783 | 1773 | 74 | Havana | Stranded in storm near Gibraltar (1782) during the Great Siege, captured by the British. British *San Miguel* (74). Sold 1791. | |
| 177 ANGEL de la GUARDA | – | 1773-1810 | 1773 | 74 | Cartagena | BU 1810 | |
| 178 SAN EUGENIO | – | 1775-1804 | 1775 | 80 | Ferrol | BU 1804 | |
| 179 SAN RAMON | – | 1775-1810 | 1775 | 68 | Havana | Wrecked Cadiz Bay 1810 | |
| 180 SAN DAMASO | – | 1776-1797 | 1776 | 74 | Cartagena | Scuttled to block harbour entrance at Trinidad, later raised by the British. British *San Damaso* (74). Prison hulk 1800, sold 1814 | |
| 181 SAN ISIDORO (2) | – | 1776-1794 | 1776 | 64 | Castellammare | A Neapolitan warship exchanged (together with No 182) in 1776, for 3 Spanish frigates: *Santa Teresa*, *Santa Dorotea* and *Santa Clara*. Wrecked off Catalonia (1794) | |
| 182 SAN LEANDRO (1) | – | 1776-1784 | ? | 64 | Castellammare | See above. Sold 1784 | |
| 183 PURISMA CONCEP-CION | – | 1779-1810 | 1779 | 112 | Ferrol | Wrecked Cadiz Bay 1810 | A 3-decker |
| 184 MIÑO | – | 1779-1814 | 1779 | 54 | Ferrol | BU 1814 | |
| 185 SAN JUSTO (2) | – | 1779-1824 | 1779 | 74 | Cartagena | BU 1824 | |
| 186 CASTILLA (4) | – | 1780-1808 | 1780 | 64 | Ferrol | Hulked 1808. Wrecked Cadiz Bay 1810 | |
| 187 SAN FELIPE APSOTOL | – | 1781-1794 | 1781 | 64 | Ferrol | Sold to Dutch Navy 1794, renamed *Overijssel* (64/68), captured by the British 1795. British *Overijssel* (64). Hulk 1810, sold 1822 | |
| 188 SANTO DOMINGO (2) | – | 1781-1807 | 1781 | 64 | Cartagena | BU 1807 | |
| 189 SAN JULIAN (2) | – | 1781-1830 | 1781 | 60 | Cartagena | BU 1830 | |
| 190 SAN FERMIN | – | 1782-1808 | 1782 | 74 | Pasajes | BU 1808 | |
| 191 SAN SEBASTIAN | – | 1783-1799 | 1783 | 74 | Pasajes | Transferred to France 1799 in exchange for *Censeur* (see No 220), renamed *Alliance*. Stricken 1807 | |
| 192 SAN JOSE (2) | – | 1783-1797 | 1783 | 112 | Ferrol | Captured by the British at Cape St Vincent (1797). British *San Josef* (112). Hulk 1836, BU 1849. | A 3-decker |
| 193 SANTA ANA (2) | – | 1784-1812 | 1784 | 112 | Ferrol | Stricken 1812 | A 3-decker |
| 194 BAHAMA | *San Cristobal* | 1784-1805 | 1784 | 74 | Havana | Captured by the British at Trafalgar (1805). British *Bahama* (74). Prison hulk 1806. BU 1814 | |
| 195 SAN ILDEFONSO | – | 1785-1805 | 1785 | 74 | Cartagena | Captured by the British at Trafalgar (1805). British *San Ildefonso* (74). Depot hulk 1808, BU 1816 | |

| Name | Also called | Service | Ld. | Guns | Yard | Fate | Remarks |
|------|-------------|---------|-----|------|------|------|---------|
| 196 SAN ANTONIO (3) | – | 1785-1801 | 1785 | 74 | Cartagena | Transferred to France 1801, renamed *Saint Antoine*. Captured by the British 1801, renamed *San Antonio* (74). Prison hulk 1808, sold 1828. | |
| 197 CONDE de REGLA | – | 1786-1811 | 1786 | 112 | Havana | BU 1811 | A 3-decker |
| 198 MEJICANO | *San Hipolito* | 1786-1815 | 1786 | 112 | Havana | Sold 1815 | A 3-decker |
| 199 SALVADOR del MUNDO | – | 1786-1797 | 1786 | 112 | Havana | Captured by the British at St Vincent (1797). British *Salvador del Mundo* (112). Prison hulk 1798. BU 1815 | A 3-decker |
| 200 SAN LEANDRO (2) | – | 1787-1812 | 1787 | 64 | Ferrol | Stricken 1812 | |
| 201 REAL CARLOS | – | 1787-1801 | 1787 | 112 | Havana | Blew up in night action off Gibraltar 1801, 22 survivors | A 3-decker |
| 202 SAN FULGENCIO | – | 1787-1814 | 1787 | 64/68 | Cartagena | Stricken 1814 | |
| 203 SAN TELMO | – | 1788-1819 | 1788 | 74 | Ferrol | Lost with all hands off Cape Horn (1819) | |
| 204 S PEDRO ALCANTARA (2) | – | 1788-1815 | 1788 | 64 | Havana | Accidentally burned off coast of Venezuela (1815) | |
| 205 S FRANCISCO de PAULA (2) | – | 1788-1823 | 1788 | 74 | Cartagena | BU 1823 | |
| 206 EUROPA (2) | – | 1789-1801 | 1789 | 74 | Ferrol | Stricken 1801 | |
| 207 ASIA (3) | – | 1789-1825 | 1789 | 64 | Havana | Crew mutinied at Marina Is (Pacific Ocean), set officers ashore, sailed ship to Mexico and handed her over to the Mexicans 1825. BU 1830 | |
| 208 S HERMENE-GILDO | – | 1789-1801 | 1789 | 112 | Havana | Blew up in night action off Gibraltar 1801, about 25 survivors | A 3-decker |
| 209 INTREPIDO | – | 1790-1801 | 1790 | 74 | Ferrol | Transferred to French 1801, renamed *L'Intrepide*. Captured by the British at Trafalgar. Sank in the storm 1805. | |
| 210 SOBERANO (2) | – | 1790-1809 | 1790 | 74 | Havana | BU 1809 | |
| 211 REINA LUISA (renamed FERNANDO VII 1809) | – | 1791-1815 | 1791 | 112 | Ferrol | Wrecked off Bougie, Algeria 1815 | |
| 212 CONQUISTA-DOR | – | 1791-1801 | 1791 | 74 | Cartagena | Transferred to French 1801, renamed *Le Conquerant*. Stricken 1804. | |
| 213 PELAYO | – | 1792-1801 | 1792 | 74 | Havana | Transferred to French 1801, renamed *Desaix*. Stricken 1804 | |
| 214 LE FERME | – | 1793-1808 | 1785 | 74 | France | Stricken 1808 | French *La Ferme*, renamed *Phocion*, 1792. Handed over to Spanish at Havana by her Royalist officers 1793. |
| 215 MONARCA (2) | – | 1794-1805 | 1794 | 74 | Ferrol | Captured by the British at Trafalgar, wrecked in the storm which followed, 1805. | |
| 216 MONTAÑES | | 1794-1810 | 1794 | 74 | Ferrol | Wrecked in Cadiz Bay 1810 | |
| 217 PRINCIPE de ASTURIAS (2) | *Los Santos Reyes* | 1794-1812 | 1794 | 112 | Havana | Stricken 1812 | A 3-decker |

| Name | Also called | Service | Ld. | Guns | Yard | Fate | Remarks |
|---|---|---|---|---|---|---|---|
| 218 NEPTUNO (3) | – | 1795-1805 | 1795 | 80 | Ferrol | Damaged at Trafalgar and wrecked in the storm which followed | |
| 219 ARGONAUTA (1) | – | 1798-1805 | 1798 | 80 | Ferrol | Captured by the British at Trafalgar, sank in the storm | |
| 220 CENSEUR | – | 1799-1799 | 1782 | 74 | France | Found to be rotten. Never served. BU | French ship of the line transferred to Spain 1799 in exchange for *San Sebastian* (See No 191 |
| 221 ARGONAUTA (2) | – | 1806-1810 | 1789 | 74 | France | Wrecked in Cadiz Bay 1810 | French *Argonaute*, exchanged for *Vencedor* (See No 127) |
| 222 HEROE | – | 1808-1839 | 1801 | 80 | France | Stricken 1839 | French *Heros*, captured by the Spanish at Cadiz 1808. |
| 223 ALGECIRAS | – | 1808-1826 | 1804 | 80 | France | Stricken 1826 | French *Algeciras*, captured by the Spanish at Cadiz 1808 |
| 224 NEPTUNO (4) | – | 1808-1820 | 1803 | 80 | Toulon | BU 1820 | French *Neptune*, captured by the Spanish at Cadiz 1808 |
| 225 PLUTON (renamed MONTAÑES) | – | 1808-1816 | 1805 | 74 | Toulon | BU 1816 | French *Pluton*, captured by the Spanish at Cadiz 1808 |
| 226 FERNANDO VII (2) | – | 1819-1823 | 1813 | 74 | St Petersburg | Stricken 1823 (rotten) | Russian *Neptun* (or *Neptunus*). Sold to Spain 1819 |
| 227 ALEJANDRO I | – | 1819-1823 | 1813 | 74 | Arkangelsk | Stricken 1823 (rotten) | Russian, *Dreszden* sold to Spain 1819 |
| 228 NUMANCIA I | – | 1819-1823 | 1813 | 74 | Arkangelsk | Never served (rotten). BU 1823 | Russian *Ljubeck* sold to Spain 1819 |
| 229 ESPAÑA (2) | – | 1819-1821 | 1811 | 74 | Arkangelsk | Never served (rotten). Stricken 1821 | Russian *Nord Ayde* or *Severny Orel*, sold to Spain 1819 |
| 230 VELASCO (2) | – | 1819-1821 | 1813 | 74 | Arkangelsk | Never served (rotten). Stricken 1821 | Russian *Epifania* (or *Krestshenie Gospodne* sold to Spanish 1819 |

BU = Broken up. NS = Nuestra Señora. Sta = Santa. Sto = Santo.

NOTE – SPANISH SHIPS OF THE LINE LAID DOWN BUT NOT COMPLETED:
1.  When the French invaded the Basque Provinces in 1719, they burned on the stocks, at Pasajes, six new ships of the line (names unknown).
2.  The same year, British troops landed at Santoña and destroyed on the stocks three ships of the line (names unknown).
3.  At Ferro in 1754, the *Arrogante* (74) was accidentally burnt on the stocks.
4.  At Havana in 1762, the *San Carlos* (80) and the *Santiago* (80) were destroyed on the stocks by the British.
5.  At the time of the French invasion (1808), two ships were building at Ferrol: *Emprendedor* (86) and *Tridente* (76), and one ship *Real Familia* (114) was building at Havana. Due to the invasion, work was stopped and the three ships were later broken up on the stocks.

After 1796 no ships of the line were built in Spain or Cuba until the *Reina Isabel II* (launched at Cadiz in 1853) and *Rey Francisco de Asis* (launched at Ferrol in 1854). Both were 86-gun ships, and the last Spanish Ships of the line.

MAIN SOURCES
G de Artiñano *Arquitectura Naval Española (En Madera)*, Madrid 1920.
R de la Guardia *Datos para un Cronicón de la Marina Militar de España*, second edition, Madrid 1921.
C Fernandez Duro *Armada Española desde la Union de los Reinos de Castilla y Aragon*, 9 vols, Madrid 1895.
J March y Labores *Historia de la Marina Real Española*, Madrid 1854.
J Gella Iturriaga *La Real Armada de 1808*, Madrid 1974.
Admiral Fr de Paula Pavia 'Noticia circunstanciada de los Navíos, Fragatas, Urcas, Corbetas Bergantínes y Vapores que ha tenido la Marina Española desde 1700 a 1875' (nd but c1878–1880), Museo Naval, Madrid (Manuscript No 1747).
J Montero y Arostegui *Historia ... del Ferrol*, Madrid 1859.

The compiler wishes to thank the staff of the Museo Naval, Madrid, and in particular the former Director, Captain José Maria Zumalcárregui, Spanish Navy (Ret).

# INDEX